James H. Sollow

THE ALABAMA CLAIMS

American Politics and
Anglo-American Relations, 1865–1872

Also by Adrian Cook

The Armies of the Streets: The New York City Draft Riots of 1863

THE ALABAMA CLAIMS

American Politics and
Anglo-American Relations, 1865–1872

ADRIAN COOK

Cornell University Press

ITHACA AND LONDON

Copyright © 1975 by Cornell University

All rights reserved. Except for brief quotations in a review, this
book, or parts thereof, must not be reproduced in any form without
permission in writing from the publisher. For information address
Cornell University Press, 124 Roberts Place, Ithaca, New York 14850.

First published 1975 by Cornell University Press.
Published in the United Kingdom by Cornell University Press Ltd.,
2-4 Brook Street, London W1Y 1AA.

International Standard Book Number 0-8014-0893-8
Library of Congress Catalog Card Number 74-10408

Printed in the United States of America by Cayuga Press, Inc.

To a signalman of the
Great Western Railway
1902—1964

Contents

Few military victories have been as complete as the Union triumph in the American Civil War. A government with such an achievement to its credit, with the largest army in the history of the world at its command, should have experienced no difficulty in getting its own way in foreign affairs. Yet the Alabama Claims — the American demands for compensation from Great Britain for unneutral acts during the Civil War — were not settled for seven years after the end of the fighting, and relations between the two countries were gravely strained. When the Americans were ready to strike a bargain, the British recklessly and arrogantly refused. When Palmerston and Russell, blind old men who had failed to learn the lessons of their humiliation by Bismarck over Schleswig-Holstein, passed from the scene and the British finally adopted a new policy of friendship with all nations and entangling alliances with none, the Americans raised their demands and asked for infinitely more than any nation could yield. How the claims were finally settled, why the process of adjustment took so long, and why the world's first great international tribunal of arbitration almost collapsed in an ignominious squabble form the story of this book.

The settlement of the Alabama Claims was complicated by a number of factors: traditional American distrust and dislike of Britain, Fenian hopes of enlisting the aid of the United States in the struggle for Irish independence, American dreams of adding Canada to the Union, nascent Canadian nationalism. I have dealt with such matters only insofar as they affected the settlement of the Alabama Claims. Neither government could operate as a free agent. American negotiators always had to think of how domestic public opinion would react to their policies; after the Second Reform Act, British diplomats had to observe a similar caution. Left to themselves, the U.S. secretary of state and the British foreign secretary could have settled the Alabama Claims in short order at any time from 1869 to 1872. But the intervention of Senator Charles Sumner in 1869 raised the expectations of American public opinion to such heights of fantasy that it proved tortuously difficult to arrange an equitable agreement. The settlement of the Alabama Claims provides a nineteenth-century demonstration of a disagreeable truth that has become all too obvious in the twentieth century: how difficult it is to pursue a sane foreign policy in a democracy.

I have contracted many debts of gratitude during the preparation of this book, and it is a great pleasure to be able to thank all those who have helped me. Professor David Herbert Donald and Professor W. R. Brock were always unstintingly generous of their time and aid, and I owe them both a great deal. I am also especially indebted to Professor Oliver MacDonagh, Professor H. C. Allen, Mr. R. N. Gooderson, Professor Ibby Nathans, Mrs. Mildred M. Panetti, and Mr. and Mrs. John G. Grimmer. Among all the long-suffering and helpful library staff whom I pestered, those in the Manuscripts Division at the Library of Congress were particularly gracious. The British Association for American Studies award of a Rockefeller Grant Fellowship enabled me to do most of the research on the American side, and subventions from the University of Reading Research Board helped me in the final preparation of the manuscript. To all, my thanks.

Reproduction of Crown-copyright records in the Public Record Office, London, appear by permission of the Controller of H. M. Stationery Office. Quotations from material in the Boston Public Library appear by permission of the Trustees, and quotations from the papers of Charles Sumner by permission of the Harvard College Library. Quotations from the Adams Papers are from the microfilm edition, by permission of the Massachusetts Historical Society, which also allowed me to quote from the Papers of George Bemis. Quotations from the Ignatius Donnelly Papers appear by permission of the Minnesota Historical Society; those from the L. P. Morton Papers by permission of the Manuscripts and Archives Division, The New York Public Library, Astor, Lenox and Tilden Foundations; from the William H. Seward Papers and the Thurlow Weed Papers by permission of the University of Rochester Library; from the Gladstone Papers in the British Library by permission of Sir William Gladstone; from the Clarendon Papers in the Bodleian Library by permission of the Earl of Clarendon; from the Iddesleigh Papers in the British Library by permission of the Rt. Hon. the Earl of Iddesleigh; and from the Hamilton Fish Papers in the Library of Congress by permission of Hamilton Fish. Portions of this book originally appeared, in somewhat different form, in the *Australian Journal of Politics and History,* Vol. 12, and the *Maryland Historical Magazine,* Vol. 61, and I am grateful to the editors of those learned journals for permission to reprint material here.

ADRIAN COOK

Henley-on-Thames

THE ALABAMA CLAIMS

American Politics and
Anglo-American Relations, 1865–1872

CHAPTER 1

Introduction

The morning of July 29, 1862, dawned pale and cloudy[1] as the 290th ship built in Laird Brothers' Birkenhead yard moved down the Mersey estuary toward the sea. Those who watched her did not suspect that they were witnessing the birth of the most successful privateer of modern times. For No. 290 was the Confederate States steamer *Alabama,* setting out on a cruise that was to last nearly two years and decimate American shipping. During the first year of her voyage, the *Alabama* captured forty-eight Northern merchant ships; but after she left Simonstown in Cape Colony on August 14, 1863, and sailed east, she took only ten prizes before being sunk by the U.S.S. *Kearsarge* off Cherbourg on June 19, 1864. Dreading the elusive raider, Northern shipowners either laid their vessels up or transferred them to foreign flags. In four years, 1861-1864, 750 ships, representing a total burthen of 481,332 tons, were transferred. In 1860 two-thirds of the commerce of New York was carried in American bottoms, but by 1863 three-quarters of it came in foreign ships.[2]

1. *The Times* (London), July 30, 1862.
2. Raphael Semmes, *Memoirs of Service Afloat during the War between the States* (Baltimore: Kelly, Piet, 1869), *passim.* James Russell Soley, *The Navy in the Civil War: The Blockade and the Cruisers* (London: Sampson Low, Marston, 1898), pp. 190-192. *Papers Relating to the Foreign Relations of the United States, Transmitted to Congress with the Annual Message of the President, December 2, 1872. Part II,*

The *Alabama* was not the only Confederate ship to sail from a British port. There were the *Florida,* the *Rappahannock,* the *Georgia.* The last of these, the *Shenandoah,* provided a grisly postscript to the war by refusing to surrender after Appomattox and burning a large part of the American whaling fleet in the Bering Sea during the early summer of 1865. Her commander, James I. Waddell, brought her into Liverpool and, by claiming that he had no definite news of the fall of Jefferson Davis' government until June 28, escaped scot-free.[3]

The Confederate commerce raiders were the most lurid, but not the only, example of the unneutral British acts and friendliness toward the South that infuriated the Union. The British subscribed heavily to the Confederate cotton loan.[4] Blockade runners set out from the Mersey, the Clyde, and the Thames rivers in hundreds,[5] and the British interpretation of the neutrality laws "converted the port of Nassau into an insurgent port, which could not be blockaded by the naval forces of the United States."[6] From the safety of Canada, Southern agents seized shipping on the Great Lakes and in November 1864 shot up the town of St. Albans, Vermont, and robbed three banks before disappearing over the border to be arrested briefly before quick release by a flagrantly biased judge.[7]

The British government seemed actively hostile to the Union

Papers Relating to the Treaty of Washington. Volume III, Geneva Arbitration, Containing the Argument of the United States; Argument of Her Britannic Majesty's Government; and Supplementary Statements or Arguments made by the Respective Agents or Counsel (Washington: Government Printing Office, 1872), pp. 574-575, 622-623, 187 (hereafter cited as *Foreign Relations, 1872*).

3. Soley, pp. 183-186, 213-215, 219-220.

4. E. D. Adams, *Great Britain and the American Civil War* (London: Longmans, Green, 1925), II, 158-160.

5. Soley, pp. 36, 158 ff.

6. *Foreign Relations, 1872,* p. 93.

7. *Papers Relating to Foreign Affairs Accompanying the Annual Message of the President to the First Session Thirty-ninth Congress* (Washington: Government Printing Office, 1866), pp. 5-8, 15-17, 37-38.

from the very beginning of the war. George M. Dallas, the retiring American minister in London, was assured that the British attitude toward secession would not be determined before his successor arrived, and the new secretary of state, William H. Seward, decided to take advantage of this pledge to formulate his policy in a calm, unhurried fashion. Yet before Charles Francis Adams, the new minister, could reach London, the Foreign Office issued the Neutrality Proclamation which granted the Confederacy equal belligerent rights with the Union.[8]

Besides breaking their promise, it appeared that the British had rushed to acknowledge the Confederates upon partial and imperfect information. Lord John Russell, the British foreign secretary, rationalized this action by pointing to Jefferson Davis' call for privateers and to Abraham Lincoln's proclamation of a blockade of Southern ports. To treat Confederate privateers as pirates would be to intervene in the war on the Northern side, and if British ships sailing to the South were liable to search and seizure by Union ships, they had to be given the status of neutrals. Americans argued, though, that since the mails and telegraph between New York and Washington were cut by Southern sympathizers in Baltimore on April 19, 1861, and not restored until the 30th, only an imperfect and fragmentary copy of Lincoln's proclamation could have reached England before May 10. But Russell was discussing a neutrality proclamation with the Admiralty, the French government, and Southern emissaries as early as May 1. And all this at a time when the South had not a single ship afloat.[9]

Despite American diplomats' prodigious labors in gathering the most damning evidence, British official tardiness and narrow interpretation of the letter of the law meant that the Confeder-

8. Charles Francis Adams, Jr., *Charles Francis Adams* (London: Duckworth, 1900), p. 158.

9. *Foreign Relations, 1872*, pp. 24-31; Martin B. Duberman, *Charles Francis Adams, 1807-1886* (Boston: Houghton Mifflin, 1961), pp. 259-261.

ate cruisers escaped from British ports with ease. When the *Alexandra* was seized and her ostensible owners prosecuted, the chief baron so charged the jury that they had no alternative but to acquit, and Adams presented an ultimatum that went to the brink of war in 1863 to stop the Laird rams from sailing. No matter how often they had infringed the neutrality statutes, the commerce raiders were nearly always welcome at British colonial ports, and passengers on British ships cheered the *Alabama* to the echo as she passed.[10]

"The great body of the aristocracy and the wealthy commercial classes," wrote Charles Francis Adams, "are anxious to see the United States go to pieces."[11] In Parliament, a Conservative member, Sir John Ramsden, jubilantly announced that the great Republican bubble had burst, and he was greeted with cries of approval.[12] John Laird brought cheers from the Tory benches when he declared that he would rather his name be handed down to posterity as the builder of a dozen *Alabamas* than as a man who glorified worthless foreign institutions which reduced liberty to an absurdity. Speeches made by government ministers showed no friendliness toward the United States. Palmerston asserted on June 30, 1863, that the Union no longer legally existed. America, he said, was not divided into a legitimate government and a rebellion, but was merely two belligerents. Russell repeatedly argued that the Union could never be restored and that bloodshed, misery, and destruction would be the only fruits of the war. Gladstone's notorious declaration, in a speech at Newcastle on October 7, 1862, that the Confederate leaders had made an army, were making a navy, and had made what was more than either, a nation, touched off a flurry of

10. E. D. Adams, II, pp. 35, 120-135 *passim,* 152, 161, 185, 195-196. C. F. Adams, Jr., p. 309. Brougham Villiers and W. H. Chesson, *Anglo-American Relations, 1861-1865* (London: T. Fisher Unwin, 1919), p. 72.

11. W. C. Ford, ed., *A Cycle of Adams' Letters, 1861-1865* (London: Constable, 1921), I, 220.

12. *The Times* (London), May 28, 1861.

excited speculation that England would recognize the Confederacy.[13]

Only a few of the great newspapers and magazines — the *Daily News,* the *Morning Star,* the *Westminster Review,* and the *Spectator* — supported the Union.[14] At least one paper, the Edinburgh *Caledonian Mercury and Weekly Herald,* was ruined by popular rejection of its pro-Northern policy.[15] *The Times,* the most famous and powerful newspaper in the world, ridiculed Northern deeds and vigorously supported the South. Charles Mackay, its American correspondent after the spring of 1862, was a Confederate sympathizer and was selected by John Delane, the paper's editor, for that reason. "Why," asked John Walter III, the "Thunderer" 's proprietor, "should we be so very anxious to see the Union preserved? What has it done to command our sympathy?"[16]

America felt betrayed, insulted, and injured. At no time since the close of the War of 1812 had Anglo-American relations been worse than they were at the end of the Civil War.

A hearty dislike of Britain came naturally to Americans. "Nothing," Alexis de Tocqueville wrote after his visit in 1831-1832, "can be more virulent than the hatred which exists between the Americans of the United States and the English."[17] Hatred of England was a badge of loyalty, a common factor unifying the disparate American society, and a constant spur to make America greater. If a country has no history to act as a source of national pride and emotion, it must hold up the

13. *Foreign Relations, 1872,* pp. 40-44. Duberman, p. 295.

14. Duberman, p. 273.

15. W. Ritchie to C. F. Adams, June 16, 1866, Adams Papers. Consulted on microfilm at Eisenhower Library, Johns Hopkins University, Baltimore, Md.

16. *History of 'The Times'* (London: Office of *The Times,* 1939), III, 364-366, 376-378. Donaldson Jordan and E. J. Pratt, *Europe and the American Civil War* (Boston: Houghton Mifflin, 1931), p. 80.

17. Alexis de Tocqueville, *Democracy in America,* trans. by Henry Reeve, rev. by Francis Bowen, introd. by Daniel C. Gilman (New York: Century, 1898), p. 91.

image of its enemies. A hatred of the oppressive despotism whose chains they had broken supplied Americans with a national identity and a patriotic rallying point.

As the United States grew and prospered, nationalist feeling mounted. A new generation grew up, and the Revolutionary tradition, with its violent Anglophobic connotations, became institutionalized and idealized. Parson Mason Weems and his cherry tree may have become a joke in the twentieth century, but in the early 1800s Weems' biography of Washington served a vital purpose. He and his confreres provided heroes for a new nation, models of classical virtue and republican dignity for a people cut off by their own volition from their sources of tradition and legend. Heroes represent what should be, not what is or what was, and Weems' deified Washington was what every American aspired to be.[18]

The Revolution and its heroes quickly became immortalized in poetry, art, and architecture. Even before Washington's death, his birthday was often celebrated, and until after the Civil War this was the only national holiday besides Independence Day. Few Fourth of July orations were complete without a romantic account of colonial and Revolutionary history, rendered with a heavy slant in favor of the American patriots.[19] Until after the Civil War, the nation's most prized document was the Declaration of Independence, not the Constitution. America's first great national historian, George Bancroft, saw God working out his purposes through American history and linked the Revolution to a tradition of liberty reaching back to the dawn of history.[20]

---

18. Merle Curti, *The Roots of American Loyalty* (New York: Columbia University Press, 1946), pp. 58-59, 134-135, 140. I am not, of course, suggesting that Anglophobia was the *only* element in American patriotism, but it was certainly a very powerful one.

19. A typical example is to be found in the Des Moines, Iowa, *Daily Bulletin,* July 6, 1869: Representative John A. Kasson's oration to the German School Association, "The Progress of America and American Ideas."

20. Dixon Wecter, *The Hero in America: A Chronicle of Hero-Wor-*

Americans rejected past ties with Britain, and in the early days of the republic seemed to want to differentiate themselves from the country with which they still had much in common. The prominent Federalist Fisher Ames remarked in 1805 that Americans had come to regard English boasts of personal freedom as proof of their acceptance of tyranny; lack of a written English constitution as complete absence of governmental guarantees; and English vitality and vigor as the last feverish writhings of a sick and dying society.

The War of 1812 naturally stimulated Anglophobia.[21] The United States fought no other major war in the first half of the century, except the Mexican adventure of 1846. Then the country's existence was not at stake, nor was the life of the people affected by privation and attack. A great weight of popular tradition and militant patriotism settled upon the two wars with England. Native Americans cherished the spirit of '76, and immigrants were presented with a simplified set of loyalties. Nearly two million Irish,[22] white-hot with hatred of England, formed the advance guard of American Anglophobia.

The casting of Britain as a villain was unassailable. No other great power possessed colonies on the North American continent; the only other potential enemy was weak, complaisant Spain. The remote central European empires rarely entered the American consciousness; Russia came to be regarded as the most friendly of all the European powers.[23] France was forgiven every-

---

ship (New York: Scribner's, 1941), p. 3. George Bancroft, *History of the United States of America, from the Discovery of the Continent* (New York: Appleton, 1885).

21. Curti, p. 153.

22. In 1860 there were 1,611,304 Irish-born people living in the United States. United States Immigration Commission, *Statistical Review of Immigration, 1820-1910* (Washington: Government Printing Office, 1911), p. 416. This does not take account of their children, nor of the children of earlier immigrants.

23. Vera Michaels Dean, *The United States and Russia* (London: Oxford University Press, 1947), pp. 7-8. Thomas A. Bailey, *America Faces Russia: Russian-American Relations from Early Times to Our Day* (Ithaca, N.Y.: Cornell University Press, 1950), pp. 12-107, *passim.*

thing by the Revolutionary tradition. Napoleon III's Mexican puppet empire was universally denounced, and Charles Sumner, chairman of the Senate Foreign Relations Committee, thought that there was a real danger of war with France.[24] But there was no animus against the French nation. General Ulysses S. Grant regarded Maximilian's expedition to Mexico not as an act of the French people, who were brave friends and true allies, but as one of the nefarious schemes of "Louis Napoleon," who he thought would soon be overthrown.[25] A few influential men, such as the great Boston capitalist John Murray Forbes,[26] or a newspaper like the Baltimore *Sun*,[27] might hold France as guilty as England in her wartime behavior, but this view did not find wide acceptance. Charles Sumner admitted that both England and France had erred in conceding belligerent rights to the Confederacy, but he ignored Napoleon III's hostile diplomacy and declared that England alone had built privateers and blockade runners. The American public gave little attention to France's wartime policy, but gathered a vague impression, based on memories of the Revolutionary alliance, of a good feeling between the two countries.[28]

In the years after the Civil War, the long anti-British tradition in American life gave added force and rancor to the resentment stemming from the United States legitimate grievances. Americans of the 1860s, wrote the historian James Ford Rhodes, had learned at school, from "crude historical study of the Revolution

---

Thomas A. Bailey, "The Russian Fleet Myth Re-examined," *Mississippi Valley Historical Review*, 38 (1951-1952), 81-90; Frank A. Golder, "The Purchase of Alaska," *American Historical Review*, 25 (1919-1920), 411-425.

24. Charles Sumner to Richard Cobden, March 27, 1865; Sumner to John Bright, Nov. 5, 1865, Bright Papers.

25. General Horace Porter, *Campaigning with Grant*, ed. with introd. and notes by Wayne C. Temple (Civil War Centennial Series, Bloomington: Indiana University Press, 1961), p. 256.

26. John M. Forbes to Charles Sumner, Oct. 31, 1869, Sumner Papers.

27. March 15, 1869.

28. Edward L. Pierce, *Memoir and Letters of Charles Sumner* (Boston: Robert Brothers, 1894), IV, 406. C. F. Adams, Jr., pp. 153-154. W. H.

and the War of 1812, that England was a natural enemy."[29]
"The American people," said the *Illinois Daily State Journal*
in its editorial upon Sumner's denunciation of England in April
1869, "remember that their Pilgrim ancestry sought a wilderness
for the enjoyment of religious and civil liberty, and from whence
they went; they remember the history of the times of the Revolution, for it was written with British steel in the priceless blood
of seven years' relentless, bitter warfare; they remember Bunker
Hill, Yorktown and other notable fields of blood; they remember
1812, with its blood and carnage — all is fresh, undying *present*
history to them."[30]

The common language and cultural tradition that should
have brought Britain and America closer together, only helped
to make their enmity more fierce during the Civil War. The two
countries were just close enough in thought, feeling, and outlook
to give Americans a deep interest in what Englishmen thought,
and just alien enough to make it hard, sometimes impossible,
for Americans to comprehend the processes behind the formation
of that opinion. Each confident in the absolute justice of its
cause, both North and South naturally expected unanimous
sympathy and complete support.

Northern antislavery men, who had received inspiration, encouragement, and help from Britain before the war, were particularly disillusioned by their idol's fall, when Britain, in their eyes
cold-bloodedly, rejected their fervent efforts toward emancipation and "allied itself in sympathy with a rebellion that was
undertaken in the interests of slavery and prosecuted for the
perpetuity and enlargement of the system of human bondage."[31]

Russell, *My Civil War Diary*, ed. by Fletcher Pratt, introd. by D. W.
Brogan (London: Hamish Hamilton, 1954), p. 14.

29. James Ford Rhodes, *History of the United States from the
Compromise of 1850* (London: Macmillan, 1895), III, 517. Rhodes
was a contemporary, born in 1848.

30. April 22, 1869; see also *New York Herald*, Feb. 11, 1871; *Washington Daily Morning Chronicle*, June 17, 1872.

31. Senator Henry B. Anthony of Rhode Island, on Dec. 9, 1867, U. S.
Congressional Globe, 40 Cong., 2 sess., p. 85. Hereafter cited as *Cong.
Globe*.

William Howard Russell, the great war correspondent of *The Times*, was surprised at the unanimity with which members of Lincoln's cabinet, assumed that England was bound, by her antislavery antecedents, to discourage the South and favor the North.[32] James Ford Rhodes, looking back on these years, thought the English argument that slavery was not the cause of the war, "wilful blindness."[33]

In the hysterical atmosphere of a desperately hard-fought war, Americans saw Britain blacker than she deserved. There was a universal conviction that perfidious, jealous Albion had seized the opportunity of 1861 to break a rival in power, a competitor in commerce, and a menace to aristocratic institutions. The policy of Palmerston, Russell, and Gladstone seemed to have all the marks of a sustained and premeditated attempt to smash the Union; never "in the history of political turpitude had any brigand of modern civilization offered a worse example." Only after many years, and then slowly and unwillingly, did Americans come to realize that the actions of the Palmerston ministry had proceeded as much from muddle and vacillation as from malevolence and viciousness.[34] To a certain extent Americans had looked for English hostility. "The English are gushingly unhappy as to our family quarrel," a South Carolina lady noted in her diary on March 4, 1861. "Magnanimous of them, for it is their opportunity."[35] Talking to members of the New York Press Association, William Howard Russell found them convinced that Britain would act only on sordid motives.[36]

Palmerston was certainly anti-American, and pleased to see the country divided. But, as prime minister of a shaky coalition

32. Russell, who was generally pro-Northern, left America in the spring of 1862, and had nothing to do with *The Times* later reporting of the war. Jordan and Pratt, p. 80; Russell, pp. 29-30.

33. Rhodes, IV, 79.

34. *The Education of Henry Adams: An Autobiography* (Boston: Houghton Mifflin, 1918), pp. 149-166.

35. Mary Boykin Crestnut, *A Diary from Dixie*, ed. by Ben Ames Williams (Boston: Houghton Mifflin, 1961), p. 11.

36. Russell, p. 14.

government, he could not afford to raise a storm and was always cautious in his American policy. Russell and Gladstone both inclined to the North from dislike of slavery, but neither had the slightest hope that the union would ever be restored. The Whig politicians were uneasy about their dealings with America after the movement toward manhood suffrage. Severely limited as reformers, they could see only that America had thrown its government to the mob. The Whigs never understood nationalism; the central tenets of their faith were the freedom of the individual and its political corollary, the right of revolution. This was why Russell helped Count Cavour to unify Italy in 1860, and why he could never penetrate the motives of Abraham Lincoln as he could comprehend those of Jefferson Davis. In the critical months of 1862, when recognition of the Confederacy and mediation were discussed, Russell and Gladstone were the extremists and Palmerston the moderate.[37]

To despair of Northern success did not necessarily mean to be pro-Confederate. When Gladstone made his Newcastle speech, he firmly believed that he was acting as a friend of the North, helping the distracted nation to accept what its stubborn pride would not let it admit, that the struggle was over.[38] Though a number of eminent peers sympathized with the North, and the Conservative party was by no means united on the American question, most of the aristocracy favored the South. William Howard Russell advised Sumner that behind most British attacks upon the Union cause lay a fear of "Brightism and republicanism at home."[39] John Dalberg Acton, not yet Lord Acton, admitted to Robert E. Lee after the war that a great part of the British

37. Russell had rebuked Ramsden for his speech. Duberman, pp. 261, 277. E. D. Adams, I, 28. Jordan and Pratt, pp. 23-25. A. Wyatt Tilby, *Lord John Russell: A Study in Civil and Religious Liberty* (London: Cassell, 1930), pp. 189-190, 201-202.
38. John Morley, *The Life of William Ewart Gladstone* (London: Macmillan, 1903), II, 81.
39. Wilbur Devereux Jones, "The British Conservatives and the American Civil War," *American Historical Review,* 58 (1952-1953), 527-543. Jordan and Pratt, p. 59.

sympathy for the South had been selfish and insincere. "It sprang," he thought, "partly from an exultant belief in the imminent decline and ruin of Democratic institutions, partly from the hope that America would be weakened by the separation, and from terror at the remote prospect of Farragut appearing in the channel and Sherman landing in Ireland."[40]

The commercial classes also tended to side against the Union, guided by a dislike of the Northern tariff and by hopes of capturing the Southern market. Many of this class would have welcomed mediation; they were really interested in trade, and the less that was interrupted by war the better. By its insistence that it was fighting for nothing but the preservation of the Union, the federal government managed to dissipate a good deal of the support given to it at the beginning of the war by people of antislavery convictions. But the Emancipation Proclamation rallied sympathy to the Union from the lower and middle classes with striking effect.[41] John Bright, Richard Cobden, James Stansfeld, and other radicals were always for the Union.

Americans might acknowledge this sympathy, but their mood toward Great Britain remained sullen and antagonistic. Much might have been urged in Britain's favor. Britain assented, in the cases of her own ships *Springbok* and *Peterhoff,* to the doctrine of "continuous voyage," which meant that the Confederates could not obtain war supplies by consigning them through neutral ports in Mexico or the West Indies.[42] The government refused to allow Confederate privateers into British ports and fully recognized the Federal blockade of the South. The authorities were slow and dilatory in the *Alabama* affair, but orders for detention were eventually issued, and the vessel would have

40. John Dalberg Acton to R. E. Lee, Nov. 4, 1866, printed in Douglas Southall Freeman, *R. E. Lee: A Biography* (New York: Scribner's, 1934), IV, Appendix IV, p. 516.

41. Duberman, pp. 265-269, 299. Rhodes, IV, 77, 349-354.

42. J. G. Randall, *Lincoln — the President* (London: Eyre and Spottiswoode, 1952), III, 334-335.

been seized if the Queen's Advocate had not suddenly become insane. Russell had already decided to stop the Laird rams before the United States ultimatum of 1863 reached him. The British government did try to do its duty as it saw it, but it was hamstrung by a law which drew a fine distinction between building a vessel and equipping it for war: the Confederate raiders, built as warships but supplied with guns and shells outside the British jurisdiction, were immune. Palmerston's ramshackle party could not be relied upon to support an amending bill created by foreign pressure. The prime minister had already discovered this, to his cost, in 1859, when after the Orsinis had hatched their plot to assassinate Napoleon III in London, he brought in the Conspiracy to Murder Bill — and found himself voted out of office by an aggressively British Parliament.

So frigid was the British government toward the Confederate emissaries in London that, in late 1863, James Murray Mason left the city in disgust and the British consuls in the South, still occupying an anomalous position, were expelled. The Federal government never treated the Confederates as rebels: captured soldiers were treated as prisoners of war, and no one was ever hanged for his part in the struggle. In fact, the Federal attitude did not substantially differ from the British. Britain had good reasons for issuing the Neutrality Proclamation in May 1861: the friends of the Union in the cabinet had pressed it most strongly, thinking that strict neutrality would favor the North. And the government acted none too soon: on May 21, 1861, Northern ships captured a British schooner for trying to run the blockade. It is doubtful whether Washington would ever have welcomed the Proclamation. The North did not really want strict neutrality from Britain; it wanted help against the Confederacy.[43] As Wil-

43. *Ibid.*, II, 34-35; III, 315-334. Randall, *Lincoln the Liberal Statesman* (London: Eyre and Spottiswoode, 1947), p. 140. Allan Nevins, *Hamilton Fish: The Inner History of the Grant Administration* (New York: Dodd, Mead, 1937), pp. 142-147. Duberman, pp. 258-333. San Francisco *Daily Alta California,* May 10, 1869.

liam Howard Russell observed, "A neutral who tries to moderate the violence of either side is very like an ice between two hot plates."[44]

But Americans did not consider any mitigating circumstances. Together wth their many serious and genuine grievances, they nourished others based upon unreasonable demands and misunderstandings. They remembered only the *Alabama* and the blockade runners, *The Times* and Sir John Ramsden, and they nursed a deep sense of national injury:

> "Ef I turned mad dogs loose, John,
> On *your* front-parlor stairs,
> Would it jest meet your views, John
> To wait an' sue their heirs?
> > Ole Uncle S. sez he, 'I guess
> > I on'y guess,' sez he,
> > 'Thet, ef Vattell on *his* toes fell,
> > 'Twould kind o' rile J.B.,
> > Ez wal ez you an' me!"

> "We know we've gut a cause, John,
> Thet's honest, just an' true;
> We thought 'twould win applause, John,
> Ef nowheres else, from you.
> > Ol Uncle S. sez he, 'I guess
> > His love of right, 'sez he,
> > 'Hangs by a rotten fibre o'cotton:
> > There's natur' in J.B.,
> > Ez wal ez you an' me!"[45]

44. Russell, p. 79.
45. James Russell Lowell, "Jonathan to John," *The Bigelow Papers,* prefatory note by Ernest Rhys (London: Walter Scott, n.d.), pp. 168-169, 171.

CHAPTER 2

The End of Adams' Mission

In early 1865 the minister of the United States encountered
a new and unaccustomed cordiality in London society. British
feeling in favor of the Union mounted victory by victory, and
even *The Times* was chastened.[1] Yet at the same time, Charles
Francis Adams found greater uneasiness and alarm in the country
than at any time since the *Trent* affair had brought the North
and Britain to the brink of war four years earlier. Fear that
Union victory would be followed by a war of revenge against
Britain and France was widespread; the Confederate propaganda sheet the *Index* and some virulently pro-Southern papers
like the *Owl* advocated preventive war and an alliance with
the tottering Confederacy.[2] The panic reached its height in late
February and early March 1865, then it was temporarily quieted
by a Parliamentary debate expressing hope and assurances of
future friendship with America and by the announcement that
the Rush-Bagot agreement for the neutrality of the Great Lakes

1. Charles Francis Adams to William H. Seward, Feb. 2, 10, March
9, April 20, 1865, Diplomatic Despatches. C. F. Adams to C. F. Adams,
Jr., Feb. 10, March 10, 1865; C. F. Adams to Brooks Adams, Jan. 5, 1866,
Adams Papers.
2. Adams to Seward, Feb. 9, 10, 16, 23, March 2, 16, 30, April 28,
1865, Diplomatic Despatches. C. F. Adams to C. F. Adams, Jr., Jan. 27,
Feb. 3, 10, 17, March 10, 1865; Adams Diary, Jan. 31, Feb 7, March 5,
1865, Adams Papers. Benjamin Moran to Sumner, March 6, 1865; James
Phalen to Sumner, Feb. 13, 1865, Sumner Papers.

was to be preserved. But fear still lingered, to issue again in April and in June.

Even in December 1865 the remnants of the Confederate propaganda machine still inspired malicious reports calculated to stir up trouble between the two countries.[3] Earlier in the year they had successfully encouraged English dread. The directors of England's greatest banking house, Baring's, worried about protecting their American interests in the event of war, and Adams was sufficiently alarmed by press reports and the stories retailed by both the Prince de Joinville and a Juarista agent of a French war fleet that was preparing to attack America that he raised the matter with Lord Russell. Although reassured, Adams still cautioned Secretary of State Seward against any action, even the presentation of the United States war claims, that might frighten the British public.[4]

The Minister was a member of America's most distinguished family. His father and grandfather had been presidents. Correct, restrained, with a penetrating intellect, Adams was one of the ablest diplomats ever to represent America abroad. During the war he performed his task supremely well; afterward the initiative passed to Washington and the newly laid cable permitted closer supervision of negotiations, so his talents were not exercised to their full extent. Seward was a very different type of man. Energetic, ambitious, volatile, his quick mind too often led him to a superficial assessment of a problem, and his shallow judgment too often resulted in an unprincipled *Realpolitik* that missed the underlying verities of a situation. Throughout his career, Seward was at his best when controlled and advised by an alter ego, such as Thurlow Weed, John Quincy Adams, or Abraham Lincoln. After the war he was without such a guide, and his actions suffered in consequence.

3. Adams to Seward, March 14, 16, 30, April 7, Dec. 1, 1865; Adams to W. Hunter, June 2, 1865, Diplomatic Despatches. C. F. Adams to Henry Adams, March 11, 1865, Adams Papers.

4. Adams to Seward, March 9, 1865, Diplomatic Despatches. Adams Diary, Jan. 31, Feb. 14, 1865.

By midsummer 1865 the danger of a collision was over. The concession of belligerent rights to the Confederates was partly withdrawn on May 11 — although Adams remarked that he could only regret that what might have been a manly and honest correction of a hasty blunder had not been spontaneously presented as a peace offering — and it was finally abandoned on June 2. By then, the minister told his son, there was nothing left to cause future dissension. The arguments about the claims had been drawn up and presented by both sides. "Nothing remains but arbitration, which need not be determined upon for some time to come."[5]

In reality, the situation was less rosy than Adams' letter indicated. He had already remarked upon Lord Russell's nervousness and dread of large American claims.[6] In early May this dread, coupled with a strong desire to justify his own actions, had inspired the foreign secretary to seize the ground of negotiation before Seward could stake a formal claim. He told Adams that Great Britain could never admit that her duties as a neutral were to be measured by American losses in trade and commerce. The only question to be decided was whether or not Britain had preserved a faithful and diligent neutrality, and to that question he returned a resounding yes.[7] Once assured by Sir Frederick Bruce, the British minister in Washington, that Britain's complete refusal to compensate for the ravages of the Confederate cruisers would not mean war, only Washington's threat of like behavior when Britain was a belligerent,[8] Russell felt able to go farther. In a letter to Adams of August 30 he raked up an old American proposal of October 23, 1863, for "any form of

5. Adams to Hunter, May 18, June 8, 1865, Diplomatic Despatches. C. F. Adams to C. F. Adams, Jr., June 9, 1865, Adams Papers.

6. Adams to Seward, Feb. 9, 1865, Diplomatic Despatches.

7. Lord Russell to Adams, May 4, 1865, encl. in Adams to Hunter, May 11, 1865, Diplomatic Despatches.

8. Russell considered this "quite fair." Russell to Austen H. Layard, Aug. 19, 1865, Layard Papers.

arbitration," probably for the sole purpose of burying it again.

"Her Majesty's Government," announced Russell, "are the sole guardians of their own honour." To ask a foreign government to decide if the British had been right or wrong in their behavior would insult national dignity and character. The Crown law officers were better interpreters of British statutes than any arbitrator. He would not agree to pay compensation for the acts of Confederate cruisers, nor would he submit the question to arbitration. All he offered was a commission to consider the Civil War claims of both nations, with the proviso that the two governments should agree beforehand upon the claims to be presented. Russell made it clear that he did not mean to consent to the inclusion of the Alabama Claims. In other words, remarked Adams, Russell agreed to refer British claims to arbitration and returned a polite refusal to include American losses. "Wonderful liberality!"[9] Not surprisingly, Seward refused the offer of a joint commission and later, on November 4, informed the British government that henceforward he would not accept arbitration as a solution.[10]

On October 18, 1865, the aged Lord Palmerston died, and Russell succeeded to the premiership. Adams was untroubled by any regrets for Palmerston, who he had always regarded (incorrectly) as "the most ill-affected to America out of all the Cabinet Ministers." Russell, though far from being a great man, he thought morally much superior. With Lord Clarendon,

9. Russell to Adams, Aug. 30, Oct. 14, 1865, encl. in Adams to Seward, Sept. 7, Oct. 19, 1865, Diplomatic Despatches. Adams Diary, Oct. 14, 1865. Russell decided to write his dispatch of August 30 without consulting the cabinet and sent it over the objections of several ministers. Gladstone, though he regarded arbitration as "unreasonable," wanted the door left open for future discussions. Clarendon thought the American question the most important then outstanding and was eager for a settlement. Gladstone to Russell, Sept. 2, 6, 1865, Gladstone Papers. Clarendon to Edmund Hammond, Sept. 4, 1865, Hammond Papers, FO 391/4; Russell to Hammond, Sept. 18, 1865, Hammond Papers, FO 391/7.

10. Seward to Adams, Sept. 27, Nov. 4, 1865, Diplomatic Instructions, Great Britain, State Department, R.G.59, N.A. (hereafter cited as Diplomatic Instructions).

who entered the Foreign Office, Adams' New England conscience stirred. "Easy, frank, prompt and courteous, the contrast with the more dry homely and yet not unkind, the stiff and yet honest bearing of Lord Russell, is striking. Pleasanter, perhaps a trifle less true, I suspect to be the difference."[11]

Adams thought that the new foreign secretary might prove more conciliatory than the old. Russell's flat refusal to include American losses in arbitration he found generally regretted, and he heard a rumor that Clarendon had intended to make the delivery of the recalcitrant *Shenandoah,* which had struck her flag at Liverpool in October, the occasion for a soothing note.[12] But Clarendon only moved to propose that both Britain and America should revise their neutrality laws and disclaim national liability in case of future *Alabamas.* Adams did not expect Seward to agree, for it simply would secure Britain from the consequences of her wartime acts without admitting her guilt, while America abandoned the basis of justice for her claims and lost all chance of profiting from the British precedent. However, he consented to refer the matter to Washington in February 1866. As he expected, Seward refused to hear of it and sent word that the validity of U.S. claims must be recognized before any negotiations could begin. And when Adams learned that Clarendon, despite his discouraging answer, had ordered Bruce to press the suggestion, he dismissed the whole proposal as a measure of publicity. Clarendon, he believed, wanted to show Parliament that something was being done to relieve the unease felt about Russell's slamming of the diplomatic door and hoped to make America seem unreasonable in adopting Russell's tactics.[13]

11. Adams to Seward, Oct 19, 1965, Diplomatic Despatches. Adams Diary, April 24, Oct 19, Nov. 6, 1865, Jan. 27, June 26, 1866. C. F. Adams to C. F. Adams, Jr., Oct. 20, 1865; Henry Adams to C. F. Adams, Jr., Oct. 20, 1865, Adams Papers.
12. Adams to Seward, Oct. 19, 1865, Diplomatic Despatches. Adams Diary, Nov. 18, 1865.
13. Adams to Seward, Feb. 15, 1866, Diplomatic Despatches. Seward to Adams, March 5, 1866, Confidential, Feb. 16, 1866, Diplomatic In-

For the remainder of Russell's ministry the American question slumbered. Adams thought British public opinion more and more favorable to the United States and British politicians sensitive to American strictures. The newer members of Parliament he found alive to the importance of an Anglo-American *rapprochement*. Nevertheless, Adams felt that cordiality would not be restored for many years and that Clarendon was doing nothing to help.[14]

On June 18, 1866, Russell's ramshackle administration fell, and the Conservatives formed a minority government, with the Earl of Derby as prime minister and Lord Stanley, his son, as foreign secretary. Seward chose this moment to take the offensive. On July 7 he asked Adams to probe the British attitude toward a settlement, and on August 27 he sent a summary of the American claims, with definite instructions to reopen negotiations. The United States, he wrote, thought that a settlement was "urgently necessary" if friendly relations were to be re-established, and he was willing to have British claims, mostly for British property in the South destroyed by the Union army, considered in "one comprehensive settlement." Seward explained that he was driven to take up the question again by the subsidence of the political excitement which had disturbed both Britain and the United States. Really, he wanted to test the new government and hoped to tap the British eagerness for a settlement. Lord Stanley had already announced the appoint-

---

structions. Adams Diary, Feb. 9, 11, March 5, 1866. Adams did the foreign secretary an injustice; he genuinely wanted a settlement and better relations between Britain and America. But he believed Britain's wartime conduct to be blameless and suspected the Americans were trying to pick a quarrel. In April 1866, he suggested that both nations should wipe out all claims between them and start afresh. Clarendon to Hammond, Sept. 4, Oct. 14, 23, 1865, Hammond Papers, FO 391/4. Clarendon to Bruce, Nov. 25, 1865, April 28, 1866, Clarendon Papers, Bodleian.

14. Adams to Seward, Jan. 4, June 28, 1866, Diplomatic Despatches. Adams to George Bancroft, March 2, 1866, Bancroft Papers. Adams Diary, Feb. 11, 22, 1866, Adams Papers.

ment of a royal commission to inquire into, and perhaps revise, the neutrality laws, and the British were full of gratitude for the United States prompt suppression of attempts to raid Canada by the Fenians, the Irish-American revolutionaries who were then at the height of their career. The French had agreed to withdraw from Mexico, and fears of war across the Rio-Grande and on the Atlantic were dead.[15] Bearing in mind Seward's later desire for the annexation of Canada, it is just possible that he had this in his mind, too, and wanted to act before the process of confederation could be completed.

Certainly the secretary of state displayed some impatience when he learned that holidays would prevent Derby's cabinet from considering American matters until the end of October. There was no more important issue, he told Adams; the minister should at all times impress the British "with the conviction of the importance of an early disposition of the question."[16]

Meanwhile, semiofficial articles began to appear in *The Times* looking to a reconsideration of the claims, and Lord Derby made a conciliatory speech at the Guildhall dinner. Unofficially, Lord Stanley inquired if the Americans had any plan of settlement ready.[17] Adams thought that the main difficulty facing the Derby government was to find a way of withdrawing gracefully from Russell's extreme position. Stanley's response of November 30 did make a strong defense against Seward's detailed list of British sins. It maintained, too, the refusal to admit British liability for any of the claims. But Stanley made the vital concession: he agreed to arbitration and proposed a general reference of all British and American war claims, with two conditions. Both nations must agree upon the points to be decided, and he

15. Seward to Adams, Aug. 27, July 30, 1866, Diplomatic Instructions. Adams to Seward, July 26, Aug. 23, 1866, Diplomatic Despatches.
16. Seward to Adams, Oct. 8, 1866, Diplomatic Instructions. Adams to Seward, Sept. 21, 1866, Diplomatic Despatches.
17. Adams to Seward, Nov. 23, 1866, Diplomatic Despatches. Benjamin Moran to C. F. Adams, Oct. 4, 30, 1866, Adams Papers.

would not admit the matter of Britain's recognition of the Confederacy as a belligerent power to arbitration. Seward, while admitting that it was the sovereign right of any nation to make such a recognition, claimed that the British action had been unnecessary and premature, giving vital encouragement to dissident Southerners and leading directly to the launching of the commerce raiders.[18] Upon this rock the negotiations were to splinter.

Seward's reply to Stanley was made on January 12, 1867. Once more, he fought over the well-trodden ground of British aid to the cruisers and the Queen's Proclamation of Neutrality. As to Stanley's tentative offer of a settlement, the secretary replied that he thought it would be easier and better if Great Britain acknowledged and paid the claims outright. But if the British really wanted arbitration, he would not object. He would expect, though, to refer the whole quarrel, just as it was found in the diplomatic correspondence, together with whatever other evidence either party wanted to present. He wanted no conditions, no restrictions, no limitations. To knock Stanley's reservations about the Neutrality Proclamation on the head again, Seward added that the United States would not excuse any question on the plea of national honor, though they would not insist that the arbitrator should rule on a point of national pride or honor alone. The elder Adams thought Seward's dispatch "scarcely conciliatory . . . throws us back again I fear to our old position," and his son Henry wrote that "Seward makes a hitch, it appears, in re Ala. et al. . . . I don't think so well as I did of our prospect of settling it all up. Another damned rope's-end let loose to trip us up."[19]

But, as Adams guessed, early in February, Seward was nervous about American public opinion.[20] In December and over the new

18. Lord Stanley to Sir Frederick Bruce, Nov. 30, 1866 (two), FO 5/1326. Seward to Adams, Aug. 27, 1866, Diplomatic Instructions.

19. Seward to Adams, Jan. 2, 1867, Diplomatic Instructions. Adams Diary, Jan. 28, 1867. Henry Adams to C. F. Adams, Jr., Feb. 1, 1867, Adams Papers.

20. C. F. Adams to C. F. Adams, Jr., Feb. 8, 1867, Adams Papers.

year, Senator Charles Sumner found him carefully watching for any signs of change, and the secretary of state had actually asked Bruce, the British minister in Washington, not to give him an official copy of Stanley's November 30 offer so that he could continue to deny that he had received any such proposal. Early in the new year, Seward had come to the conclusion that America would not accept arbitration by "a commission of wise men" — jurists — and there were difficulties in selecting a Power who would be both fair and acceptable to both sides."[21] From this preoccupation with what the public would accept may be traced the tone and the demands of his January 12 dispatch.

On March 28, Seward wrote again, saying that Stanley's proposal could not be accepted, since his condition of a "technical definition" of all the claims to be arbitrated would permit a belief in America that just claims were being railroaded out of court. He expressed anxiety about the time factor, saying that continued delay might mean that the matter could not be settled by a "friendly correspondence." Congressman Nathaniel P. Banks of Massachusetts, fresh from a disastrous career in the army, was trying to recapture his prewar eminence by twisting the lion's tail. He had produced a bill to replace the stringent American neutrality laws with weaker ones based on the lax British statutes. Under such laws Irish rebels, such as the Fenians, would be able to launch their own commerce raiders from American ports, and Seward warned that Banks' bill might well pass, in the wake of overwhelming American sympathy for the anticipated Irish rebellion. Finally, he enclosed copies of Banks' House resolutions objecting to the confederation of Canada and expressing sympathy with the liberty-seeking peoples of Ireland and Canada, with another resolution opposing the payment of foreign war claims. This should have worried Seward, but not to such an extent. His admission at the end of the dis-

21. Charles Sumner to George Bemis, Dec. 24, 30, 1866, Jan. 13, 1867, printed in Edward L. Pierce, *Memoir and Letters of Charles Sumner* (Boston: Robert Brothers, 1894), IV, 308-309, 312.

patch that "I may, indeed, entirely misunderstand the situation there [in Britain]" confirms the impression that he was trying to frighten the British government into giving him a favorable answer.[22]

Adams, disturbed, went to the Foreign Office to see Stanley, only to learn that Bruce had delayed presenting the British answer of March 9. If it had been presented, said Seward later, he would not have written his dispatch of March 28. But he felt obliged to refuse Stanley's tentatives. Arbitration of British liability for the Alabama Claims, excluding the question of the Neutrality Proclamation, with reference of the claims to a mixed commission if Britain should be found guilty and ordered to pay, was the British proposal. The commission should decide all other claims, too. To Seward, this was unsatisfactory: he could not agree to isolate the Alabama Claims.[23]

Stanley did not give up. Convinced that Seward had misunderstood him, he sent a restatement of the British position to Bruce, with instructions to try again.[24] Seward waited two months before he replied on August 12, and during that time he launched a new policy.

Earlier in the year Seward had negotiated the purchase of Alaska and announced openly that his purpose was to increase American influence in British Columbia and hasten the day when Canada and the United States would be joined. In this way, he said, causes of irritation between Britain and the United States would be removed.[25] To John Bigelow the secretary remarked that the purchase was part of a grand design of negotia-

22. Seward to Adams, March 28, 1867, Diplomatic Instructions. On Banks, see Fred Harvey Harrington, *Fighting Politician, Major-General N. P. Banks* (Philadelphia: University of Pennsylvania Press, 1948).

23. Stanley to Bruce, March 9, 1867, FO 5/1327. C. F. Adams to Seward, April 15, 1867, Diplomatic Despatches. Seward to Adams, April 16, May 2, 1867, Diplomatic Instructions.

24. Stanley to Bruce, May 24, 1867, FO 5/1327.

25. J. M. Callahan, *American Foreign Policy in Canadian Relations* (New York: Macmillan, 1937), p. 307.

tions which he hoped to bring to a successful end.[26] The Senate's ratification of the Alaska Treaty on June 30 removed the last obstacle to a diplomatic offensive on this subject. A day or two before, Charles Francis Adams, Jr., found him "all agog" about Alaska and was told that "the Alabama Claims would soon be settled, but *now* they could only be settled in one way, by such acquisition from England as would enable us to round off our North-Western territory."[27]

Minister Adams, however, was not affected by Seward's rosy visions. To the secretary's feelers on the question, Adams briskly replied that he did not think any new element could advantageously be introduced into the negotiations. The Derby government was satisfied with repairing Russell's blunder and had united English opinion in support of its stand. "In my belief," he summed up, "the maintenance of the connection with Canada is a matter of pride with the British nation which will only be made the more stubborn in resistance to change by the smallest indication on our part of a disposition to impair it."[28]

Adams seems to have thought that this settled the matter, but evidence suggests that Seward kept the idea of annexation in mind until well into 1868. His dispatch of August 12 seems extraordinarily vague, full of high-flown generalities and totally ignoring Stanley's previous caveats. The conclusion that he was trying to prolong the negotiations artificially in order to bring the British round to his own covert purposes is inescapable.

Neither Adams nor Lord Stanley saw it this way. Going over it together and weighing every word, they decided that "it proposed a fair chance of making a harmonious result." Seward had declared that he understood Stanley to offer arbitration on the question of the responsibility of the British government for the American losses. This was reasonable enough, he thought,

26. Diary of John Bigelow, April 3, 1867, Bigelow Papers.
27. C. F. Adams, Jr., to C. F. Adams, June 29, 1867, Adams Papers.
28. Adams to Seward, Aug. 2, 1867; C. F. Adams to C. F. Adams, Jr., July 15, 1867, Adams Papers.

but the actual proceedings and relations of the British government must be included in the adjudication and there must be no restrictions upon the terms of the arbitration. Although he spoke in wide and general terms, Seward was obviously trying to reintroduce the subject of the Neutrality Proclamation, which Stanley had already thrown out of the dispute. Why the latter saw some hope in the dispatch is not altogether clear, unless he thought that Seward was trying to leave room for compromise or retreat by being deliberately vague and evasive. He promised to discuss the two crucial paragraphs with his cabinet colleagues and return a definite answer. Before Adams left, the two discussed the choice of an arbitrator. Stanley felt that some limitation on the field of arbitration was essential, but agreed that perhaps this could be trusted to the umpire. There were only four strong powers that could take this role; America would not trust France, England would not accept Russia. Prussia and Austria remained. Adams replied that the United States would be perfectly willing to agree to either, and on this optimistic note the conversation ended.[29]

At their next meeting, on October 30, Stanley said that there was nothing left to argue about. The British people would accept an adverse judgment, but they would not hear of the submission of the Neutrality Proclamation to arbitration. No one in the country, not even John Bright, would agree to that. Seward replied almost immediately that the American people were as unanimous as the British in maintaining their beliefs. The point could not be conceded; it need cause no surprise that John Bright should react as an Englishman rather than as an American. In a letter to Charles Sumner, Seward expressed himself more freely. Bright he found "illogical." The Neutrality Proclamation was "unnecessary, ungracious, unfriendly, irritating and injurious," and he thought it twice as difficult for him to retreat, in the face

29. Seward to Adams, Aug. 12, 1867, Diplomatic Instructions. Adams to Seward, Sept. 13, 1867, Diplomatic Despatches. Adams Diary, Sept. 10, 1867.

of American public opinion, as it would be for the British to give way.[30]

With the rejection of the British offer in his pocket, Adams waited upon Lord Stanley on Christmas Eve. The American made no secret of his conviction that the negotiation was over and that nothing could be done until the new administration took office in fifteen months. To Adams' surprise, Stanley then produced a proposal from Seward to take all matters in dispute between the two countries — the Alabama Claims, the naturalization question, the San Juan water boundary, the fisheries — and make them the subject of a general negotiation. "I saw very clearly," wrote Adams in his diary, "the drift of this to be a bargain for the British territory in the North West, or the West India islands more or less in lieu of all demands. Mr. Seward's thirst for more land seems insatiable. I did not however hint at any such thing to his Lordship, for I know how entirely it would block up every avenue." Stanley did not understand the underlying implications of the offer. In the end it was taken into advisement and was ultimately dropped.[31]

Charles Francis Adams always thought that Seward had trifled with the great opportunity he was offered when Derby's government first took office. He doubted that the question of the Neutrality Proclamation could be arbitrated. Even if it could, Adams wondered whether the United States should question a sovereign right in this way and risk tying its own hands in the future. But in December 1867 his keen disappointment made

30. Adams Diary, Oct. 30, 1867. Seward to Adams, Nov. 16, 1867, Diplomatic Instructions. Seward to Sumner, Dec. 6, 1867, encl. in Sumner to Bright, Dec. 10, 1867, Bright Papers. The formal refusal of the British offer was made on November 29. Seward to Adams, Nov. 29, 1867, Diplomatic Instructions.

31. Adams Diary, Dec. 24, 1867. Adams to Seward, Dec. 24, 1867, Diplomatic Despatches. Seward to Adams, Jan. 13, 1868, Diplomatic Instructions. Seward wrote to Adams reporting sentiment in the Bahamas for annexation to the United States and suggesting them as payment for the Alabama Claims on Nov. 22, Diplomatic Instructions.

him attack both sides in the pages of his diary. Only a thin veil of pride separated the two. If Seward had admitted the right of Great Britain to decide when a neutrality proclamation should be issued and questioned only whether the way in which this one had been exercised had encouraged lawbreakers;[32] if the English had admitted that a little haste in the proclamation's issue should have meant greater vigilance thereafter, a settlement would have followed. "As it is, new parties must come in to tie the broken thread."[33] Adams had already sent in his resignation; the remainder of his term proved quiet, and in May 1868 he sailed for home.

32. As he almost had done in his original dispatch of Aug. 27, 1866.
33. Adams to Seward, April 15, 1867, Diplomatic Despatches. C. F. Adams to Henry Adams, Dec. 24, 1867, Adams Papers.

CHAPTER 3

In Brief Authority: Reverdy Johnson

When the news came that Charles Francis Adams was to leave the post he had filled so long and so well, a number of people in high places expected Seward to take the London mission. Impeachment of President Andrew Johnson was already under way; there were persistent rumors that the secretary and the president did not agree and that the Democrats would not give whole-hearted support to an administration which retained Seward. His old political manager, Thurlow Weed, favored his appointment and wrote him a letter advocating it which could be shown to the president to clinch the matter. But Seward would not hear of it, and Andrew Johnson had settled upon General George B. McClellan, commander of the Army of the Potomac during the first eighteen months of the war[1] and the Democratic nominee in 1864, almost as soon as he heard of the vacancy. Seward put forward two or three names, notably Hamilton Fish, but Johnson had made up his mind and nominated McClellan.[2] As might have been anticipated, the Senate

1. Not counting McDowell's First Manassas forces, nor Pope's Army of Virginia.
2. Thurlow Weed to Seward, Feb. 3, 1868; Seward to Weed, Feb. 5, 1868, Seward Papers, *Diary of Gideon Welles*, ed. by Howard K. Beale and Alan W. Brownsword (New York: Norton, 1960), III, 256-257, Jan. 11, 1868. John Bigelow, *Retrospections of an Active Life* (Garden City, N.Y.: Doubleday, Page, 1913), IV, 155, Diary, Feb. 21, 1868. LaWanda and John H. Cox, *Politics, Principle and Prejudice, 1865-1866: Dilemma*

majority would not have him. The president then selected
Reverdy Johnson, senator from Maryland, and this time the
Senate concurred.

Johnson seemed an excellent choice. He was the acknowledged
leader of the American bar; he had been a senator twice,
Zachary Taylor's attorney-general, and a strong Unionist in a
state dangerously attracted to secession. In Congress he had
emerged as the ablest of the War Democrats, and his vote for
the Military Reconstruction bill, lest the Radicals should be
driven into something worse, showed a disposition to accept
the results of the war three years before Clement L. Vallandig-
ham advocated the "New Departure." But in the intellectually
bankrupt Democracy of 1865-1870, with its standpat policy
of "the Constitution as it is, the Union as it was and the niggers
as they were," Johnson was accused of currying Radical favor
to have his son-in-law confirmed as United States attorney for
Maryland,[3] and the legislature of his state refused to re-elect him.
The president, remembering his services during impeachment,
was more forgiving.

In July, Charles Francis Adams told a correspondent that
"Mr. Reverdy Johnson, the new Minister, is now about to go
out under very favorable circumstances,"[4] and the diplomatic
outlook had indeed brightened since January. For the last two
years of his service in London, Adams had been vexed by problems connected with naturalization. The United States and
Great Britain held two conflicting views of the nature of allegiance. The British still maintained the feudal doctrine of indefeasible nationality: once a subject, always a subject, an un-
alterable status. On the other hand, the United States, a nation
of immigrants, affirmed the absolute rights of expatriation and
naturalization. Any man could throw off his old allegiance and

of *Reconstruction America* (New York: The Free Press of Glencoe, 1963),
p. 59.

3. *Diary of Gideon Welles,* pp. 55-56, March 2, 1867.

4. C. F. Adams to A. J. McClure, July 13, 1868, Adams Papers.

take up a new one, limited only by the laws of the country in which he made his home.[5]

Such matters might have remained in the realm of theory, had it not been for the Fenian efforts to raise rebellion in Ireland. In 1866 and 1867 large numbers of Americans were arrested in Ireland, many of them naturalized citizens. The British, well aware of American sensitivity to slights on their national dignity and wishing to avoid trouble, acted in conciliatory fashion. Most of the arrested Americans were quickly deported, and only nine of those most deeply involved in the Fenian rising of 1867 were brought to trial. But their incarceration raised a storm of protest in America, made more intense by Fenian propaganda which emphasized their gallant Civil War records and which created the impression that they were being imprisoned not for acts of treason in Ireland, but for words spoken and deeds done in the United States. Naturalization as U.S. citizens was no defense in the British courts, said the Fenians, for these Irishmen were born subjects of Queen Victoria, and their allegiance was indefeasible.[6]

Protest meetings were held throughout the United States, and a flood of petitions descended upon Congress.[7] "No subject has ever shown greater unanimity of opinion than this demand for the protection of American citizens resident or travelling in foreign states," summed up a report of the House Committee on Foreign Affairs.[8] Seward told Adams that the British action "has awakened a general feeling of resentment and deeply wounded our pride of sovereignty. The people are appealing to

5. Adams to Seward, Feb. 22, 1866, Diplomatic Despatches.

6. Seward to Adams, Sept. 20, 24, Oct. 3, 31, Nov. 15, 18, 27, Dec. 14, 1867, Diplomatic Instructions. Adams to Seward, Aug. 23, Sept. 3, Oct. 10, 12, 19, Nov. 1, 5, 16, 18, 29, Dec. 21, 24, 1867, Diplomatic Despatches.

7. *Cong. Globe*, 40 Cong., 2 sess., pp. 5-6, 128, 268, 316-317, 342, 385, 403, 417, 420, 433, 452-453, 636, 637, 638, 649, 650, 673, 675, 687, 764, 765, 781-782, 815, 1334, 1759, 2165, 3364.

8. Quoted by Representative Charles W. Willard of Vermont on Feb. 15, 1870, *Cong. Globe,* 41 Cong., 2 sess., Appendix, p. 97.

this government throughout the whole country, from Portland to San Francisco and from St. Paul to Pensacola."[9] Fortunately for the cause of peace, Lord Stanley did not long maintain the vast British pretensions. Early in 1868 he agreed to give up all claims to indefeasible allegiance and sign a naturalization treaty similar to the one the United States had just negotiated with the North German Confederation, though he insisted on waiting for the report of a Royal Commission on the naturalization, inheritance, and succession laws before actually drawing up terms.[10]

In his original proposal to make a treaty with England like the one the United States had negotiated with Bismarck, Seward had added that he would reserve his suggestions on the Alabama Claims, "because the views I shall have occasion to submit on those subjects will be greatly influenced by the result of the anticipated proceedings in regard to naturalization."[11] A few days later the Secretary outlined to Edward Thornton, the new British minister in Washington, a four-stage plan to end all disagreement between Britain and America. A treaty like the North German one should settle the naturalization question; the San Juan water boundary should be referred to the arbitration of Switzerland.[12] A "sparing and prudent" clemency would be

9. Seward to Adams, Jan. 13, 1868, Diplomatic Instructions.
10. Adams Diary, Feb. 15, 1868. Adams to Seward, Feb. 18, March 28, April 11, 1868, Diplomatic Despatches. Seward to Adams, Feb. 14, March 7, 1868, Diplomatic Instructions. Telegrams from Edward Thornton to Stanley, March 8, 11, (two), 1868; Thornton to Stanley, March 14, 21, 1868, FO 5/1356. Stanley to Thornton, March 16, 1868, FO 5/1126.
11. Seward to Adams, March 7, 1868, Diplomatic Instructions.
12. This dispute concerned San Juan Island, the military key to Vancouver Straits. In the treaty negotiated by President James K. Polk and Secretary of State James Buchanan with Lord Aberdeen to settle the Oregon boundary crisis, the dividing line between Vancouver Island and the mainland was declared to be "the middle of the channel" which ran between them. Britain declared that this was the one to the east of San Juan; the Americans argued that it was the strait to the west. The quarrel remained unsettled for some years until the island was

exercised toward the Fenian prisoners; and "the existing irritation will be so far relieved that I think it beyond doubt that we
can provide for adjusting the Alabama and other claims in a
manner practically unobjectionable in either country."[13] Seward
managed to convince Thornton that his proposition on the
claims would be "acceptable." But what would that proposition
have been?[14]

In July, Seward suggested that all claims, British and American, should go before a joint commission like the one set up
in 1853 to adjudicate claims by Americans against Britain and
by Britons against the United States.[15] This is probably what
he would have offered in the spring. If he was bluffing when he
promised favorable terms after a naturalization treaty was
signed, he certainly carried the deception unusually far: "I
have a hope that all our difficulties with Great Britain may now
be settled," he wrote in a private letter to Henry S. Sanford,
the American minister in Brussels.[16] Everything indicates that
Seward was quite sincere in his offer. In the first week of February he was inveighing against Stanley's conditions;[17] his change
of mind by July is easily explained by his ambition to negotiate
a settlement. More difficult to explain, we know that in late
January, Seward was still thinking of taking British Columbia
as the equivalent of the Alabama Claims. At that time he expected the British to agree to his December idea of a negotiation in which "all grievances on both sides would be thrown

populated, and a sudden crisis erupted in 1859 when an American shot
a pig belonging to the Hudson's Bay Company. Joint military occupation
followed, and the two countries agreed to submit the matter to the decision of the president of the Swiss Confederation. The outbreak of the
Civil War prevented this.

13. Seward to Adams, March 23, 1868, Diplomatic Instructions.
14. Telegrams from Thornton to Stanley, March 20, 1868, FO 5/1129.
15. Seward to Reverdy Johnson, July 20, 1868, Diplomatic Instruc-
tion.
16. Seward to Sanford, March 23, 1868, Seward Papers.
17. Seward to Hinton Rowan Helper, Feb. 5, 1868, Seward Papers.

into a heap, and one would be taken out to balance another
until all were disposed of," and he believed this was the way
he would obtain a territorial accession.[18] Yet something besides
Lord Stanley's casual rejection of the scheme on February 15[19]
must have made Seward drop the idea of annexation.

What made Seward adopt an expansionist policy in the first
place? Gideon Welles thought he aimed to run for president
on the Democratic ticket, with territorial expansion as his cry.[20]
The possibility of his nomination was certainly discussed by
people close to Seward, but there is no evidence to show that
he ever thought of it. Thurlow Weed held it impossible,[21] and
Seward should have too: no newspaper ever even mentioned
his name in that connection, and if the Democrats thought of
seizing the middle ground by nominating a conservative Republican, the man they mentioned was Chief Justice Salmon
P. Chase, or, fleetingly, Charles Francis Adams.[22] It is much
more likely that Seward was quite simply bidding for popular
favor once more, as the Russian Minister Edouard de Stoeckl
thought during the Alaska negotiation, and was fulfilling his
desire to make a great record as secretary of state.[23] During the
spring of 1868 it must have been evident to him, first, that the
British would not lightly give up Canada, and second, that
expansionism was not proving the tonic he had hoped either

18. *The Diary of Orville Hickman Browning,* ed., introd., and notes
by James G. Randall (Springfield, Ill.: Trustees of the Illinois State
Historical Library, n.d.), II, 177, Jan. 28, 1868.
19. C. F. Adams to Seward, Feb. 18, 1868, Diplomatic Despatches.
20. *Diary of Gideon Welles,* pp. 106-107, 120, 125, 163, June 14,
26, July 2, Aug. 9, 1867.
21. *Bigelow, Retrospections,* IV, 182, Diary, May 19, 1868.
22. Charles H. Coleman, *The Election of 1868: The Democratic Effort
to Regain Control.* (New York: Columbia University Press, 1933), p.
185.
23. Frank A. Golder, "The Purchase of Alaska," *American Historical
Review,* 25 (1919-1920), 425. *Diary of Gideon Welles,* p. 504, Jan. 12,
1869.

for his popularity or his reputation. Ratification of the Alaska purchase had been a struggle; the Senate had conspicuously ignored the treaty for the sale of the Danish West Indies ever since December; and ridicule was mounting.

Meanwhile, Seward put pressure on Stanley to sign a naturalization treaty right away. Objections which the Crown law officers had made to terms similar to the United States–North German ones were bounced back at once with a rebuttal, and three days later the secretary proposed that "the great principle of expatriation and naturalization" should be laid down immediately and other details left until later.[24] Seward instructed Adams to tell Lord Stanley that American opinion would grow no easier to placate and that in Britain the Irish church fracas obviously threatened political stability and would disturb diplomatic negotiations.[25] On May 27, Seward ordered Benjamin Moran, chargé d'affaires in London after Adams' departure earlier that month, to sound Stanley again about signing a treaty like the North German one. "Had such a treaty been in existence," he ended, "I think it would have avoided most of the trouble and difficulties which have arisen between the two governments during the last three years."[26] Late in June, Seward sent Moran a House resolution requesting the president to take measures for the release of two of the Fenian prisoners; the secretary added a long remonstrance about the English obstinacy and alluded to the reprisals bill. And he repeatedly warned that Stanley's attitude was a "serious embarrassment" to him in preserving the peace on the Canadian border, where a new Fenian *razzia* was expected. Delay, Seward repeated, was hazardous; the issue was a gift to agitators. Upon one occasion, he even told Thornton that "whatever danger there may be of a

24. Telegram of Thornton to Stanley, March 27, 1868, FO 5/1129. Thornton to Stanley, March 30, 1868. FO 5/1356.
25. Seward to Adams, April 24, 1868, Diplomatic Instructions.
26. Seward to Moran, May 27, 1868, Diplomatic Instructions.

disturbance of the peace of the frontier at the present time, that danger is altogether due to British policy on naturalized citizens' rights."[27]

But none of this made any impression on Stanley. Negotiating before the Royal Commission on the laws of naturalization reported was putting the cart before the horse, he told Moran. And, in any case, there would be no time in the current session to pass an act giving legislative force to the recommendations of a treaty. A treaty alone was worse than useless, and the best thing to do was to let it wait until the new session of Parliament in November.[28]

Naturalization was uppermost in Seward's mind when he wrote Reverdy Johnson's instructions in July. The United States, the secretary said, preserved a rigid neutrality toward the Fenian movement. But this involved so much difficulty and inconvenience that the U.S. was entitled to a similar consideration and liberality from Great Britain. Instead, the British were acting in a way that would result in an "extensive and profound alienation" of the two countries. Great Britain's policy of procrastination did her no good and only crippled attempts to spread cordiality and good feelings in America. Naturalization was the most important question outstanding and must be settled before any of the other sores could be healed. Should Stanley agree, the American treaties with the North German Confederation, Bavaria, and Württemberg should be used as a model in negotiating.

After solving the naturalization question, the San Juan problem should be taken; the United States was willing to refer this to arbitration. Only then was Johnson to turn to the Alabama Claims. Seward thought that, without reviewing previous discussions (which would bring up the Neutrality Proclamation), the two countries might agree on a joint commission. (This

27. Seward to Moran, June 22, 1868, Diplomatic Instructions. Notes of Seward to Thornton, May 28, June 9, 1868, Notes to the British Legation.
28. Moran to Seward, June 16, 1868, Diplomatic Despatches. Stanley to Thornton, June 16, 1868, FO 5/1356.

would leave the terms of reference open and let the commission itself decide whether to include the timing and effect of the Neutrality Proclamation in the arbitration.) But Johnson was only to sound Lord Stanley about this course and was not to commit the United States to it. Since he was only to introduce this after San Juan and naturalization were safely tucked away, it seems unlikely that Seward really expected to gain an Alabama Claims settlement in the seven months left to him, although he hoped the new administration and the reformed British government could start relations with a clean slate.[29]

When Reverdy Johnson arrived in London in mid-August, he found court and Parliament scattered and both the Queen and Lord Stanley on the Continent. It was September 10 before he met the foreign secretary, the 14th when he was presented to the Queen, and the 25th by the time negotiations started.[30] In the meantime, Seward had fired off two more complaints about the "entire in-attention" of the British to his protests about the naturalization issue, the difficulties of repressing the Fenians under such circumstances, and the inflammability of American public opinion. It was vital, he wrote, that the naturalization quarrel should be settled before Congress met in December.[31]

However, when he heard that Parliament could not pass a naturalization law until the spring, Seward gave Johnson the power to go on with the other negotiations once he was convinced that a satisfactory arrangement could be made on the first question. But he made a large reservation: such negotiations could not be completed or considered binding until either a naturalization treaty or a law was safely delivered.[32] Johnson tried to persuade Stanley into a convention with the argument

29. Seward to Johnson, July 20, Sept. 23, 1868, Diplomatic Instructions.

30. Johnson to Seward, Aug. 29, Sept. 15, 25, 1868, Diplomatic Despatches.

31. Seward to Johnson, Aug. 27, Sept. 23, 1868, Diplomatic Instructions.

32. Johnson to Seward, Sept. 12, 1868, Diplomatic Despatches. Seward to Johnson, Sept. 23, 1868, Diplomatic Instructions.

that the British should put their desire for a settlement on record and that it need not go into effect until the Royal Commission reported and Parliament acted. But Stanley would have none of this, and Johnson had to be satisfied with a protocol of principles, which the two signed on October 9.[33]

In this document, said Henry Adams, "the British Government abandoned all its old theories of citizenship, and conceded all, and more than all, that had ever been asked by the United States."[34] Its terms were wider than the North German ones; there was no five-year waiting period after naturalization before the country of birth abandoned its claims. A native subject of Great Britain who had become naturalized in the United States ceased to hold any allegiance to the Queen, and if he ever re-entered British jurisdiction the authorities were bound to consider him "in all respects and for all purposes" an American citizen.[35] Seward thought the protocol "brief, simple, effective, and therefore as satisfactory as any arrangement that could be made without waiting for legislation," and he commended Johnson.[36]

The minister then turned to the San Juan dispute, and in a week had signed a protocol for its settlement, by arbitration.[37] Seward, excited, cabled, "Can you hasten claims convention?"[38] He had probably wished that the Alabama Claims could be liquidated but had not believed this was likely in the short time remaining of his term. Seward was proud of his record as secretary of state, of the number of treaties he had negotiated —

33. Stanley to Thornton, Oct. 9, 1868, FO 5/1356. Johnson to Seward, Sept. 25, Oct. 7; 9, 1868; Telegram of Johnson to Seward, Oct. 9, 1868, Diplomatic Despatches. Telegram of Seward to Johnson, Oct. 7, 1868, Diplomatic Instructions.

34. Henry Adams, "The Session," *North American Review*, April 1869, p. 630.

35. Johnson to Seward, Oct. 9, 1868, Diplomatic Despatches.

36. Seward to Johnson, Oct. 26, 1868, Diplomatic Instructions.

37. Johnson to Seward, Oct. 17, 1868, Diplomatic Despatches.

38. Telegram of Seward to Johnson, Oct. 25, 1868, Diplomatic Instructions.

as many as had been made during the whole previous existence of the Republic — and of his diplomatic prowess.[39] It was only natural that he should jump at the chance of settling the Alabama Claims.

Johnson had already asked for power to sign a claims convention modeled on the 1853 treaty and had inquired if he could consent to leave everything to the king of Prussia's arbitration. Seward agreed that the instrument should follow the 1853 agreement, but ordered Johnson to refrain from naming the arbitrator. The convention would have to go before the Senate and the country, and objections would inevitably be raised to anyone named in advance. When the convention went into effect the two governments could always tell the commissioners to agree upon an arbitrator acceptable to both of them.[40] With this in mind, Johnson went ahead at incredible speed. In a mere ten days the convention was made and on November 4, Johnson wrote Seward that he had just emerged from final consultations with Stanley and Attorney-General Sir John Karslake. The Queen and the cabinet had to examine their work, but otherwise it was all over but the signing. The minister explained that he had hurried the negotiation to get it over while the Disraeli government still retained its feeble grasp on office. Though he knew the Liberals would look favorably upon an accommodation with America, he feared they might ask for modified terms and throw the negotiations back to the start.[41] So far, everything was perfect. And then, suddenly, things began to go wrong.

Seward received the San Juan protocol and immediately cabled that the president of the Swiss Federal Council must

39. *Diary of Gideon Welles,* pp. 76, 504, March 30, 1867, Jan. 12, 1869.

40. Two telegrams of Johnson to Seward, Oct. 20, 1868, Diplomatic Despatches. Telegram of Seward to Johnson, Oct. 24, 1868, Diplomatic Instructions. Telegram of W. Hunter to Seward, Oct. 20, 1868, Seward Papers.

41. Johnson to Seward, Nov. 4, 1868, Diplomatic Despatches.

be named as the arbitrator. Probably he wanted to present the agreement as exactly the same one that the Senate had approved in 1860. Stanley made no objection to this, and the change was formalized in a supplementary protocol.[42] Then, on November 11, without having received the full text of the claims convention, Seward cabled that it was "absolutely essential" that the commission that would be formed sit in Washington. Johnson replied that he would try to secure this, but the idea was completely new to him. He had agreed to London as the meeting place of the commission because most of the claims would be concerned with the Confederate cruisers, and all the evidence was in England. The umpire would almost certainly be a European head of state, and much time would be lost in communicating with him from Washington. There was nothing about this in his instructions; and Johnson, with the expertise of the great courtroom lawyer, flourished a dispatch which Seward had written to Adams in 1862 saying that choice of a meeting place was not important enough to insist on if an agreement was made to arbitrate.[43] Stanley once more proved complaisant, the alteration was made, and things began to look bright again. On November 24, Johnson cabled asking whether the San Juan protocol could be made a convention, an obvious step toward a full and final settlement. No answer came and, puzzled, he cabled once more on the 26th.[44] Later that day his answer came, a real bombshell: "Let San Juan rest. Claims convention unless amended is useless."[45]

42. Telegram of Seward to Johnson, Nov. 7, 1868, Diplomatic Instructions. Telegram of Johnson to Seward, Nov. 7, 1868; Johnson to Seward, Nov. 10, 1868, Diplomatic Despatches.

43. Telegrams of Seward to Johnson, Nov. 11, 12, 1868, Diplomatic Instructions. Telegrams of Johnson to Seward, Nov. 12, 16, 24, 1868; Dispatches of Johnson to Seward, Nov. 14, 23, 1868, Diplomatic Despatches.

44. Telegrams of Johnson to Seward, Nov. 24, 26, 1868, Diplomatic Despatches.

45. Telegram of Seward to Johnson, Nov. 26, 1868, Diplomatic Instructions.

Seward managed to give his fellow cabinet members the impression that Reverdy Johnson had bungled the negotiations. Orville Hickman Browning, secretary of the interior, found Seward "greatly disappointed." He "announced the failure of the negotiations for the settlement of the Alabama Claims, saying that Mr. Johnson had exceeded his instructions and assented to terms which were inadmissible . . . Mr. Johnson's failure to bring the matter to a satisfactory conclusion had made him sick."[46] Gideon Welles, viewing the scene with more malice, thought that Seward had "a queer expression on his countenance" when he entered the cabinet room. The two of them were the first arrivals, and Welles asked Seward what was wrong. The secretary of state said he was "sick, quite sick." He had got "the damnedst strange thing from Reverdy Johnson for a protocol." He submitted the document to the president and cabinet "with a lugubrious look which cannot be described. Intended to be sad and grieved, but with a lurking laugh. . . . The whole thing, he said, was wrong, contrary to instructions, must be sent back."[47]

Seward told Johnson that use of the cable had proved deceitful. He expected Johnson to adhere more closely to the 1853 convention than he had and wrote his cable dispatches under that impression. However, these telegrams might have been interpreted by Johnson as approving his course.[48] Johnson did not exceed instructions because he had none on the Alabama Claims and only inadequate ones on San Juan. The true burden of responsibility for the muddle and mistakes of the Johnson negotiations must fall on Seward. He gave only an outline as a guide and encouraged Johnson to press on at frantic speed, instead of ordering him to cable the convention part by part for approval. Despite his long tenure in the State Department, Seward was

---

46. *Diary of Orville Hickman Browning,* pp. 227-228, Nov. 24, 1868.
47. *Diary of Gideon Welles,* p. 468, Nov. 24, 1868. Hearing such reports, Reverdy Johnson protested to Seward, Nov. 28, 1868, Diplomatic Despatches.
48. Seward to Johnson, Nov. 27, 1868, Diplomatic Instructions.

not practiced in negotiating constructively from a distance. He had gained his diplomatic experience during the war years, when the sole questions of policy were deterrent: to stop the powers of Europe from aiding the Confederacy. He either negotiated treaties himself (like the purchase of Alaska) or he gave his plenipotentiaries a general statement of what he wanted and accepted what they could get (like the Bancroft-Bismarck naturalization treaty). This system was bound to come to grief sooner or later, and it was Reverdy Johnson's bad luck that the disaster happened to him.

Between November 24 and 27, the members of the cabinet considered the terms of the Johnson-Stanley convention. Gideon Welles went to see the president and found him anxious to submit the treaty as it was. He was not sure what Seward thought was wrong with it, and Welles advised him to wait until the Friday cabinet meeting when the secretary of state would present his draft dispatch to Reverdy Johnson.[49]

When Friday came, the gravamen of Seward's objections proved to be that the treaty discriminated against the Alabama Claims. It provided that a joint commission should be set up to consider all British and American claims. These, of course, included the Alabama Claims. But, before they came before the commission, the two governments could fix upon a head of state as an arbitrator, to whom these claims alone would be referred if the four commissioners could not unanimously agree upon them. Seward said this singled out the Alabama Claims invidiously; all the others were to be decided by a majority vote of the commissioners, and if there was deadlock an arbitrator, chosen either by their agreement or by lot, should decide.[50]

Such a limitation could not be accepted; the Alabama Claims

49. *Diary of Gideon Welles,* pp. 469-470, Nov. 25, 1868.

50. Seward to Johnson, Nov. 27, 1868, Diplomatic Instructions. Seward wanted to put all the claims on the same footing to avoid the criticism that more was being done for British claims against America than for the Alabama Claims. Thornton to Clarendon, Jan. 5, 1869, Clarendon Papers, Bodleian.

should be treated just like the others. Again, the article dealing with evidence required that only the official correspondence about the Alabama Claims should be presented to the commissioners or the arbitrator, though they could call for verbal argument or additional evidence if they wanted to. Seward thought that either government should be left free to submit evidence and argument as it liked. In making these objections, Seward was wasting his time. The future showed that Reverdy Johnson's convention had many faults, but Seward did not discover them. His amendments of minor matters of procedure left the flawed principles untouched.

Seward's draft came under heavy fire from his colleagues. The president especially appreciated the British agreement to arbitrate. All the cases would have to go to the arbitrator, and it did not matter whether one or all of the commissioners sent them there. Browning and Attorney-General William M. Evarts would have liked the terms modified so that the only discrimination as to the Alabama Claims should be in the selection of a head of state as arbitrator.[51] Secretary of the Treasury Hugh McCulloch wanted to know whether Seward would accept the protocol if he could not get better terms, but the latter confidently replied that the English would certainly yield. Finally, the president said that a decision on the dispatch would be made the following Tuesday. Seward was up in arms at this, wanted to cable that afternoon, and claimed he could get a favorable answer within the week. The president asked Welles into the library and told him that "he wished the subject disposed of during his Administration or that the Senate should be responsible for the delay." Welles replied that he had no great confidence in Seward; nevertheless, he would be offended if others tried to rule him, and he might as well be given a chance to see what he could get. The president agreed, and, going back into the council room, he told Seward to cable.[52]

51. *Diary of Orville Hickman Browning*, p. 228, Nov. 27, 1868.
52. *Diary of Gideon Welles*, pp. 470-471, Nov. 27, 1868.

Within a few hours, the new terms were on their way to Reverdy Johnson, who was sorely puzzled and could think of nothing that he had done wrong. Seward added that he considered the changes essential to ratification by the Senate and auhorized Johnson to apologize to the British and tell them that there had been a genuine misunderstanding. If Stanley agreed to the changes, Seward thought it would be better to make a protocol rather than a convention: a welcome sign of caution. Yet, in his cable, he stressed that "time is important." It had already run out; the Disraeli government had only days to live, and Gladstone, with Lord Clarendon as his foreign secretary, took office on December 10.[53] Consequently, the claims convention had to wait, and George Bancroft, United States minister to the North German Confederation, trying to pump the British ambassador in Berlin, complained that "in an hour's conversation, I could not get one word out of him on the subject."[54]

Neither Stanley nor Clarendon took kindly to Seward's proposed changes. They agreed that the Alabama Claims raised such issues that an arbitrator of dignity, authority, and stature was needed, and that either government would find it easier to defer to the judgment of a head of state than they would to an ordinary arbitrator's, however eminent he might be.[55] Clarendon offered a watered-down version of the original: if the four commissioners, or two of them, found themselves unable to decide any claim and thought that it should be left to the arbitration of a foreign state, they should report this to their govern-

53. Telegram from Seward to Johnson, Nov. 27, 1868; Seward to Johnson, Nov. 27, 1868, Diplomatic Instructions. Johnson to Seward, Nov. 28, 1868, Diplomatic Despatches. Edmund Hammond to Thornton, Dec. 19, 1868; Clarendon to Thornton, Dec. 26, 1868, Clarendon Papers, Bodleian. Clarendon was against making a protocol first because he did not want the treaty to face the Senate twice.

54. George Bancroft to Seward, Dec. 19, 1868, Seward Papers.

55. Johnson to Seward, Dec. 5, 16, 1868, Diplomatic Despatches.

ments, who would agree upon a suitable head of state within six months.[56]

This provided for the Alabama Claims, implicitly, rather than explicitly. Seward wanted a fuller version; the commissioners should first name someone as arbitrator, and any claim they could not decide upon would go to him. On any and every claim, the arbitrator could be a head of state, and in choosing him the commissioners could refer to their governments for instructions; the two governments should agree on someone within six months. If they failed to do so, each pair of commissioners should name someone, who could be a head of state or not, just as they chose. When they found themselves unable to pronounce upon a claim, lots should be cast to decide which arbitrator, the British nominee or the American, should make the ruling.[57]

Clarendon did not mind the first part of this, but he said that the second part, concerned with what should be done if the two governments did not agree upon an arbitrator, was impossible. It questioned the good faith of the nations by implying they might not be able to agree on such a matter. And no head of state would accept a call from the commissioners, thinking it discourteous to the governments to take up such a charge. Neither would the foreign secretary make the agreement a protocol, instead of a convention. Seward's suggestion that it should be signed in Washington he thought an insult to Stanley and the Derby-Disraeli government. He was fully supported on all these points by the cabinet.[58] Privately, Johnson warned Seward that the British suspected he did not want a settlement by arbitration. The minister had succeeded in removing this impression for the time being, but it remained in the British mind, strengthened by the unfortunate appointment of a known Fenian

56. Telegram from Johnson to Seward, Dec. 18, 1868, Diplomatic Despatches.
57. Seward to Johnson, Dec. 20, 1868, Diplomatic Despatches.
58. Johnson to Seward, Dec. 23, 24, 1868, Diplomatic Despatches.

to be United States consul at Leeds. The cabinet was united in the opinion that Seward was asking for more than could be honorably conceded, more than was necessary for a settlement, and no one believed so more strongly than such friends of America as John Bright and the Duke of Argyll.[59]

There, from Christmas until the middle of January, the negotiations rested, since the steamer carrying Reverdy Johnson's dispatches was delayed. When an answer eventually came from Seward, it contained a complete capitulation on terms. He disputed only a few matters of phrasing.[60] These were quickly arranged, and on January 14 the three treaties dealing with naturalization, San Juan, and the claims were signed.

The claims convention provided "a full and final settlement." All claims by citizens of Great Britain or the United States upon the other country were to go before a commission of four, two from each country. The commission would sit at Washington. The commissioners were to agree upon an arbitrator, and any claim they could not decide was to be submitted to his final decision. If they could not agree upon one person, each side was to appoint an arbitrator, and lots should be cast to decide which arbitrator should rule on each disputed claim. But if the commissioners, or any two of them, wished a head of state to arbitrate any claim (this meant the Alabama Claims), they should report this to their respective govern-

59. Johnson to Seward, Dec. 26, 1868, Seward Papers.
60. Seward to Johnson, Jan. 12, 1869, Diplomatic Instructions. However, when he first saw the British reply, Seward despaired of achieving a treaty that would satisfy both the government in London and the Senate in Washington. Their proposal, he said, would be interpreted as distinguishing between the Alabama Claims and the other claims, and neither the Senate nor the American people would approve that. Thornton also detected wounded vanity in Seward's attitude, for he had been "extremely proud" of his December 20 formula, "though it is in general miserably weak and confused." After many objections and much talk, "not of an entirely pleasant nature," the secretary of state finally gave in. Thornton to Clarendon, Jan. 12, 1869, Clarendon Papers, Bodleian.

ments, who, in their turn, were to appoint one within six months. As to evidence, the commissioners and the ordinary arbitrators were to be given the official correspondence between the two governments on the claims and any statements either nation wanted to make, and they were to hear one person advocate the case of each side on every claim. The head of state, however, was to be given only the written evidence. If a decision involving compensation was arrived at by either kind of arbitrator, the amount was to be set by the commissioners. If they could not agree, it was to be decided by the arbitrator who handed down the decision.[61]

For all his quibbling and objections, Seward had gained remarkably little. Instead of being made the subject of an explicit reservation, the Alabama Claims were now dealt with by an implicit understanding. Both Stanley and Clarendon had yielded on the Neutrality Proclamation, which would obviously be brought into the arbitration by the Americans. But they had saved British face by not letting it in openly themselves, and they were free to complain about its introduction if necessary. The vital point was that the British government had not admitted that a former ministry had been biased against, or actively hostile to, the United States.

Reverdy Johnson was firmly convinced that the convention gave America all she wanted and had no doubt that it would be ratified by the Senate.[62] But criticism of its terms began as soon as they were known. John M. Forbes, seizing upon the provision to select arbitrators by lot, if necessary (as it certainly would have been), wrote of "Seward's *gambling* treaty. . . . Just imagine old Reverdy Johnson, or Seward himself throwing the dice as each claim came up, to determine whether it should go to the Yankee umpire or the Blockade Raising Umpire! or in other words whether each claim should be paid or go into the

61. Johnson to Seward, Jan. 15, 1869, Diplomatic Despatches.
62. Johnson to Seward, Jan. 13, 1869, Seward Papers. Johnson to William Pitt Fessenden, Nov. 13, 1868, Fessenden Papers.

---

fire! I really think this gambling scheme ... well worthy of a certain class of old Washington Politicians of the (I hope) bygone type of Slidell and Co."[63]

When Seward first brought up the claims convention in the cabinet, Gideon Welles had told him that if the British were allowed to claim for captured blockade-runners, it should not be signed. Evarts estimated such British claims against the United States at $100 million, the American shipping losses at only $8 million. Meeting Seward on December 4, Welles asked him point-blank about the convention: "Does it embrace claims of Englishmen for cotton and other property captured or destroyed during the War?" Seward replied emphatically, "No, it does not." "And, of course," continued Welles, "this shuts off any claim for prizes condemned in our courts." "Shuts off all," said Seward, "they do not come within the treaty," and he added that nothing which came within the United States' admiralty or local jurisdiction was to be included in the arbitration. Within enemy's limits, the British suffered like other belligerents. Welles told Seward the Johnson-Clarendon Convention was wholly adverse to America. The secretary of state's only defense was that he could not have secured a treaty unless it included all claims on both sides.[64]

The New York *Evening Post* said the claims for the British blockade-runners and the plundered American merchantmen were treated as exactly equal. The claims for confiscated blockade-runners were "ludicrous." If the blockade was lawful, they were forfeit by the laws of war. If it was not, they were smugglers and forfeit by the revenue laws. Even worse, the treaty did not even mention the question of international law upon which the American claims depended: was a government responsible for a warlike expedition fitted out in its own ports

63. John M. Forbes to Sumner, Feb. 1, 1869, Sumner Papers.
64. *Diary of Gideon Welles*, III, 470, 474, 506-507, Nov. 25, Dec. 4, 1868; Jan. 15, 1869.

against a friendly power? Lord Stanley, standing at the dispatch box, had admitted that it was, but the treaty did not.[65]

Seward had adopted a reckless and dangerous course. He habitually talked big, bigger than truth, and this explains his conversation of December 4 with Welles. But, having been warned of the danger, why did Seward do nothing about it? Possibly he expected the arbitrator to throw out such British claims. If so, he was sailing dangerously near the wind, remembering the system of choice by lots; and though the submission of those claims to the head of state would have solved that problem, the very fact of their admission would have given them some chance of award. Seward was naturally inclined toward optimism,[66] and this explains his behavior when negotiating and his surprise later when the convention was not ratified by the Senate. But his conduct over the British claims can less be called optimism than a pathological desire to look on the bright side, a refusal to face facts.

The Johnson-Clarendon Convention was a bad treaty. The machinery it set up was cumbersome, slow, and so involved that it would have stood a good chance of creating more disputes than it settled. It was desperately vague on points of crucial importance, the system of choice by lots was ridiculous, and it made no provision for international law for the future. At the very least, the British claims should have been restricted to real estate and property in British hands on April 15, 1861. Nevertheless, if the Senate vote had been taken solely on the merit of its terms, the convention might well have passed. Charles Sumner wrote that it would have been ratified almost unanimously at any time during 1868, and Henry Adams agreed with him.[67] American public opinion was aroused against the convention by other things besides its own nature.

65. Jan. 23, 1869.
66. Frederick Bancroft, *Life of William H. Seward* (New York: Harper, 1900), I, 194-196, 198.
67. Hamilton Fish to John C. Hamilton, April 22, 1869, Fish Papers,

The major one was the behavior of Reverdy Johnson. Though no one admitted it at the time, the minister had shown great ability and shrewdness in conducting a difficult negotiation, and the misconceptions of the agreement were Seward's, not his. Johnson was kind, genial, pacific, easily flattered, disliked quarreling, and was inclined to be sentimental. American reaction to the news of his appointment and his farewell to the Senate had convinced him that the country was behind him.[68] Well they might: his fellow senators, who sincerely respected his erudition and honesty, unanimously confirmed the nomination without the usual reference to a committee and, at the conclusion of his valedictory speech, "the Senators rose simultaneously and advanced towards the retiring Senator to grasp him by the hand and wish him success in his new sphere of public duty."[69] Republican newspapers welcomed his appointment;[70] even the *New York Herald* found him "satisfactory."[71] Johnson did not realize that the Senate only confirmed him because they thought he was the best they would get from Andrew Johnson. As *Harper's Weekly* pointed out, "If the only points to be considered were personal fitness and intellectual accomplishment, the United States could have no better minister." But he was not representative of the nation.[72]

Reverdy Johnson left America with the impression that public opinion was at his beck and call; though he knew Andrew Johnson was finished in national politics, he told Thomas H. Dudley, United States consul at Liverpool, that he expected to hold the

---

L. C. Sumner to Bright, Jan. 17, 1869, printed in Edward L. Pierce, *Memoir and Letters of Charles Sumner* (Boston: Robert Brothers, 1894), IV, 368. Henry Adams to Bright, May 30, 1869, Bright Papers.

68. C. F. Adams to W. R. Forster, June 4, 1869, Adams Papers.

69. *Cong. Globe,* 40 Cong., 2 sess., p. 3870, July 9, 1868.

70. San Francisco *Daily Evening Bulletin,* June 15, 1869. Newbury *Aurora of the Valley and Vermont Cultivator,* June 27, 1868.

71. July 22, 1868.

72. July 4, 1868.

English mission for five years.[73] He reached England to find the warmest and most cordial of welcomes, even in pro-Confederate Liverpool.[74] It is surprising that his head was not turned far more than it was; Johnson was not a people's politician, for this was long before the popular election of senators, and to this unaccustomed mass adulation he reacted, as most people would, a little foolishly. Johnson decided that the whole population of Britain wanted to be friends with America and that it was his duty to promote this "friendly international feeling." But he soon came across Englishmen who did not share such feelings — and treated them as though they did. He hobnobbed with Lord Wharncliffe, erstwhile head of the Southern Rights Association, shook hands with Laird, the unabashed and unrepentant builder of the *Alabama,* sat through an anti-American tirade by J. A. Roebuck at the Cutler's Banquet in Sheffield, and took the chair at the dinner of a company headed by Emile Erlanger, negotiator of the Confederate cotton loan.[75]

When news of such doings reached America, public opinion was outraged. Edwin M. Stanton fumed that the Senate should have voted to send Reverdy Johnson to the infernal regions, not to England. "He did not know what use it was to have a hell except to roast such men as Johnson."[76] A constituent of Charles Sumner's called the minister "too eager for self-popularity to be . . . judicious," and another declared that diplomacy "can

73. Reverdy Johnson to Sumner, Oct. 10, 1868, Sumner Papers. Adams Diary, Nov. 16, 1868.
74. Johnson to Sumner, Oct. 10, 1868, Sumner Papers. Reverdy Johnson, *A Reply to a Recent Speech of Sir Roundell Palmer on the Washington Treaty and the Alabama Claims* (Baltimore: John Murphy, 1871), p. 37. Johnson to Seward, Aug. 19, 1868, Seward Papers. Johnson to William Pitt Fessenden, Nov. 13, 1868, Fessenden Papers.
75. Bertrand C. E. Steiner, *Life of Reverdy Johnson* (Baltimore: Norman Remington, 1914), p. 243. Johnson to Fessenden, Nov. 13, 1868, Fessenden Papers. Johnson to Sumner, Oct. 10, 1868, Sumner Papers. Benjamin Moran to Thurlow Weed, Jan. 9, 1869, Weed Papers.
76. Samuel Hooper to Sumner, Nov. 17, 1868, Sumner Papers.

all be done without the intervention of a large number of dinners, hugh [sic] sirloins of roast beef — immense plum puddings — any quantity of port wine, and a diarrhoea of after-dinner speeches."[77] Joseph Medill, publisher of the *Chicago Tribune,* announced that "the people are utterly disgusted with Reverdy Johnson and his 'Alabama' negotiations"; Horace Greeley denounced the minister.[78] A joint resolution was introduced in Congress requesting the president to recall Reverdy Johnson for conduct "prejudicial to the interests and dignity of this nation."[79]

If the North, still preoccupied with the problems caused by the Civil War, had known more of what was going on in London, its reaction might have been even more violent. "Our visitors," wrote the secretary of legation, "are Geo. N. Sanders, Wigfall, Benjamin and men of that stamp — indeed only rebels and rebel sympathizers."[80] This was only natural to a Maryland Democrat: these men had been Johnson's friends before the war, and they were his friends now. Johnson's trouble was that he simply was not representative of American opinion.

By early 1869 he was losing his hold on British feeling. "I do not see a great deal of our friend Reverdy," wrote Freeman H. Morse, United States consul-general in London, "He is away so much on the swing round the circle . . . meetings got up for him to dilate on the soothing theme of peace and international love. Socially he is genial, agreeable and entertaining, and I like him much, but he is altogether too fond of making speeches and entertains too high an opinion of his own. He thinks every one of his public utterances has a tremendous influence in form-

77. M. C. Laycock to Sumner, April 14, 1869; J. G. Dudley to Sumner, April 15, 1869, Sumner Papers.

78. Joseph Medill to Sumner, Dec. 2, 1868, Sumner Papers. Diary of John Bigelow, Oct. 29, 1868, Bigelow Papers.

79. *Cong. Globe,* 40 Cong., 3 sess., p. 10. Representative Daniel J. Morrell of Pennsylvania on Dec. 7, 1868.

80. Benjamin Moran to Thurlow Weed, Jan. 9, 1869, Weed Papers. Judah P. Benjamin to Reverdy Johnson, Nov. 12, 1868, Johnson Papers.

ing and cementing friendship between the two nations. At first his speeches really had considerable and favorable influence on the English mind. But he has so overdone it, that, with the unfavorable criticism at home, but little heed is now paid to any speech he may make.[81] "He talks too much and is being laughed at in Society," said another diplomat. "And then his colleagues also laugh at him."[82]

Johnson remained oblivious to all this. He wrote home justifying his behavior, explaining, for example, that he had not heard Roebuck's speech properly and had replied to it as soon as he read it in the papers next day.[83] Seward, the one person who might have warned the minister about the damage he was doing and made him change his course, went to great lengths to reassure him. All ministers, the secretary said, had to run a gauntlet of press criticism. Factional bitterness was high; the public did not expect a successful end to the negotiations and believed that Johnson had added humiliation to failure. The opposition would howl again when they saw the treaties, as they and their like had done all through United States history. But all would be well. "The treaties will prove satisfactory in the end, and the wisdom of the speeches you have made will thus be fully vindicated by the achievements which follow them."[84] Reverdy Johnson lapped up this encouragement and became quite convinced that the "better and wiser part" of the American press was with him. He told Senator William P. Fessenden that only some papers under Fenian control were censuring him.[85]

Johnson had the wide Atlantic between himself and reality; Seward's remarks show that he was wildly out of touch with

81. Freeman H. Morse to Fessenden, Jan. 20, 1869, Fessenden Papers.
82. Benjamin Moran to Thurlow Weed, Jan. 9, 1869, Weed Papers.
83. Johnson to Sumner, Oct. 10, 1868, Sumner Papers. Johnson to Seward, Oct. 7, 1868, Seward Papers.
84. Seward to Johnson, Oct. 26, 1868, Johnson Papers. Seward to Johnson, Oct. 7, 1868 (Unofficial), Diplomatic Instructions.
85. Johnson to Seward, Nov. 7, 1868, Private, Diplomatic Despatches. Johnson to Fessenden, Nov. 13, 1868, Fessenden Papers.

public opinion. From the day it was published, informed politicians knew that the convention could not be ratified. "At present," Ben Butler told someone who wanted to retain him as attorney when the claims came to be adjudicated, "there is not the remotest possibility of a settlement."[86] An Ohio representative asked Charles Francis Adams for some information to use in a speech on the convention; a few days later, he wrote again and told him not to bother, as the treaty was "wholly discarded." Henry Wilson thought it might not get one vote.[87]

A few Southern and Democratic newspapers welcomed the treaty and defended Reverdy Johnson,[88] but nearly all the great New York papers condemned his work. The *Tribune* greeted it as "an utter failure, a fraud on American claimants, and a treaty which the Senate will overwhelmingly refuse to sanction";[89] the *Herald* called it "mixed-up and unsatisfactory ... like the two Johnsons, Andy and Reverdy, a failure";[90] the *Evening Post* wanted it thrown in the wastebasket immediately.[91] The moderate Republican *New York Times* had to execute an awkward and humiliating retreat after proclaiming the convention's terms "eminently favorable,"[92] and even the *World,* the leading Democratic paper of the nation, was forced to admit that popular sentiment was almost universally against the agreement.[93] The *Sacramento Daily Union* dismissed the convention as incomprehensible;[94] the *Washington Daily Morning Chronicle* thought

86. B. F. Butler to L. Roseth, Jan. 27, 1869; L. Roseth to Butler, Jan. 22, 1869, Butler Papers.

87. Samuel Shellabarger to C. F. Adams, Feb. 10, 19, 1869, Adams Papers. Thornton to Clarendon, Jan. 26, 1869, Clarendon Papers, Bodleian.

88. Baltimore *Sun,* Jan. 20, 23, 1869. *Mobile Daily Register,* Feb. 25, 26, May 18, 29, 1869.

89. Jan. 22, 1869.

90. Feb. 5, 1869.

91. Feb. 26, 1869; see also *New York Evening Mail,* Jan. 27, 1869.

92. Jan. 19, 27, 30, Feb. 1, 1869.

93. April 14, 1869.

94. Feb. 9, 1869.

it gave "no absolute assurance of anything."[95] George B. Upton got Sumner to introduce a petition in Congress remonstrating against equating British claims with American losses caused by pirates which were British-built, British-manned, British-armed, and British-protected. At the same time, he had the speeches of Cobden, William E. Forster, and Sir Francis Baring on the Alabama Claims, saying Britain was guilty of unneutral behavior, printed ("with a little introduction of my own") to make the British offences clear and sent Sumner a batch of them for distribution to colleagues.[96]

Seward, convinced of his own rectitude to the last, told Reverdy Johnson that the opposition to the convention was pure party spite, just like the attempt at impeachment. Ignoring other causes of complaint, he wrote that "the only pretence of a logical principle which is made for the new issue is that Great Britain owes the United States for injuries committed by the recognition of the rebels as a belligerent power, and compensation beyond the mere damages of aggrieved merchants and seamen; that the injury is of a nature which cannot be estimated in pecuniary damages; atonement ought therefore to be demanded in the form of an acknowledgement of that wrong with a concession of territory."[97]

Johnson had already dismissed these objections with the arguments that the demand was totally new, that a nation's honor could have no compensation in money, and that the United States had held no direct interest in the ships and goods destroyed by the Confederate raiders. He replied to Seward that if these were the demands to be made on the English, the Alabama Claims would never be settled.[98] But during the next three days

95. April 14, 1869.

96. *The Times,* Feb. 19, 1869. Upton to Sumner, Feb. 20, 1869, Sumner Papers.

97. Seward to Johnson, March 3, 1869, Seward Papers.

98. Johnson to Seward, Feb. 17, 1869, Diplomatic Despatches. Johnson to Seward, March 19, 1869, Seward Papers.

he decided to make one last effort to save the convention. He went to the Foreign Office on March 22 and proposed an amendment to the treaty allowing claims by the two governments to be admitted. Clarendon gave him no encouragement; Gladstone thought that he had taken "a great and indeed an outrageous liberty" in making a proposal without the sanction of his government (Grant had been inaugurated, and Reverdy Johnson was on the verge of resigning), and the idea died stillborn.[99]

It is doubtful if anything would have arrested the bloodthirsty pursuit of the convention. It was voted down on April 13. Goldwin Smith told Charles Francis Adams, Jr., that one of the Republican senators who had voted against impeachment "and among whom I suppose if anywhere, independence is to be found," had confessed privately that he had voted against the treaty because it was so unpopular, though he thought America would never get a better one.[100] "A single benighted Senator, a Kentuckian,"[101] Thomas C. McCreery, voted in favor, 54 against. Sumner's great speech against the treaty supplied a rationale, but many contemporaries mentioned Reverdy Johnson's behavior first when they listed causes.[102] Also, there was

99. Clarendon to W. E. Gladstone, March 22, 26, 1869; Gladstone to Clarendon, March 30, 1869, Gladstone Papers. When the new secretary of state, Hamilton Fish, heard what Johnson had done, he sent a swift reproof. Johnson to Fish, April 9, 16, 1869, Diplomatic Despatches. Telegram from Fish to Johnson, April 12, 1869, Diplomatic Instructions.

100. Of the seven, only four voted on the convention. Grimes of Iowa was abroad; Van Winkle of West Virginia and Henderson of Missouri had failed to win re-election to the Senate in March 1869. Fessenden was against the convention. Fessenden to Hamilton Fish, May 23, 1869, Fish Papers, L.C. This leaves Ross of Kansas, Fowler of Tennessee, and Trumbull of Illinois. The latter seems the most likely person to be interested in foreign affairs. Goldwin Smith to C. F. Adams, Jr., May 25, 1869, Adams Papers.

101. The Diary of George Templeton Strong: Post-War Years, 1865-1875, ed. by Allan Nevins and Milton Halsey Thomas (New York: Macmillan, 1952), pp. 244-245, April 16, 1869.

102. Sumner to Bemis, May 25, 1869, printed in Pierce, p. 393, Lowell to Leslie Stephen, April 24, 1869, printed in Letters of James Russell

a feeling of holiday in the air. After four long years Andrew Johnson was out. The Republicans in Congress wanted nothing more to do with him or any of his works. They had no desire to give him and Seward, who, with his usual complete failure to understand the facts of life during Reconstruction, had expected to add enough middle-of-the-road Republicans to the Democratic vote for ratification, a posthumous triumph.[103] Nor did the Democrats want to lash themselves to a political corpse. In the White House the Radicals had a man regarded with a respect and reverence rarely accorded to any mortal: "To doubt Grant was to doubt Christ,"[104] and the feeling was overwhelming that he should be entrusted with the English questions. With hardly a regret, the Johnson-Clarendon Convention was ignominiously pushed into its grave.

Meanwhile, the members of Andrew Johnson's administration straggled to their homes, and a phase of Anglo-American diplomacy closed. How well had the men of 1865-1869 done? Of the British foreign secretaries, Lord Russell, pigheaded, obstinate, and stupid, was by far the worst. He surely committed a colossal blunder by not offering a settlement in the summer or autumn of 1865. The war spirit of earlier months was passing away and as Sumner said, "at that time we would have accepted very little."[105] Clarendon's record was a little better, for he did not press the naturalization question to a break, even though he

---

Lowell, ed. by C. E. Norton (London: Osgood, McIlvaine, 1894), II, 29. Henry Adams to John Bright, May 30, 1869, Bright Papers. *Mobile Daily Register,* March 20, 1869. Montgomery *Alabama State Journal,* March 16, 1869. San Francisco *Daily Alta California,* May 4, 1869.

103. Bigelow, *Retrospections,* pp. 219-220, Diary, Sept. 24, 1868. *New York Times,* March 22, 1869, *New York Herald,* April 14, 1869. *Springfield Weekly Republican,* Jan. 23, 1869.

104. Elizabeth N. Barr, "The Populist Uprising," in *A Standard History of Kansas and the Kansans,* II, 1115-1195, quoted in Wilfrid E. Binkley, *American Political Parties, Their Natural History* (New York: Alfred A. Knopf, 1943), p. 292.

105. Sumner to John Lothrop Motley, July 6, 1869, printed in Pierce, p. 384, n. 1. *North American Review,* April 1865, pp. 235-351. San Francisco *Daily Evening Bulletin,* May 4, 1865.

lacked the courage to abandon his predecessor's stand on the claims. Stanley performed well in many respects; his policy was flexible, and he shunned extremism. But he, too, missed an excellent opportunity to clear up all the disputes that vexed Anglo-American relations. It is unlikely that a treaty with England would have passed the Senate in 1866 or 1867. With repression in Ireland and, in 1866, vital elections looming, the enemies of Britain could have easily mustered eighteen senators, one-third and enough to defeat a treaty. In early 1868, on the other hand, a treaty ending both the Alabama Claims and the naturalization controversy might well have been ratified. If Stanley had conceded in January what he refused until October, if the respected Adams, not Reverdy Johnson, had put his name to the terms, four years of exacerbation, alarm, and threats might have been avoided.

The two men who deserved most credit for their part in the transatlantic diplomacy of those years were Seward and Sir Frederick Bruce. Bruce played the moderator to perfection, doing his utmost to steer the home government out of dangerous waters and presenting the British viewpoint with such understanding of the Johnson administration's political difficulties that Seward was never embarrassed. Seward, though often ill-advised, deluded by hopes of flattering success and popularity, and needlessly exacting, never stooped to take the easy way out. He could have been the leader of an Anglophobe crusade, the darling of the Fenians, the idol of the Democrats. Instead he doggedly pursued a policy which, with all its faults, was at least honest. Much divided the British and American governments in the postwar years, but, thanks to Seward, they never ceased to trust each other.

CHAPTER 4

Sumner's Speech

In March 1869, Charles Sumner seemed at the height of his power. He was unquestionably the leading Republican in Congress, the most prominent and distinguished of American politicians. No administration could afford to reckon without him. Sumner was a remarkable man, uniting a ruthless sincerity with a pure and fanatic devotion to principle. He was the finest orator in the nation; his store of learning was immense. In an age when American public life was often corrupt and frequently crude, he was decorous, honorable, honest, and cultured. With all this, he was not a great man, not as Washington, Lincoln, and Robert E. Lee were great. Sumner had no humility and no sense of humor, and without such qualities saints become prigs. He was egotistical, self-complacent, and arrogant; he treated everyone as his inferior and could not stand opposition of any kind.

Sumner's inability to compromise finally ruined him as a politician, and though he advocated many great and successful causes he never saw one settled to his liking. He never learned the art of persuasion; he was not a quick thinker and invariably came off worst in the cut and thrust of debate. Even his great speeches tended to lose their force in rococo elaborations of meaningless detail; Sumner confused learning with wisdom and information with knowledge. He succeeded to Daniel Webster's seat in the Senate, and many observers saw him as the natural heir of the titanic orators of the thirties and forties. But really he was less the heir of Henry Clay, Webster, and John C. Calhoun than a throwback to their era; he was born twenty years too late and survived, baffled, into the age of the boss and the machine politician. Abraham Lincoln once remarked that Sumner was his idea of a bishop, and perhaps it was the Massachusetts senator's tragedy that he never found a cause — or a church — into which he could sink himself completely. In another age, on a different continent, stripped of his protective pomposity, one can imagine Sumner as a second St. Bernard of Clairvaux.

The Committee on Foreign Relations had voted unanimously against the ratification of the Johnson-Clarendon Convention, and it was Sumner's duty as chairman to report the decision to the Senate and urge the treaty's rejection. For some time before the vote on the convention on April 13, rumors had been going about that he intended to make a "great speech"; newspapermen wrote to ask for advance copies, well-wishers urged him on.[1] As he rose to speak expectancy was high.

He began by saying that though the rejection of a treaty was unusual the defeat of this convention would be in the interests of peace. It did not remove the grievance it was concerned with, but left it for heartburning and rancor. Attacking the frenzied haste of the negotiation, Sumner showed that the treaty dealt only with individual American claims. It was a "capitulation." Even the Confederate bonds bought by Englishmen might be included.

The British had granted belligerent rights to the Confederates with unexampled haste. Belligerency had to be a fact before it could be recognized; belligerency on land did not necessarily imply the same condition at sea, and the Confederates had no power on the sea to be recognized. The British Neutrality

1. C. F. Adams to Henry Adams, March 17, 1869, Adams Papers. John Russell Young to Charles Sumner, March 15, 1869; Charles W. Slack to Sumner, March 17, 1869; Cephas Brainerd to Sumner, April 2, 1869; A. C. Lawrence to Sumner, March 19, 1869, Sumner Papers. Montgomery *Alabama State Journal*, March 23, 1869.

Proclamation was, therefore, completely indefensible, its only justification a technicality about the use of the word "blockade" instead of "closing of the ports" in Lincoln's proclamation of April 15, 1861. "Blockade," the British said, involved a recognition of war between two sovereign powers; yet Lincoln's proclamation itself reserved the rights of United States sovereignty and declared Confederate cruisers pirates. There were several precedents of what the great German authority, August Heffter, called "pacific blockade," or blockade without the concession of ocean belligerency. Viewing such cases, Heffter had laid down the rule that "blockade" did not necessarily constitute a state of regular war. The British, Sumner continued, allowed the *Alabama* to escape by gross negligence and renewed their guilt every time she was allowed to coal at a colonial port. The Confederate cruisers were British in every way except for their commanders. British blockade-runners, protected by the Neutrality Proclamation, brought British munitions to the South; the British government, committed to antislavery, had rushed to help a slave Confederacy.

The Johnson-Clarendon Convention contained no admission of these wrongs, provided no rule for the future, and made no reparation to the nation. For the United States had *national* claims; claims for "the rise of insurance on all American vessels; the fate of the carrying trade, which was one of the great resources of our country; the diminution of our tonnage, with the corresponding increase of British tonnage; the falling off in our exports and imports, with due allowance for our abnormal currency and the diversion of war." The cost of the ships lost, plus the destruction of the American mercantile marine's prospects (it was growing at the rate of 5 percent a year before the war), would alone come to $110,000,000.

To this point, Sumner had done little more than restate the familiar American grievances, although his claim for the destruction of the mercantile marine as an entity was novel. Next he produced an entirely new and devastating charge — that the secessionists were originally encouraged by hope of support from England and that their conviction was strengthened by the Neutrality Proclamation. The Confederacy was fed to the end by British supplies, aided by British blockade-runners, and stimulated into frantic life by every report from the British-built cruisers. British intervention added years to the war. "The Rebellion was suppressed at a cost of more than four thousand million dollars, a considerable portion of which has been already paid, leaving twenty-five hundred millions as a national debt to burden the people. If through British intervention, the war was doubled in duration, or in any way extended, as cannot be doubted, then is England justly liable for the additional expenditure to which our country was doomed." He did not say that America *would* make such a claim, but he felt she had a perfect right to do so.[2]

The speech was immediately, wildly popular. Senator Henry B. Anthony sent a page scurrying across the floor of the chamber carrying a crumpled envelope with "That was a great speech" scrawled across the front.[3] Other senators, John Sherman, Allen G. Thurman, Eugene Casserly, and John P. Stockton took the floor to endorse Sumner's views.[4] By a unanimous vote, the Senate removed the injunction of secrecy from the speech, and even men like Fessenden, whose dislike for Sumner was notorious, stopped to congratulate him.[5] A deluge of letters, many from distinguished figures like Gerrit Smith, Frederick Douglass, Parke

2. "Claims on England: Individual and National," Speech on the Johnson-Clarendon Treaty in Executive Session of the Senate, April 13, 1869, in *The Works of Charles Sumner* (Boston: Lee and Shepard, 1880), XIII, 53-93.

3. Sumner kept the envelope among his correspondence with the note "From H. B. Anthony, who was in the chair, 13th April, 1869" written on it, Sumner Papers.

4. *Springfield Weekly Republican,* April 24, 1869.

5. Sumner to George Bemis, May 25, 1869, Bemis Papers.

Godwin and John M. Forbes, descended upon the senator.[6] The reaction of the press was overwhelmingly favorable.[7]

Much of the comment on the speech was well-considered and restrained. The consensus among a majority of Republican newspapers was well put by the *Wilmington* (Delaware) *Daily Commercial*. "We are not going to war to collect the bill. We know too well the cost of monitors, and the expense of maintaining a regiment of troops. We do not need the money. Secretary Boutwell, with an honest administration, is reducing our debt, every month. So we simply present our claim, with the items specified; we show the proof that these were damages done through the inefficiency, if not by the approval, of the British Government; and then we simply wait."[8] When England next went to war a swarm of American *Alabamas* and *Shenandoahs* would decimate her commerce; and the United States would meet her every complaint by pointing to the conduct of her own government in 1861-1865.[9] Some believed that England

6. Gerrit Smith to Sumner [July 16 ?], 1869; Frederick Douglass to Sumner, April 26, 1869; Parke Godwin to Sumner, May 1, 1869; J. M. Forbes to Sumner, April 17, 1869, Sumner Papers. Altogether, Sumner received 135 congratulatory letters about the speech, far more than he got on any other question between 1865 and 1872.

7. *Chicago Republican*, April 19, 1869; Montgomery *Alabama State Journal*, April 21, 1869; Springfield *Illinois State Journal*, April 22, 1869; *Washington Daily Chronicle*, April 14, 16, May 20, 1869; *Sacramento Daily Union*, April 28, 1869; *Springfield Weekly Republican* April 24, 1869; *Hartford Daily Courant*, April 15, 1869; New York *Dispatch*, April 18, 1869; *New York Times*, April 16, 1869; Des Moines, Iowa, *Daily State Register*, April 27, 1869; New York *Evening Post*, April 15, 1869; *Harper's Weekly* (New York), May 1, 1869; *New York Herald*, April 14, 15, 16, 17, 1869; San Francisco *Daily Evening Bulletin*, April 28, 1869.

8. May 4, 1869.

9. In the same vein: New York *Sun*, April 19, 1869; *Chicago Republican*, April 15, 1869; New York *Evening Post*, March 19, May 20, 28, 1869; New York *Commercial Advertiser*, April 21, May 1, 18, 1869; *New York Evening Mail*, March 3, April 22, May 29, 1869; *Washington Daily Chronicle*, April 17, 28, May 5, 14, 15, 1869; San Francisco *Daily*

would never allow matters to go that far: the Liberals were in power, and Gladstone and Bright would surely admit British guilt and would understand that Sumner's indictment was not half as bitter or caustic as their dead friend Cobden's had been.[10]

Few of these papers went into detail about the claims they wished to present to the British, and there is evidence that not all this bloc of Republican opinion wanted to press for the huge sums Sumner had mentioned. A New York state senator wrote to Sumner that though he fully approved the speech, "I suppose, in the interests of peace, we shall find it best to accept a limited reparation."[11] The Yonkers, N.Y., *Statesman* wrote that "we are not really going to ask for that little 'moral debt' of two thousand millions,"[12] and even the truculent and irascible *Illinois State Journal* thought that the question might be settled without the payment of a cent more than enough to cover the private claims if England would only apologize and make the offer at once.[13] The old abolitionist Edmund Quincy favored this course, too, though he was convinced that the national claims Sumner had put forward were just.[14] The *Alta California* was emphatic that America had not yet decided how much to ask for. Sumner's "florid calculations" represented the maxi-

---

Alta California, April 15, May 4, 13, 1869; *Sacramento Daily Union,* April 16, May 13, 1869. Private correspondence taking the same attitude: J. G. Dudley to Sumner, April 15, 1869; David C. Humphrey to Sumner, April 17, 1869; Horace Binney Sargent to Sumner, April 27, 1869, Sumner Papers. E. Quincy to R. D. Webb, May 4, 1869, Dept. of Rare Books & Mss., Boston Public Library.

10. *Washington Daily Chronicle,* April 15, 1869; *Wilmington Daily Commercial,* April 14, 1869; *Harper's Weekly* (New York), June 26, 1869.

11. L. H. Morgan to Sumner, April 28, 1869, Sumner Papers.

12. June 17, 1869, encl. in J. Edwards Clark to Hamilton Fish, June 23, 1869, Fish Papers, L.C.

13. Springfield *Illinois State Journal,* May 1, 1869.

14. E. Quincy to R. D. Webb, June 10, 1869, Dept. of Rare Books & Mss., Boston Public Library. The same attitude was taken by a lawyer who wrote to Sumner, Dexter A. Hawkins to Sumner, May 25, 1869, Sumner Papers.

mum demand that could be made. No one expected payment of the whole amount, and the Massachusetts senator's calculations were quite arbitrary. British perfidy had lengthened the war, no doubt, and infused it with unusual bitterness and animosity. But who could say that two years, not one, were added to the war in this way, and, as a consequence, whether John Bull should assume half, or only a quarter, of the war debt?[15] Against this must be set the fervent attitude of a newspaper like the *Washington Daily Morning Chronicle*. The sum of the damages, it admitted, was portentous. But the account was a true one; only bungling, piecemeal diplomacy had given the world the idea that the American claims were a bagatelle of three or four million pounds. The real material injuries, the journal added, were nothing compared with the moral damages: the attempt upon the existence of republican institutions.[16]

But there was another bloc of opinion. Although Sumner believed that he was acting in a cause of peace, the rejection of the treaty and his forceful restatement of American grievances effectively declared open season for Anglophobe assaults. Just before he was due to speak, John Scott of Pennsylvania rejected a proposal to postpone the vote by pointing out that April 13 was the anniversary of the bombardment of Fort Sumter and that it was highly appropriate to mark the day by killing a treaty made in the interests of a power which for four long years had done nothing that was not calculated either to help the Confederates or to injure those who were fighting them.[17]

John Meredith Read, Sr., the leader of the Philadelphia bar, was stimulated by the speech to write two polemics on "Hasty Belligerency" and the escape of the *Alabama* which charged that England had plotted to divide the United States into three or

15. San Francisco *Daily Alta California*, May 4, 13, 27, 1869. The San Francisco *Daily Evening Bulletin* wrote that, despite the enormity of the outrage, the consequential claims could not be ascertained and could not, therefore, be paid, May 3, 1869.
16. May 5, 14, 1869.
17. *Washington Daily Chronicle*, April 15, 1869.

four pitiful, weak confederacies.[18] A Pennsylvania newspaper
wanted to keep the claims unpaid and the precedent in force
until American privateers could take revenge upon Britain.[19]
A New York journalist denounced papers like Henry Raymond's
Times with its "infinitely infernal lickspittle leaders" and asked:
"How would it do to fulminate against these Anglico-American
doughfaces again — either here or in Boston?"[20] The shipowner
George B. Upton told Sumner that his estimates of the lost
ships' worth was far too low, and Thomas Dawes Eliot, five-term
congressman from Massachusetts, wanted to revive an old plan
for the United States government to act as judge in its own case
and issue drafts on the British government, payable in sterling
after twenty years, with interest at 3 percent per annum. What
if Britain would not pay? "Then bring an action against her
at the tribunal of nations, and collect by reprisals." But she
would pay.[21]

In Congress, Zachariah Chandler demanded that Britain cede
Canada as payment of the Alabama Claims. Sumner, said the
Michigan senator, had shown Britain responsible for half the
expenses of the Civil War. Now was the the time to settle the debt.
The United States could not allow an enemy and an enemy's
base so near. In words that recalled Henry Clay, Chandler
boasted that the sixty thousand Michigan volunteers could com-

18. J. M. Read, Sr., to Sumner, June 9, July 2, 1869, Sumner Papers.
19. Wilkes-Barre *Record of the Times,* encl. in A. L. Maxwell to
Hamilton Fish, July 2, 1868, Fish Papers, L.C.
20. Frank W. Ballard to Sumner, May 26, 1869; Thomas Williams to
Sumner, June 19, 1869; Samuel C. Frey to Sumner, March [error for
April ?], 17, 1869; M. Wakeman to Sumner, April 14, 1869; George
Ashley to Sumner, June 17, 1869; Henry C. Lawes to Sumner, May 3,
1869; Henry S. Sanford to Sumner, May 12, 1869, Sumner Papers. Anon.
letter to Hamilton Fish, signed "A Voice from the Rocky Mountains,"
May 13, 1869, Fish Papers, L.C.
21. Sumner had valued the ships sunk by the Confederate raiders at
$40 a ton; Upton thought that $70 would be nearer the mark. Upton
to Sumner, April 19, 1869, Sumner Papers. T. D. Eliot to Sumner,
Sept. 5, 1869, enclosing a clipping from the *Boston Daily Advertiser,*
Feb. 7, 1866.

plete the conquest in thirty days. In a war against Britain the United States was bound to emerge victorious: "There will be no war on land, and not much on water."[22]

Another scheme was offered by Ben Butler in an interview published in the *New York Times* on Monday, May 24. Butler said that he would give the British plenty of time to think things over. In six months or so, if they offered no settlement, the United States should issue a proclamation of nonintercourse. Deprived of a market for her manufactures, Britain would be full of unemployed workmen rioting for bread and threatening revolution. Under such circumstances, the British would settle the Alabama Claims in no time.

Butler's proposal aroused no interest at all, for reasons well put by Ignatius Donnelly: "Fancy a western farmer impoverishing himself to spite some nabob in Manchester or Sheffield. Fancy him as the auctioneer cries going-going-going-what shall we have for this superior farm team — fancy him grinning and saying, 'Ha! Ain't I giving it to John Bull?' Why General B might just as well stick one of his hind legs into the fire and burn it off to spite with the foul smell his enemy across the street."[23]

Chandler's plan of annexation was more persuasive and more dangerous. The idea of securing Canada predated the Declaration of Independence; the spirit of manifest destiny moved strong in American minds, and nearly every American believed that, sooner or later, union would come. Great newspapers like the *New York Herald* and the *Tribune* had advocated it, on and off, ever since the end of the war, and the opposition to confederation in Canada convinced many people that the hour of continental consolidation was at hand. In the first months of 1869 annexation was mentioned in papers far and wide. The Springfield *Illinois State Journal* said that the American people

22. *Cong. Globe,* 41 Cong., Special sess., p. 730, April 19, 1869.
23. Diary, Oct. 10, 1869, Donnelly Papers.

would welcome it almost to a man.[24] The Montgomery *Alabama
State Journal* carried articles on the annexation movement in
Nova Scotia and expressed the opinion that the whole of Canada
would soon follow.[25] The *Sacramento Daily Union* said the same
thing.[26]

The idea of exchanging Canada for the Alabama Claims
followed naturally. Joseph Medill, publisher of the *Chicago
Tribune* and a violent hater of Britain, was a zealous expansionist, who regarded the cession of Canada as the only adequate
"attonment" Britain could make for her wartime treachery.[27]
The eminent lawyer Elias Hasket Derby sent letters, statistics,
and clippings to try and bring Sumner over to such a policy
and urged him to suggest it to Bright or Gladstone.[28] The huge
sums of money, mentioned by Sumner and by Chandler, gave
the scheme currency. Another politician made it the occasion
for his last appearance on the stage of American history. Robert
J. Walker, two-term Jacksonian senator from Mississippi, Polk's
secretary of the treasury, and territorial governor of "bleeding
Kansas," was a lifelong expansionist, and now, in his final illness,
set out to do for Canada what his open letter of 1844 had done
for Texas. On Wednesday, April 7, the *Washington Daily
Morning Chronicle*, which had already published several articles
on the likelihood of annexation,[29] carried a letter from Walker
"to a friend in New York" denouncing the Johnson-Clarendon
Convention, charging that England was liable for the American
losses of "commerce, tonnage, and revenue, the driving of our
flag from the ocean, and the prolongation of the war," and
setting out three possible solutions. One was war, which Walker

24. Jan. 23, 1869.
25. March 22, 27, 1869.
26. April 3, 13, 1869.
27. Medill was even willing to offer a *pourboire* of $100 or $200
million to save Britain's face. Medill to Sumner, Dec. 2, 1868, Sumner
Papers.
28. Derby to Sumner, April 12, 13, 1869, Sumner Papers.
29. March 20, April 3, 4, 1869.

hoped would be avoided. Another was to submit all claims, national and private, to fair arbitration. A third was for Britain to give her North American colonies their independence and allow them to make any alliances they liked. This was only a preliminary: on Friday, April 23, the *Chronicle* printed Walker's main effort as a special supplement. It took the form of a letter to the chairman and secretary of the Nova Scotia League, an annexationist group in Halifax, and filled eleven and a half columns. Toward the end, Walker pronounced against exchanging the provinces for the Alabama Claims. England would never allow it, the United States should not ask it: Canada must come of her own free will. Whether he was merely bowing to Nova Scotian dislike of being transferred like so many sacks of potatoes (he had, of course, already found a way around this obstacle in the third point of his April 7 letter), there can be no doubt that so important a manifesto spread the idea of annexation just when the Alabama Claims were in the public eye. The *Chronicle* itself had already linked the two: in reviewing Sumner's speech, it had remarked that though it did not require Britain to give up her American possessions, before the business was finished she probably would come to think that the cheapest way out.[30] Other papers were far more eager.[31] In New York the three largest-selling papers, the *Sun,*[32] the *Herald,*[33] and the *Tribune*[34] all came out for this solution.

Just as many newspapers denounced and ridiculed the idea on the grounds that the British, with their traditional policy of keeping all they had and getting all they could, would never

30. April 14, 1869; also, April 12, 1869.
31. Springfield *Illinois State Journal,* April 9, 1869. *Sacramento Daily Union,* April 23, May 4, 1869.
32. Candace Stone, *Dana and the Sun* (New York: Dodd, Mead, 1938), p. 325.
33. Feb. 13, 18, May 8, 1869.
34. Jan. 22, Feb. 3, 22, April 5, 21, 1869. This solution also appeared in Sumner's correspondence: O. W. Wright to Sumner, April 16, 1869; E. R. Wiswell to Sumner, July 22, 1869, Sumner Papers.

agree to it[35]; that the provinces were bound to join the Union eventually, by the laws of commerce, and that there was no reason to buy a certainty[36]; that Canada should be acquired from the Canadians, not from the British[37]; and finally, that the republic was big enough already.[38] None of this opinion reached Britain, where news of Sumner's speech and Chandler's call for the cession of Canada caused a sensation. The British, of course, were well aware that the convention was most unlikely to be ratified,[39] but the novelty of Sumner's charges and the huge amounts he mentioned, followed by Chandler's demands and the intemperate language of some of the newspapers, produced a state of consternation.

For some days, said the American consul-general in London, the British thought "war was next to certainty."[40] John Jay, on his way to take up the position of minister to Austria, described their reaction as "panic."[41] "I hear the wildest expressions from men we have always looked to for moderation and friendliness," wrote George W. Smalley, the London correspondent of the *New York Tribune.*[42] United States bonds tumbled 5 percent.[43] *The Times* called the manner of Sumner's speech "passionate" and his allegations "flagrantly unfounded." "Had a speech of such extravagance been made by a statesman of equal eminence in either House of the British Parliament, it

35. Washington *National Intelligencer,* March 20, 1869.

36. *Chicago Republican,* April 13, 15, 1869. *Springfield Weekly Republican,* Jan. 9, 1869.

37. San Francisco *Daily Alta California,* May 5, 1869.

38. *Florence* (Alabama) *Journal,* May 6, 1869.

39. Clarendon to Thornton, Jan. 16, 30, 1869, Clarendon Papers, Bodleian.

40. Freeman H. Morse to William Pitt Fessenden, May 17, 1869, Fessenden Papers.

41. John Jay to Hamilton Fish, May 11, 1869, Fish Papers, L.C.

42. George W. Smalley to Sumner, May 14, 1869, Sumner Papers.

43. James W. Grimes to Fessenden, May 10, 1869, printed in William Salter, *The Life of James W. Grimes, Governor of Iowa, 1854-1858; A Senator of the United States, 1859-1869* (New York: Appleton, 1876), pp. 370-371. Also, Morse to Fessenden, May 15, 1869, Fessenden Papers.

would not only have been repudiated on the spot, but would have permanently injured the political reputation of its author."[44] Goldwin Smith made matters worse when he wrote to the *Beehive*, a London workingman's paper which had asked him for an article about prospects for British emigrants in America, that Sumner's speech had roused such feelings of hostility to Britain and the preservation of friendly relations was in such peril that he advised emigrants to go elsewhere.[45] Senator James W. Grimes of Iowa, traveling in Europe for his health, felt obliged to write a letter to *The Times* assuring its readers that the United States had no desire to go to war and that the Senate's vote on the convention only concurred with Sumner's conclusions, not with his reasoning.[46] Writing to Fessenden, Grimes told him that he could have no idea of the tumult created by the speech. The friends of America found themselves in a false position, and Bright denounced Sumner "quite violently, for a Quaker. . . . It has really been looking blue here for a week."[47]

When news of this furore reached America, public opinion tried to make it so plain that there was no need for alarm that Sumner asked a few of his acquaintances if the country was "going back" on him.[48]

Most of the moderate opinion that had welcomed Sumner's speech held firm to the principles he had set out, only trying to persuade the British that there was no danger of war.[49] Wil-

44. May 2, 1869.
45. *Springfield Weekly Republican,* May 22, 1869.
46. May 12, 1869.
47. Grimes to Fessenden, May 10, 1869, printed in Salter, pp. 370-371. Also, George W. Smalley, *Anglo-American Memories* (London: Duckworth, 1911), I, 110. Motley to Fish, June 2, 1869, Unofficial, Diplomatic Despatches. Clarendon to Thornton, May 1, 1869, Clarendon Papers, Bodleian.
48. Timothy O. Howe to Sumner, June 6, 1869; Frank Ballard to Sumner, May 26, 1869, Sumner Papers.
49. *Sacramento Daily Union,* May 19, 1869; New York *Evening Post,* May 12, 1869; *New York Tribune,* May 24, 1869; San Francisco *Daily Alta California,* May 4, 13, 27, 1869; *Hartford Daily Courant,* May 20, 22, 26, 1869; *Harper's Weekly,* May 29, 1869.

liam Lloyd Garrison, worried in case a future Fenian agitation might use Sumner's arguments to carry the United States into a war with England, did what he could to restore calm by writing an article in the New York *Independent*. He pointed out that Sumner was only one of many senators and that he spoke only for himself. There was no need for alarm yet, for his views were not necessarily those of the administration; and Garrison sent off copies to his old English comrades in the fight against slavery.[50] The influential *Springfield Weekly Republican,* while fully sustaining Sumner's view of the dispute, thought it was unreasonable to expect that England would submit at once to such humiliation. It anticipated a long war of nerves before she caved in. There would be no shooting war, for the United States was never more peacefully inclined. But England had to forget that she had done America a favor by agreeing to the Johnson-Clarendon Convention. It had been wholly inadequate, and Sumner's views were supported by the whole nation. The British should face reality. In 1861-1865 they had done some things to America which they now regretted and wanted to pay for. But as their offer was unequal to American demands and was contemptuously rejected, they wanted to deny that they ever did anything wrong. If this was so, why had they been trying to apologize ever since the fall of Richmond? In searching for justification, they were quibbling like chancery lawyers and hiding behind technicalities in a way unworthy of a great nation. The *Republican* hoped to see the day when England would realize that Sumner's speech was the work of "a considerate and dispassionate friend" and turn to considering its wise and temperate suggestions.[51]

50. William Lloyd Garrison to Wendell Phillips Garrison, June 30, July 4, 1869; W. L. Garrison to Oliver Johnson, June 20, 1869, Garrison Papers. As he admitted to Sumner, Garrison did not know that Grant and John Lothrop Motley had seen and approved the speech, nor that the Senate had been so united in its commendation, when he wrote the article. W. L. Garrison to Sumner, June 26, 1869, Sumner Papers.
51. *Springfield Weekly Republican,* April 24, May 8, 15, 22, June 5, 19, 1869.

While American opinion was trying to calm the British, the unfortunate Goldwin Smith came in for a good deal of abuse as an irresponsible agitator, a learned fool, and a sufferer from morbid delusions of persecution for his *Beehive* letter.[52] "Did Goldwin think we meant to *eat* those immigrants when they got here?" a mutual acquaintance asked Sumner.[53] The *Springfield Weekly Republican* declared that it could not be more surprised if he had written that he did not dare to go to a dinner party in Ithaca for fear of being scalped by the other guests, or that the sachems of Tammany painted their faces and performed a war dance in moccasins around an enormous fire in Central Park.[54]

The professor was wiser than his detractors. The tide of hostile feeling was strong, and many Americans were quite delighted by the British scare. Charles Nordhoff, managing editor of the New York *Evening Post,* told Sumner that his speech had given the British the worst fright they had had since the Indian Mutiny.[55] James Gordon Bennett of the *Herald* "talked with great exultation" of the British reaction, gloating over "how Sumner and I have frightened him and irritated him as he has

52. *Washington Daily Chronicle,* May 24, 1869; *Hartford Daily Courant,* May 22, 1869; San Francisco *Daily Alta California,* June 1, 1869; New York *World,* May 22, 1869; *New York Herald,* May 22, 1869; New York *Tribune,* May 20, 1869; Edmund Quincy to R. D. Webb, April 7, 1870, Dept. of Rare Books & Mss., Boston Public Library. John Meredith Read, Sr., to Sumner, June 12, 1869; Frank W. Ballard to Sumner, May 26, 1869; J. W. Forney to Sumner, May 28, 1869; Samuel Hooper to Sumner, June 2, 1869, Sumner Papers. A speech attacking Sumner's views which Goldwin Smith made at Ithaca on May 19 for American consumption hauled down more coals on his head. Goldwin Smith to John M. Forbes, May 28, 1869, Goldwin Smith Papers.
53. T. W. Balch to Sumner, May 29, 1869, Sumner Papers.
54. *Springfield Weekly Republican,* May 22, 1869.
55. Charles Nordhoff to Sumner, June 14, 1869, Sumner Papers. Other letters in the same vein: H. B. Anthony to Sumner, May 31, 1869; Frederick T. Frelinghuysen to Sumner, July 5, 1869; E. S. Whittemore to Sumner, May 3, 1869; John S. Cunningham to Sumner, May 12, 1869; Alfred Willard to Sumner, May 12, 1869; Jesse French to Sumner, May 18, 1869; Dexter A. Hawkins to Sumner, May 25, 1869, Sumner Papers.

senting popular opinion here have stirred up the British lion. See how his tail wags — how he roars — and shakes his mane . . . Sumner and I have frightened him and irritated him as he has not been before for a long time."[56] In some cases the British panic seems to have increased determination to exact a heavy price. The *Bangor* (Maine) *Daily Whig and Courier* described the thunder of the British press as nothing more than an attempt to disguise the weakness of their situation. They dared not reject the American demands for fear of losing their commerce, so they were deliberately creating all the noise possible and agitating the question incessantly until an alarmed America gave them better terms.[57] The Montgomery *Alabama State Journal* agreed that the threat of war from aristocratic, arch-conservative papers like the *Pall Mall Gazette* was meaningless bluster and advised America to await in dignity "the sure redress of events."[58] England might bluster, wrote the Des Moines, Iowa, *Daily State Register*, but she must pay up — and she would.[59]

American hostility toward England increased when the Lairds, who had built the *Alabama*, wrote a letter to *The Times*,[60] claiming that they had merely carried on a normal business transaction. There had been no haste and no secrecy in the construction; the government, the public, and the American minister all knew that the ship was intended for the Confederates, and Russell had had ample opportunity to seize her. The Lairds concluded that the attacks on them were quite unjustified. They had not violated the law, British public opinion, or the practice of foreign nations. But, as the American press pointed out, this only made the British government more culpable. The *New York Tribune* called the Lairds' apologia an "attorney's quibble" and said that the British plea that they had no statute to prevent the equipping and arming of the *Alabama* only proved the incompetence of

56. S. Hooper to Sumner, May 19, 1869, Sumner Papers.
57. May 5, 1869.
58. May 25, 1869.
59. May 9, 1869.
60. May 27, 1869.

their legislators.[61] The *Herald,* too, warned that legal evasions and pettifogging would do England no good. The precedents she had created about the granting of belligerent rights and the maintenance of neutrality would prove a Pandora's box to her if she did not retract them.[62] The *Sacramento Daily Union* called the Laird letter a bombshell which must have its effect even upon America's declared transatlantic enemies. "If such facts do not call for apology and reasonable restitution, it is a perilous position for England to assume."[63]

What impelled Sumner to make the speech? His disastrous nine months' marriage was the first great shadow to fall across a brilliantly successful career, and contemporaries were not slow to suggest that the senator was taking out his private frustrations in his public life. "It is a curious coincidence that at two different periods of the history of this republic," Charles Francis Adams reflected, "the most dangerous influence to its peace and harmony should have been exercised by men without virility, and hence deprived of one great element of harmony in the creation."[64] A British diplomat on his way to the Joint High Commission in Washington wrote home that Sumner "was fool enough some year or so ago to marry a young and pretty widow. She found that he was not gifted with 'full powers' and has left him and I was told that there is a suit proceeding for dissolution a vinculo. He therefore makes up by vigour of tongue for his want of capacity in other organs."[65]

Despite such speculations, Sumner's married life can be best explained in terms of an elderly man enveloped in affairs and in himself and a self-willed, imperious woman[66] with twice the vitality of

61. June 3, 1869.
62. May 29, 1869.
63. May 31, 1869.
64. Adams Diary, June 16, 1869. The other person Adams refers to is presumably President Buchanan.
65. Lord Tenterden to Meade, Feb. 21, 1871, Granville Papers FO 29/106.
66. See David Donald, *Charles Sumner and the Rights of Man* (New York: Knopf, 1970), pp. 268-277, 289-295, 312-320.

her husband. With a man less concerned for absolutes, less morbidly sensitive, the quarrel might have been merely a "period of adjustment," for it was well known that his wife would have accepted a proposal for reconciliation.[67] But in marriage, as in politics, Sumner was unwilling to settle for anything less than perfection. And though there is no doubt that the episode left Sumner desperately conscious of his loneliness and personal unpopularity in Washington,[68] there is no reason to believe that his policy toward England (or his behavior toward Grant) would have been changed one whit if Alice Mason Hooper had never entered his life. Principle alone was his driving force; else why did he wait two years and more after the collapse of his marriage before reacting?

Sumner's eminence and his long chairmanship of the Senate Committee on Foreign Relations inevitably led to speculation that Grant might name him secretary of state or minister to England.[69] Though he probably would not have taken either post[70] when he could command more power in the Senate, Sum-

67. Diary of John Bigelow, Feb. 20, 1868, printed in John Bigelow, *Retrospections of an Active Life* (Garden City, N.Y.: Doubleday, Page, 1913), IV, 154.

68. Sumner to Longfellow, Dec. 2, 18, 1867; Jan. 15, 1868; March 18, 21, 1870; April 12, 1870; July n.d., 1870; Nov. 20, 1870; Feb. 22, 1871; March 29, 1871. Sumner to Samuel Gridley Howe, Jan. 12, May 24, 1868, Sumner Papers.

69. For Sumner as secretary of state: J. S. Prettyman to Sumner, Nov. 13, 1868; Howard M. Jenkins to Sumner, Nov. 13, 1868; Samuel Hooper to Sumner, Nov. 15, 1868; George W. Smalley to Sumner, Dec. 2, 1868; Ezra Farnsworth to Sumner, Dec. 11, 1868, Sumner Papers. Bigelow, *Retrospections,* IV, 223. For minister to England: S. Austin Allibone to Sumner, Nov. 30, 1868, Sumner Papers. For either: W. L. Garrison to Sumner, Jan. 20, 1869; John S. Cunningham to Sumner, Oct. 30, 1868; James T. Farnes to Sumner, Nov. 11, 1868, Sumner Papers. W. L. Garrison to J. G. Whittier, Jan. 26, 1869, Garrison Papers. C. A. Jellison, *Fessenden of Maine: Civil War Senator* (Syracuse, N.Y.: Syracuse University Press, 1962), p. 252.

70. Sumner to Francis Lieber, Nov. 9, 1868, printed in Edward L. Pierce, *Memoir and Letters of Charles Sumner* (Boston: Robert Brothers, 1894), IV, 372; *ibid.,* p. 371; Story of Helen Appleton, Feb. 25, 1868,

ner may have felt that an offer of the State Department from Grant would have been a compliment which he deserved. Sumner was not personally vindictive, and it is most unlikely that any feelings of wounded pride or jealousy led him to attempt to seize control of American foreign policy before Grant and his secretary of state Hamilton Fish had firmly seated themselves in power. At the same time, he may well have reflected that no one in the green and untested administration, many of its members startled by their sudden and unexpected greatness, could match his experience in handling foreign relations or his knowledge of the labyrinthine representations and negotiations over the Alabama Claims.

Sumner himself always said that he made the speech with the greatest of reluctance.[71] He had many friends in England, where he had spent some of the happiest times of his life; he firmly believed that England and America should be fast friends. He wanted "more than peace, more even than concord" between them,[72] and he had done a vast amount to defeat Anglophobe and Fenian moves in Congress.

When Senator James W. Nye of Nevada produced some pro-Fenian resolutions in 1867, Sumner objected to their consideration and "stopped speeches which some were panting to make." N. P. Banks' resolutions of sympathy with the Irish freedom fighters Sumner had referred straight to his Committee on Foreign Relations, where as he congratulated himself, "they now sleep never to know waking."[73] Banks' bill to revise the

in M. A. DeWolfe Howe, *Portrait of an Independent: Moorfield Story, 1845-1929* (Boston: Houghton Mifflin, 1932), p. 75. Diary of John Bigelow, March 24, 1869, Bigelow Papers. George S. Boutwell, *Reminiscences of Sixty Years in Public Affairs* (New York: McClure, Phillips, 1902), II, 219.

71. Sumner to George Bemis, May 25, 1869, Bemis Papers. Sumner to Hamilton Fish, Nov. 9, 1869, Fish Papers, L. C. Sumner to Longfellow, May 25, 1869, Sumner Papers. Sumner, *Works*, XIII, p. 89.

72. Sumner, *Works*, XIII, p. 93.

73. Sumner to John Bigelow, May 5, 1867, printed in Bigelow, *Retrospections*, p. 76.

neutrality laws, and incidentally open the way for the launching of Fenian *Alabamas*, was passed in the House in a "coup d'etat at the end of the session, when nobody knows what they are voting upon."[74] It came to the Senate on the afternoon of Friday, July 27, 1866; the end of the session was set for 4 P.M. on Saturday. As a matter of course, it went to Sumner's committee, and he decided to thwart the House's "mad vote" by holding it there. During the afternoon a group of Anglophobes led by Ben Wade and Chandler formed a plan to prize the bill out by a special vote and pass it. When the Senate reconvened after dinner Sumner appeared with an armful of books, announced that he was "good for five hours at least" if the bill was called up, and sat all night waiting for his opponents to show their hand. Finally, at eleven o'clock the next morning, Chandler moved to take up the bill. Sumner immediately threatened to talk out the rest of the session, and the opposition crumbled.[75]

Sumner had not done such things because he believed that Britain's wartime conduct had been right. From the earliest days of the fighting he had nourished a ferocious resentment against her policies. But he kept silence, believing that time was needed for an amicable adjustment,[76] that England would eventually realize the gravity of her offence and make a suitable apology and reparation. To this end he had urged George Bemis to write his pamphlets on the nature and duties of neutrality.[77] "I often told Sir Bruce that, notwithstanding my sense of the wrong my country had received, I would stand aside, provided the two countries could agree upon a treaty which the American

74. George Bemis to Sumner, March 21, 1867, Sumner Papers.
75. Sumner to Francis Lieber, n.d., printed in Pierce, pp. 291-292. Sumner to Bright, Aug. 17, 1866, Bright Papers. J. W. Forney to Sumner, May 30, 1867, Sumner Papers, *Cong. Globe,* 39 Cong., 1 sess., pp. 4206, 4292-4293, July 27, 28, 1866.
76. Sumner to Bright, May 27, 1867, Bright Papers.
77. Sumner to Bemis, March 28, 1865, Bemis Papers.

people could accept." This had not happened; the British had offered terms which were ludicrously inadequate to meet the American grievances, and Sumner decided that the only thing to do was to state that grievance "in length and breadth" until the British did realize it.[78]

There was nothing in the speech which Sumner made on April 13, 1869, that had not been said long before. As Senator Timothy O. Howe of Wisconsin said, in Sumner's impassioned and denunciatory 1863 Cooper Institute speech,[79] he had denounced the Neutrality Proclamation as "an insult to the National Government" and "a moral absurdity," which had been issued far too quickly. In the 1863 speech he said: "It is difficult to exaggerate the consequences of this precipitate, unfriendly and immoral concession, which has been, and still is, an overflowing fountain of mischief." The distinction between land and ocean belligerency and the claim that the Confederates could not be belligerents at sea because they had no ports or prize courts were both made in the earlier speech. And Sumner made it clear that he thought the British government's complicity in the ravages of the Confederate raiders was complete.[80] In December 1867 he told John Bright that the Neutrality Proclamation, which had made belligerents out of pirates and criminals, had been the main cause of the prolongation of the war, with all its wanton waste of blood and treasure. In the spring of 1868 he told Thornton that England had done more harm to the United States than any civilized power had ever inflicted on another without paying for it by the bloodiest of

78. Sumner to Fish, Nov. 9, 1869 Fish Papers, L. C. Sumner to Longfellow, May 25, 1869, Sumner Papers. Sumner to Adam Badeau, July 26, 1869, printed in Adam Badeau, *Grant in Peace: From Appomattox to Mount McGregor. A Personal Memoir* (London: Frederick Warne, n.d.), pp. 579-581. Henry S. Sanford to Sumner, March 13, 1869, Sumner Papers.
79. Timothy O. Howe to Sumner, May 31, 1869, Sumner Papers.
80. Sumner, *Works,* XII, 333-471.

wars and that the Queen's proclamation had cost the country millions of dollars and thousands, if not hundreds of thousands, of lives.[81]

The essentials of Sumner's speech were all raised in the diplomacy of the postwar years. "We have to thank England for not a single really energetic act of good will. That she did not take advantage of our distress to perfect the disruption of the country is deserving of no more credit than a man could claim for not striking a dagger to the heart of a neighbour lying faint by the roadside, of whom he had been jealous. The sympathy and asisstance actually given cost us all the prosperity of our commerce on the high seas for years, and an extension of the resistance on land for at least a year." This might be Sumner in 1869, but it is actually Charles Francis Adams in 1866.[82] Seward, too, had denounced the timing and effect of the British Neutrality Proclamation and charged that it protracted the Civil War.[83]

For these reasons the speech undoubtedly seemed less violent to Sumner than it did to the British. The British did react to American opinion on the speech (though not to the speech itself) a little more vigorously than they need have done. The presentation of opinion three thousand miles away, two weeks or more in transit, while short bulletins came over the cable to add information (or mystify), was necessarily inadequate, fragmentary, and partial, just as Americans received pictures

81. Sumner to Bright, Dec. 10, 1867, Bright Papers. Sumner to Fish, Nov. 9, 1869, Fish Papers, L. C. Moorfield Story to his sister Marianna, March 28, 1868, printed in Howe, p. 85. Also Sumner to Bemis, Jan. 2, 28, 1865, Bemis Papers. Sumner to Louis Agassiz, March 20, 1865, Sumner Papers.

82. Adams Diary, March 1, 1866. Also Adams to Lord Russell, April 7, 1865, encl. in Adams to Seward, April 13, 1865; Adams to Russell, May 20, 1865, encl. in Adams to W. Hunter, May 25, 1865; Adams to Russell, Sept. 18, 1865, encl. in Adams to Seward, Sept. 21, 1865, Diplomatic Despatches.

83. Notably in his dispatch of Aug. 27, 1866, to Adams, Diplomatic Instructions.

of England that were colored by the reporter's own predispositions.[84] No British paper bothered to publish Sumner's speech in full,[85] and their readers gained a sadly muddled impression of its contents. Someone wrote to Sumner in October asking for a few copies and adding that "I want them for an English friend who sails for his home on the 16th — He thinks you breathed war, but he has never seen the speech."[86] Richard D. Webb dispatched a furious letter to Edmund Quincy, in which he confused Sumner with Chandler and charged that he was talking like a slaveholder when he coolly proposed the sale of Canada and its people. Quincy replied that he would send an authentic copy of the speech, from which Webb would see that it was far less extreme than fragmentary reports and English bad conscience had made it appear and gave his opinion that Chandler was a "blatherskite."[87]

Such confusion and misrepresentation (in both England and America) enraged Sumner.[88] To fight the impression that he demanded an abject apology and exorbitant damages, he got John M. Forbes to arrange for the publication in England of a pamphlet containing his speech[89] and asked William E. Chandler, secretary of the Republican National Committee, to distribute copies of it in his home state of New Hampshire.[90] Nevertheless, the British furore was more justified than Sumner could realize, for his speech was a dangerously exaggerated and unbalanced piece of work. There is no question that the Johnson-

84. Freeman H. Morse thought that George Smalley's dispatches to the *New York Tribune* at this time on British sentiment were "gross exaggerations." Morse to Fessenden, June 23, 1869, Fessenden Papers.

85. George S. Fisher to Sumner, May 25, 1869; George W. Smalley to Sumner, Oct. 7, 1869, Sumner Papers.

86. W. W. Furness to Sumner, Oct. 5, 1869, Sumner Papers.

87. R. D. Webb to Quincy, May 28, 1869; Quincy to Webb, June 10, 1869, Dept. of Rare Books & Mss., Boston Public Library.

88. Sumner to Badeau, July 26, 1869, printed in Badeau, pp. 579-581. *New York Herald*, May 3, 1869.

89. Pierce, p. 391, n. 1.

90. William E. Chandler to Sumner, July 13, 1869, Sumner Papers.

Clarendon Convention should have been rejected, but Sumner should never have made a speech which pushed the American case so much further than it could reasonably go. If he had asked for the negotiation of a new treaty providing full and unchallengeable arbitration of the American claims for vessels sunk by the *Alabama* and her sister ships and of British claims for the destruction of property held at the outbreak of war, the dispute might have ended. But a Sumner who could have done that would not have been Sumner.

Certainly Sumner could point to similar indictments made by Seward and Charles Francis Adams, but this did not justify their accusations. He had taken every mistake, every inflation and distortion of the American case that eight years of strenuous diplomatic infighting had produced and blown them up by ten times. Of course, the United States had suffered grievous damages from Britain's actions during the Civil War; of course, she was justified in claiming reparations. But Sumner pushed the claims to their *reductio ad absurdum*. His relentlessly logical mind had practically abandoned reality as it pursued the argument from point to point. "The truth is," wrote Senator Grimes, "that Sumner has greatly injured our cause by presenting so many perfectly absurd arguments, and urging them with so much bitterness."[91]

Sumner's violent style helped to create this impression. He never had any sense of restraint and often did not realize the force of his own words;[92] as E. L. Godkin remarked, "He works his adjectives so hard that if they ever catch him alone, they will murder him."[93] Legally, too, the speech was a "mere colander."[94] George Bemis told his mother that the speech did

91. Grimes to Fessenden, May 10, 1869, printed in Salter, p. 371.

92. Henry Cabot Lodge, *Early Memories* (London: Constable, 1913), p. 280.

93. E. L. Godkin to C. E. Norton, printed in Rollo Ogden, ed., *Life and Letters of Edwin Lawrence Godkin* (New York: Macmillan, 1907), I, 304-305.

94. James Russell Lowell to his daughter Mabel, May 22, 1869,

not impress him as put with either great power or sagacity.[95] No jurist had ever distinguished between belligerency on land and on sea.[96] The British Neutrality Proclamation was perfectly justifiable, for the Union had repeatedly recognized Confederate belligerent rights. At the very moment when Sumner was speaking, the United States was prosecuting a British clothing manufacturer, Sir Peter Tait, who had contracted to supply uniforms for the Confederate Army, on the plea that the Confederacy was a de facto government, the United States was its heir, and the uniforms rightly belonged to it now.[97] As to the proclamation's timing, seventeen days before it was issued the British ship *Tropic Wind* was captured off the Southern coast and condemned as a lawful prize of war in a conviction upheld by the Supreme Court. If Great Britain had not proclaimed neutrality and recognized Confederate belligerent rights, the Union, as the sovereign authority, would have been legally liable for any damage done to British subjects, ships, or property by the secessionists. As for the doctrine of "pacific blockade," the American Civil War was far different from the action by the Allies against Turkey in 1827 or by France against Mexico in 1837-1839, which Sumner cited. Belligerency is a mere question of fact. The situation of affairs in 1861 compelled not only neutral nations, but the United States, to take legal cognizance of the fact of the Confederacy. If the recognition of belligerency caused the prolongation of the war, then the United States was as much a party to it as Great Britain, and every neutral nation in the world was as much bound to pay consequential damages.

The interpretation the Confederates chose to put upon the proclamation was no concern of the British government, and that government could not control the sympathy of its people.

printed in *New Letters of James Russell Lowell,* ed. by M. A. DeWolfe Howe (New York: Harper, 1932), p. 138.

95. George Bemis to Sarah Bemis, April 27, 1869, Bemis Papers.

96. Samuel Hooper, who approved the speech in other respects, raised this question. Hooper to Sumner, Sept. 24, 1869, Sumner Papers.

97. *Chicago Republican,* May 29, 1869.

The law can know no such offense as sympathy or solicitude for a losing, even a bad cause; active help to it is all that counts. The only legal grievance that the United States had was that Great Britain had not maintained the neutrality she had proclaimed. A demand for compensation to the value of the ships destroyed, perhaps even an additional payment for the destruction of the American mercantile marine's prospects, was perfectly justified. But a demand for consequential damages would have been ludicrous.

The effects of Sumner's speech were as unfortunate as its content. As Charles Francis Adams said, "It embodies the vague sense of injury entertained by nine-tenths of our people, and stimulates the demand for reparation as it is called far beyond even the extreme point at which he seemed to place it."[98] Until Sumner dragged the issue into the center of popular attention, most Americans probably had not given much thought to the nation's quarrel with Britain. There had been a loose idea afloat that all was not well, but very few can have followed the dispute in detail or grasped the ramifications of the principles over which Seward and Stanley were hectoring each other.[99] Now the force and authority of Sumner's rhetoric dramatized the matter, and his version of the dispute captured all minds. A Southerner wrote that during the war he had thought England rather more favorable to the Union than to the Confederacy, but after reading the speech he realized that Palmerston and Russell had done many things contrary to justice and equity.[100] "I have always felt that I was wronged as an American citizen by England," ran another letter to Sumner, "but never set down seriously to inquire wherein that wrong consisted, nor why I felt sore towards good old England. Your speech has just shown me my heart — or rather enabled me to analyse my own feelings."[101]

98. C. F. Adams to W. E. Forster, June 4, 1869, in Adams Diary.
99. David C. Humphreys to Sumner, April 17, 1869, Sumner Papers.
100. J. J. Flournoy to Sumner, Aug. 15, 1869, Sumner Papers.
101. Samuel A. Foot to Sumner, April 17, 1869, Sumner Papers.

Sumner thought he was steering the dispute into a new course that would lead straight to a final and epoch-making settlement, but he only dragged it back into the hysterical atmosphere of the war years. His objection was not that the *Alabama* had escaped the Queen's warrant, or that the *Florida* had found shelter, a welcome, and supplies at ports in the British colonies. It was that England, the home of the antislavery movement, had failed its American disciples. In 1863, Sumner had contended that "even if Rebel Slavery, coagulated in embryo government, has arrived at that *semi*-sovereignty *de facto* on the ocean which justifies belligerent rights, yet the Christian powers should indignantly decline to make the concession, because by doing so they make themselves accomplices in shameful crime." In 1869 he was still arguing the same case, in the same spirit. British policy was a "flagrant, unnatural departure from that Anti-Slavery rule, which, by manifold declarations, legislative, political and diplomatic, was the avowed creed of England . . . Rebel Slaveholders, occupied in a hideous attempt, were taken by the hand, and thus with the official protection and the God-speed of Anti-Slavery England commenced their accursed work."[102] Sumner did not speak for the American nation on a legal ground of complaint. He was the voice of the radical Northern antislavery movement, and his condemnation of England was a moral one.

It did not matter to Sumner that the United States had not really fought for the abolition of slavery. From Sumner to Appomattox, he and his Radical coterie had done so, and, quite unconsciously, he had come to assume that he represented the whole nation. Eight years of Radical propagandizing, eight years with the South absent from Congress and the Democrats reviled as traitors had convinced only part of the American electorate that the radical Republican program represented the country's best hope, but it had been totally effective with Sum-

102. Sumner, *Works*, VII, 462, XII, 71-72.

ner. From this basic mistake sprang the senator's obsession with the Neutrality Proclamation. He did not dispute its legality, he told Butler, but he deplored its effect. Without it, the building of a ship in England for the Confederates would have been illegal. It gave the South access to the shipyards and ordnance factories of England.[103] It helped the South; the South was evil; therefore the Neutrality Proclamation was evil and Britain was a criminal power.

In this respect, even so violent and prejudiced an Anglophobe as Ben Butler was more cogent and clear-minded than Sumner. He firmly believed that England had deliberately plotted to wreck the Union and that the Neutrality Proclamation was a carefully designed scheme to make Confederate privateers possible without infringing the law of nations. But he grudgingly admitted that Britain could argue that the rule of law had been preserved by the proclamation, and he made the ground of quarrel with Britain her sympathy and help to the Confederates in order to destroy the Union. Extreme, dangerous, and mendacious as Butler's doctrine was, it did at least possess the virtue of straightforwardness. And he did not make the incredible charge that the escape of the Confederate cruisers helped to prolong the war. "I do not consider," he wrote, "that the *Alabama* was even an aid to the Rebellion. She could not give the Rebels one dollar, one gun, one man; for the fight was to be decided in and around Richmond, and that she did not affect, for she did not draw from us one dollar or one man that we could have otherwise appropriated to carrying on our war."[104]

Sumner never learned that, in international law as in international politics, power is power, and must be recognized whether one likes it or not. His speech on the Johnson-Clarendon Convention was one long confusion of his private moral principles with the genuine national grievance of the Alabama Claims.

103. Sumner to B. F. Butler, June 3, 1869, Butler Papers.
104. Butler to Sumner, June 7, 1869, Sumner Papers.

Sumner pitched the American demands so high that there was no chance of negotiation unless the British made an unconditional surrender.[105] He abolished the possibility of moderation: men like Nordhoff, H. B. Anthony, and Frederick T. Frelinghuysen, who were only rather tickled by the sight of the proud and arrogant British in a fright, cheered the speech — and committed themselves to its extravagant and intransigent doctrine.[106] Even papers like the New York *Evening Post* or the *Wilmington Daily Commercial* which supported his speech in relatively restrained, moderate tones, involved themselves in making large, if not enormous demands. Sumner's violence and extremism made those who disagreed with him, like President Theodore Woolsey of Yale, appear apologists for England.[107] In their errors, the British discovered the true meaning of Sumner's demands. Though he and much of American opinion could not see it, he *had* made vast, unreasonable claims, and as the near future was to reveal he was not at all averse to accepting Canada as a *pourboire* for the meal the *Alabama* had made of the American mercantile marine. It was vastly lucky that the British did fly into a panic; without it, and the sobering effect it had upon many Americans, opinion might have gone on intoxicating itself upon Sumner's heady brew and advanced so far that negotiations would have become impossible, then or in the future. Of all observers, only Goldwin Smith read the situation correctly.[108]

Though Sumner hinted vaguely at huge demands, he supplied no means of reaching a settlement of them. Probably, as Charles

105. "If it was his desire to render friendly relations between the two countries difficult if not impossible, he may congratulate himself." Clarendon to Thornton, May 1, 1869, Clarendon Papers, Bodleian.

106. Charles Nordhoff to Sumner, June 14, 1869; H. B. Anthony to Sumner, May 31, 1869; F. T. Frelinghuysen to Sumner, July 5, 1869, Sumner Papers.

107. William Schouler to Sumner, Sept. 27, 1869, Sumner Papers.

108. Goldwin Smith to George Waring, June 20, 1869, Goldwin Smith Papers. Henry Adams to John Bright, May 30, 1869, Bright Papers.

Francis Adams said, he would have answered that it was not his business to do so: he was only a senator giving his reasons for rejecting a treaty and could not entrench upon the executive power of negotiation. But, in fact, he did not strictly observe such a course of conduct. His speech was a *diktat,* laying down the terms on which his support would be given to any future treaty. Before Grant's new and shaky administration was five weeks old, Sumner presented it with a crisis of the gravest importance.[109]

109. C. F. Adams to Henry Adams, April 21, 1869, Adams Papers. Adams Diary, April 15, 1869.

CHAPTER 5

A New Administration and a New Policy

No president has ever entered the White House enjoying as much prestige and popular favor as Grant.[1] The nation was weary of quarrels and partisan bickering, problems and yet more problems; it wanted leadership, and the man who had magically ended the war after four blood-drenched years that left the Army of the Potomac as far from Richmond as ever seemed certain to end the country's troubles, too. America was looking for a second Washington; it found the first Ulysses Grant, a man who set a new level in executive incompetency.

The trouble with President Grant was not that he thought, acted, and behaved like a soldier. True, he showed a military man's complete bewilderment at anything or anybody that could not be dressed by the right, quick march, but he could have found aides who understood the arts of persuasion and the technique of lining up a majority. He betrayed not a sign of enterprise, imagination, or thought; but he had beaten Lee and Braxton Bragg, Joseph E. Johnston and John C. Pemberton in spite of this. It has often been said that Grant could on occasions, most notably in his Vicksburg campaign, show considerable

1. John Bigelow to John Bright, Dec. 10, 1868, Bright Papers. George Frisbie Hoar, *Autobiography of Seventy Years* (New York: Scribner's, 1903), I, 245-246. *Cong. Globe,* 40 Cong., 3 sess., p. 58, Representative James G. Blaine of Maine on Dec. 10, 1868. George Bancroft to U.S. Grant, March 13, 1869, Bancroft Papers.

imagination and daring. In fact, his decision in June 1863 to cut loose from his base and march on, in defiance of all the accepted rules of war, shows great obstinacy rather than great boldness. A really daring and brilliant general, someone fit to be compared with Lee at Chancellorsville, would have marched against Vicksburg from Oxford, Mississippi, in January of 1863, instead of retreating because General Earl Van Dorn had destroyed his supply depot at Holly Springs.[2]

Grant's failure as a politician lay in acting too little like a general. The peerless leader did not lead, the great commander did not command. He had no idea of designing a course of action for the public good and then throwing all the weight of his authority and prestige behind it. He seemed incapable of taking a long view; often, incapable of taking any view at all. The obstinacy and iron will that had led him to fight it out on the Mattapony line if it took all summer were mostly directed, in the presidency, against attempts to shake him from his lethargy. For eight years, while America was changing faster than ever before, Grant made hardly a move until conditions forced him.

Hamilton Fish was Grant's third choice for secretary of state,[3] a stolid, phlegmatic, and conservative man who had figured in the Seward-Weed organization in New York. His political service as one-term governor and one-term senator had been quite undistinguished, and he had held no important office since 1857. Charles Francis Adams described him as "a man of clear judgment and plain sense with no public motives of a secondary class. Abilities, respectable, but no genius. Very suitable as a makeweight to such a man as the President, whose jealousy and impatience of superior talent are quieted by his moderation."[4] Unemotional, unimaginative, extremely obstinate when he wanted

2. *Memoirs of General William T. Sherman, by Himself* (New York: Appleton, 1875), I, 317.

3. Grant to Fish, March 10, 1869, Fish Papers, L. C. Adam Badeau, *Grant in Peace: From Appomattox to Mount McGregor: A Personal Memoir* (London: Frederick Warne, n.d.), p. 162.

4. Adams Diary, Feb. 22, 1872.

to be, Fish gave a respectable account of himself in the State Department. His policy of keeping the country out of trouble and free of entanglements fitted the times, and his deliberation, steadiness, and solidity gave dignity to a badly tarnished administration.

Grant had been opposed to any negotiations with England after his election, regarding them as an invasion of his rights. When the treaties appeared he told Sumner that the naturalization and San Juan agreements were satisfactory, but he opposed the claims convention and wanted the matter left over until he took office. Before he was inaugurated, Grant dispatched one of his private secretaries to warn Thornton that he opposed the treaty, would throw his influence against its ratification, and would exert himself to secure its revocation if it passed. In early April, Grant wrote to Fish that he thought it well to send a message to the Senate recommending the rejection of the convention.[5]

Would Fish have stopped Sumner's speech if he had acted? It is unlikely; the speech was already written, and the senator would assuredly have found some occasion to deliver it, even if the convention had been shelved without debate.[6] At any rate, Fish, doubtless considering the effect such an insult would have on the British government, did nothing.

With the speech, Sumner seized control of American policy toward England.[7] Before he delivered it, he had shown a draft to Grant, who held that England's policy during the Civil War "could not be overstated in its mischief," and had secured his

5. C. F. Adams to Henry Adams, Dec. 16, 1868, Adams Papers. Adams Diary, Dec. 10, 1868, Jan. 1, 1869. Sumner to Bright, Jan. 17-19, 1869, printed in Edward L. Pierce, *Memoir and Letters of Charles Sumner* (Boston: Robert Brothers, 1894), pp. 368-369. Badeau, pp. 153-154. U. S. Grant to Fish, April 7, 1869, Fish Papers. L. C. Thornton to Clarendon, March 8, 1869, Clarendon Papers, Bodleian.

6. Which is not very likely; the Senate might well have called for the report of the chairman of the Foreign Affairs Committee.

7. C. F. Adams to Henry Adams, April 21, 1869, Adams Papers.

approval.[8] And by April 12, the senator had won another victory: his nominee, John Lothrop Motley, the historian, was appointed minister to England.[9] The new emissary was confirmed by the Senate soon after the convention had been voted down, but Fish, against Grant's inclinations, asked him to delay his departure until mid-June to give the administration a chance to see the tone of the press and the sentiment of the country before deciding on a new course.[10] Behind this request lay the worried secretary's search for a new policy. The instructions to be given to Motley, he admitted in a letter to John Hamilton on April 22, 1869, were "a source of deep concern and embarrassment" to him. He realized the rejection of the treaty had been inevitable, but the repulse of a proposal to arbitrate meant that America had to make a new suggestion. And what that could be he did not know, for the yardstick of damages set up by Sumner was far beyond anything the British would agree to. All in all, Fish was inclined to declare a moratorium on negotiations until the British and American viewpoints drew closer together.

Fish did not differ too much from Sumner in his view of the question at this time. Private claims, he wrote, had all been satisfied by the insurance companies; the companies themselves had all raised their premiums during the war and made large profits. In an arbitration, this would certainly be urged against the claims made by the companies, so "the mere loss, from destruction of property at sea, is . . . very much diffused and it may be urged that it has ceased to belong to individuals." He thought the Neutrality Proclamation a grievous wrong, but the British would reply that America's whole history had been a

8. Sumner to Motley, May 27, 1869, printed in Pierce, p. 393. Sumner to Longfellow, May 25, 1869, Sumner Papers, Sumner to Bemis, May 25, 1869, Bemis Papers.

9. Badeau, p. 153. John O. Sargent to Reverdy Johnson, May 11, 1869, Johnson Papers.

10. Adams Diary, May 6, 1869. Fish Diary, April 20, 1869, Fish Papers, L.C. (hereafter cited Fish Diary).

tale of sympathy with rebellions and revolutions, and she could not ask compensation for having her own habitual policy applied against her. Actually, America had never been as hasty as England had in 1861, but the question of the proclamation's timing depended on individual judgment. "There are therefore two strong sides to this point of the question." The really unassailable American claims against Britain were national ones for her sympathy to the Confederacy. British unfriendliness to the Union extended the war at least a year and cost the nation her merchant navy. Such losses would come to at least $1,000,000,000, and no country would ever pay this. The only possible compensation would be territory, but the British would certainly refuse such a suggestion.[11]

Meanwhile, meeting Fish at Samuel Hooper's dinner table, Sumner had suggested that Motley should prepare a memoir of his views on the claims question. Fish agreed;[12] the delighted historian delved into the State Department archives, and on April 26 presented the secretary with a long memorandum. He reached the same conclusion Fish had in his letter of April 22: there should be a pause in negotiations "for a season." Motley's treatment of the subject followed Sumner's exactly in its assertion of consequential claims, its denial that Confederate ocean belligerency was a reality, and its attack upon the precipitate issue of the Neutrality Proclamation.[13]

But Fish gradually concluded that the right of a sovereign power to decide when a civil conflict in another country had reached a stage grave enough to require a proclamation of neutrality could not be impeached. He also disagreed with Sumner and Motley that a distinction could be made between sea and land belligerency.[14] Grant, strongly under the influence of John A. Rawlins, once his adjutant and now his secretary

11. Fish to John C. Hamilton, April 22, 1869, Fish Papers, L.C.
12. Pierce, p. 403.
13. Fish Papers, L.C.
14. Fish to S. B. Ruggles, May 18, 1869, Fish Papers, L.C.

of war, wanted to recognize the Cuban rebels and their Spanish masters as belligerents;[15] and the Cubans did not hold nearly the power and position that the Confederates had in 1861. So he, too, opposed any limitation of the right to recognize belligerency, and the first draft of Motley's instructions painstakingly avoided emphasis on this point.

Sumner saw the draft and was up in arms. "It was fatal — very," he told Motley, and he drew substitute clauses on the proclamation, which he took round to the State Department. Sumner told Fish that he would advise Motley to resign if the instructions were not changed. Next day, May 16, Sumner asked the distinguished lawyer Caleb Cushing for his help. Cushing called on Fish and then came back to dine with Sumner. The two talked over Sumner's substitute clauses, and Cushing said he thought Sumner's speech was "in complete conformity" with the law of nations, but his substitute paragraph weakened the American case. The senator replied that he knew this, but he had been trying to reconcile the administration's views with his own.

Late at night, thinking about what Cushing had said, Sumner wrote a letter to Fish withdrawing his substitute clauses. He said he had decided they were inadequate and lessened the power of the nation's case against England. Motley should be allowed to speak according to "his own enlightened discretion." But Congress should decide what to claim from England, and on what grounds, and he had no doubt its members would whole-heartedly support him. Fish, panic-stricken at this threat to lead a revolt on Capitol Hill, sent back a rather pathetic note the next morning asking Sumner to reconsider his withdrawal, saying that he had "determined to ask to introduce your suggestions, almost in totidem verbis," and adding that "we have but one object, and differ only as to some incidents — they may be of more importance than I suppose, or of less than you think, but can hardly be of sufficient importance to break up an effort

15. Sumner to Motley, May 17, 1869, printed in Pierce p. 406. Fish Diary, March 19, 1869.

at negotiation or to break down an Administration." Sumner dispatched Cushing, who had called on him just after breakfast, to the State Department, where he and the secretary spent four hours hammering out a new draft which satisfied the senator's demands.

In their final version the instructions told Motley to make it clear to the British that the rejection of the Johnson-Clarendon Convention implied no unfriendliness or discourtesy. The nation was unanimous in rejecting it, but this adverse judgment was not reached by any single train of argument, nor based on any single policy or estimate of the damages suffered by America. With this slap at Sumner, Fish said that the present was not the most favorable time for new negotiations and that he proposed a suspension of discussions until any excitement or irritation stemming from the rejection of the treaty passed away. He hoped this period of waiting would be short. Fish said he hoped that when negotiations were resumed, the two governments would agree to include discussion of a definition of the rights and duties of neutrals.

Last came the paragraphs that had caused all the trouble. Cushing managed to reconcile Sumner's demand for a strong condemnation of the British Neutrality Proclamation and the administration's desire to leave open a gap through which the United States could squeeze when it wanted to by saying that the president recognized every power's right to define its relations toward a civil conflict in another state when it had reached sufficient "complexity, magnitude and completeness." The necessity and propriety of the British proclamation were not admitted, but the United States regarded it as part of the evidence against Britain only as far as it showed the origin and direction of subsequent British policy. It was important for what it foreshadowed.

The rest of the instructions followed Sumner's substitute paragraph. Fish had wanted to distinguish between England and France, which, like Spain, had conceded Confederate belligerent rights at the same time, and Sumner had written a clause pointing out that only in England was the concession of belligerency followed by acts causing direct damage to America. "In France," as he remarked to Motley, "there was *damnum absque injuria;* in England, *damnum cum injuria.*" The instructions closed with the remark that the president was careful to make this distinction because he wanted to simplify the American charges and bring the really important ones into focus. Motley was directed to spread this view of the American case at all times, in his "social and private intercourse and conversation" as well as his official talks, and he was to stress it especially when talking to the ambassadors of countries like France and Spain, which had issued proclamations of neutrality at the same time as England. Fish did not mean to fight all the world. In retrospect, the instructions did weaken Sumner's indictment of Britain a little; anything that put less emphasis upon the Neutrality Proclamation was a step toward peace. But this was not obvious in 1869.[16]

Sumner was delighted with his victory and crowed loudly in a letter to Motley.[17] But Fish must have resented his humiliation deeply, and perhaps this contributed to the bitter, vindictive temper he displayed in his later dealings with Sumner. Privately Fish commented that he did not regard Sumner's speech as a fixed standard of demands. If the British thought of it as what most Americans "honestly believe to be the measure of our claim, but that we do not expect to be able to meet in

16. Fish to Motley, May 15, 1869, Diplomatic Instructions. (Fish let the original date of the instructions stand, although they were revised afterward.) Sumner to Fish, May 16, 1869; Fish to S. B. Ruggles, May 18, 1869; Fish to J. L. Motley, May 17, 1869; Sidney Webster to Fish, June 7, 1869, Fish Papers, L.C. Sumner to Motley, May 16, 17, 1869, printed in Pierce, pp. 405-406. Fish to Carl Schurz, May 28, 1869, Schurz Papers. J. C. Bancroft Davis, *Mr. Fish and the Alabama Claims: A Chapter in Diplomatic History* (Boston: Houghton, Mifflin, 1893), p. 33.

17. Sumner to Motley, May 17, 1869, printed in Pierce, p. 406.

full and that we do not mean to insist upon in full nor even that they recognize it in full but if they will simply admit that we think our losses approximate to something in that direction," a settlement might be reached.[18] Two days later Fish was more specific. Not every grievance was to be satisfied in damages. A single kind word of apology and regret would mean a great deal. Actual losses for property destroyed had to be paid. Consequential damages were not so easy to estimate, but "statesmanship should be able to direct negotiations to a satisfactory settlement."[19] The implication that Fish would settle for less than the huge amounts Sumner had mentioned is clear.[20]

What did Sumner expect to get from England? "You will observe," he wrote to George Bemis, about his speech, "that, while stating our case, I make no demand — not an apology or a dollar. All this I left to the diplomacy of the future."[21] It was not yet time to make demands. The first step was to make Britain see the American grievance.[22] In his speech Sumner had not said that Britain must pay the American war debt. He only argued that America would be justified in making such demands in strict equity, that this was the reckoning *sub specie aeternitatis*.[23] Sumner's aim was to start a diplomatic dialogue. He told John V. S. L. Pruyn that he expected the rejection of the treaty to lead to long discussions between the British and American governments, which might well last for years.[24]

18. Fish to Francis Lieber, June 10, 1869, Fish Papers, L.C.
19. Fish to John C. Hamilton, June 12, 1869, Fish Papers, L.C.
20. Thornton to Clarendon, June 14, 1869, Clarendon Papers, Bodleian.
21. Sumner to Bemis, May 25, 1869, Bemis Papers. Also, Sumner to Badeau, July 26, 1869, printed in Badeau, pp. 579-581. Sumner to Lieber, May 30, 1869, printed in Pierce, p. 388. R. H. Dana, Jr., to Sumner, May 22, 1872, Sumner Papers. *The Works of Charles Sumner* (Boston. Lee and Shepard, 1880), XII, 89.
22. Sumner to Fish, June 10, 1869, Fish Papers, L.C.
23. Sumner, *Works,* XII, 86, 93.
24. Reverdy Johnson to Seward, March 10, 1869, Seward Papers. He told Thornton the same thing. Thornton to Clarendon, March 8, 1869, Clarendon Papers, Bodleian.

Sumner surely expected America eventually to collect a good part, if not all, of her remaining war debt as compensation. "How the case shall be settled," he told Francis Lieber, "whether by money more or less, by territorial compensation, by apology, or by an amendment of the law of nations, is still an open question; all may be combined."[25] On June 9, Fish, acting on the course he had sketched to John C. Hamilton on April 22, sounded Thornton about exchanging Canada for the claims. The minister replied that England was not particular about keeping Canada, but could not let it go without the consent of its inhabitants.[26] Fish told Sumner about the conversation that same evening and asked him how to state the amount of American claims to the English. The senator, still anxious to bring home the nature of the American case to England, said that he would make no "claim" or "demand" at the moment, and was not disposed to mention either.[27] But on June 14, Sumner gave a dinner party. One of the guests was Caleb Cushing, a rabid expansionist, whose conversation left his host in high good humor. He wrote to Motley that England would have to yield eventually. "I do not despair," he continued, "seeing the debate end — (1) In the withdrawal of England from this hemisphere; (2) In remodelling maritime international law."[28]

There is no question that Sumner would have been glad to see Canada join the Union. In 1867 he published an article in the *Atlantic* called "Prophetic Voices about America," in which he predicted the union of North America under the leadership of the United States, quoted John Adams and Cobden on the inevitability of such a confederation, and referring to Turgot's maxim about colonies being like fruits, clinging to the

25. Sumner to Lieber, May 30, 1869, printed in Pierce, p. 388.
26. Thornton to Clarendon, June 14, 1869, Clarendon Papers, Bodleian.
27. Sumner to Motley, June 11, 1869, printed in Pierce, pp. 409-410.
28. C. F. Adams to Henry Adams, Dec. 29, 1869, Adams Papers. Sumner to Motley, June 15, 1869, printed in Pierce, p. 410.

tree only until maturity, said: "At the time Turgot wrote, Canada was a French possession; but his words are as applicable to this colony as to the United States. When will the fruit be ripe?"[29]

Sumner was not as vigorous an expansionist as Seward: he had felt very doubtful about supporting the purchase of Alaska and told John Bright, "Abstractly I am against further accessions of territory unless by the free choice of the inhabitants."[30] In September 1869 he restated this in a speech at the Republican state convention in Worcester, Massachusetts. Sumner made it quite clear, speaking in words that recalled the "Prophetic Voices" article, that he expected to see Canada and the United States one country before long. But he rejected all suggestions that Canada be handed over to pay for the claims. The great tradition of liberty from Magna Carta to the Somerset case made it impossible for England to think of such a thing, just as the great tradition of republican liberty would make it impossible for the United States to receive Canada in that way. "Territory may be conveyed, but not a people."[31] If England had offered Canada for the claims, subject to the approval of her people in a plebiscite, Sumner would have been delighted. He may well have had this in mind as a possible solution to the problem he delineated in his speech. But as his letter of May 30 to Lieber and his flexibility and open-mindedness in dealing with the Treaty of Washington show, it was certainly not the only solution he would have been willing to accept.

29. *Atlantic Monthly*, Sept. 1867, pp. 281, 283, 302-303, 305-306. Later Sumner published an expanded version of the article in book form as *Prophetic Voices Concerning America: A Monograph* (Boston: Lee and Shepard, 1874), in which there were even more references to continental union.

30. Sumner to John Bright, April 16, 1867, Bright Papers. Sumner to Longfellow, April 15, 1867, Sumner Papers.

31. "National Affairs at Home and Abroad," Speech at the Republican State Convention in Worcester, Massachusetts, Sept. 22, 1869, Sumner, *Works*, XII, 127-128.

During the summer the Alabama Claims and Sumner's speech gradually faded from public attention. The British storm and Motley's pacific instructions both helped to dampen enthusiasm. Nothing new happened in connection with the claims, and presently other matters, including the Cuban rebellion, rose to divert popular attention. The danger of a tide of extremist feeling lasted longer: in the middle of June, Charles Francis Adams heard rumors that a group of the more desperate Republicans were planning to create a war issue with England based on Sumner's speech. "Fearful of the gradual disintegration of the party from its internal dissensions, they are for forming an alliance with the Fenians, on this basis, and cutting under the democrats. The elements of this Union are to be 1st the army of the republic organization, still clinging to the habits formed in the last struggle 2nd the whole Irish army 3rd the disappointed office seekers and political camp followers 4th the Southern adventurers, as well as other classes in that region who desire to divert the public attention from its late object 5th the democratic rank and file at least to an extent sufficient to make good all losses from the respectable classes of the republicans." Butler had already fired the first salvo in his Memorial Day speech at Gloucester. The group had intended to follow it up with a pronunciamento against England by Andrew G. Curtin, the great war governor of Pennsylvania and newly appointed minister to Russia, at his farewell dinner in Philadelphia, and by giving Sumner an ovation in the West organized by Senator Nye.[32] But Grant, his attention turned toward Cuba, wanted no trouble with England, and he ordered Curtin not to speak.[33]

32. C. F. Adams to Henry Adams, June 16, 1869, Adams Papers. Such rumors also reached the papers. New York *Evening Post,* June 8, 10; New York *Commercial Advertiser,* June 10; *New York Tribune,* June 10, all reprinted in the New York *World,* June 11, 1869; also, *World,* June 15, 17, 1869. Senator Howe of Wisconsin, former Secretary Stanton, and John W. Forney, owner of the Washington *Daily Morning Chronicle* and the Philadelphia *Press,* were others mentioned in connection with the movement.

33. Sumner to Motley, June 8, 1869, printed in Pierce, p. 409.

With this, the movement came to a dead stop. Had Grant approved of it, Butler and other Anglophobes might have created a good deal of disturbance, but it is doubtful if they would have had a very deep or lasting effect. The time for that was past. If they had acted in April, when the popular excitement was at its peak, every element of the union Adams described would have been caught up in the agitation. Probably they would not have caused a war; Britain was not eager to fight, and only a little delay would have made Americans aware of their appalling naval weakness. But they might have succeeded in pressing the Ameri-- can demands so far and in embittering the controversy so much that negotiations would have been impossible and Anglo-Ameri- can relations would have been poisoned for years. Butler was not usually so slow to act, and it was fortunate that he, and those like him, were busy ingratiating themselves with the new president and struggling for patronage for three months when they might have been whipping up an Anglophobe frenzy.

In midsummer the control of American policy toward Eng- land began to change hands. Fish had possessed little real power over it, but this began to alter when Motley's dispatch re- porting his first interview with Clarendon arrived on June 23. The minister had done exactly what he had been told not to do and severely limited the absolute right of a nation to declare its neutrality or recognize belligerency by adding that "such measures must always be taken with a full view of the grave responsibilities assumed." This statement had much more in common with the principles of Sumner's speech than with the doctrines the administration had urged. Grant and Fish had both said that the Neutrality Proclamation was not important in itself, only in its demonstration of the hostility to the United States which issued later in criminal acts. Sumner had denounced the proclamation in its own right, as the concession that opened the shipyards and arsenals of England to the Confederacy, the great original wrong from which all the other crimes followed.[34]

34. Motley to Fish, June 12, 1869, Diplomatic Despatches. Fish to

Motley was closely committed to Sumner's original position before he received his instructions; a fear of imitating Reverdy Johnson's overfriendly ways, a natural tendency to extreme partisanship, and a deep-seated Anglophobia reinforced his predisposition to state the American case with all the force possible.[35]

Grant saw the dispatch and was furious. He wanted to dismiss Motley as he would have removed an insubordinate officer in the field of war, but Fish, anxious not to have a quarrel result from the first essay in foreign policy of an administration which had already lost almost all the vast stock of prestige it had started with, persuaded him not to. Perhaps he felt it was too early to risk a head-on collision with Sumner. But Motley was no longer to be trusted with any negotiations or discussions on the claims; the reply withdrew them from his care.[36]

With this, the initiative passed to Fish. Sumner's power was still great, and the secretary had to walk warily for a long time to come. But the rallying of an administration party in Congress had already begun, and in a short time Fish's personal position was greatly strengthened. Early in September, Rawlins, Grant's alter ego, died, and the way was clear for a new feeling of personal trust and reliance to develop between president and secretary. There was no personal warmth between the retiring, narrow-minded, and unpolished soldier and the cultivated successor of the patroons, but Grant came to realize that Fish

---

Motley, May 15, 1869, Diplomatic Instructions. Sumner to Butler, June 3, 1869, Butler Papers.

35. John Rose to Hamilton Fish, Nov. 3, 1869, Fish Papers, L.C. Henry Adams to C. F. Adams, Jr., Feb. 15, 1865; J. L. Motley to C. F. Adams, March 5, Sept. 15, 1865; C. F. Adams to Henry Adams, May 4, 1870, Adams Papers. Beckles Willson, *America's Ambassadors to England (1785-1929): A Narrative of Anglo-American Diplomatic Relations* (New York: Frederick A. Stokes, 1929), p. 345.

36. Badeau, pp. 201-202. Bancroft Davis, pp. 38-39. Fish to Motley, June 28, 1869, Diplomatic Instructions. Thornton to Clarendon, Sept. 21, 1869, Clarendon Papers, Bodleian.

possessed many of the qualities he lacked and the administration needed. And on July 30, Motley wrote to say that he had forgotten to mention he had shown his offending dispatch to Clarendon before sending it.[37] This letter arrived during the middle of August; Fish was about to leave for his Hudson valley home to escape the intolerable Washington heat, and it was overlooked until October. When it came to light, it gave the *coup de grâce* to confidence in Motley.

Fish exercised his new and slowly growing freedom cautiously. After June 23, he continued to do all he could to keep Sumner happy. The withdrawal from Motley of the power to negotiate was explained to him as a move prompted by the ideas that the Senate would be on hand for consultations and that the chances of settlement were better in Washington.[38] But when Sumner once more demanded that England should be confronted with the American case "in length and breadth" to make her realize the American grievance, Fish made no response. Twice Sumner wrote to urge a new statement,[39] but nothing was done until, in the middle of August, when he was staying at the secretary's home in Garrison, New York, he pointed out that Congress would expect some action on the claims. Fish, sensitive to the power of Anglophobia and the Irish vote, and perhaps thinking that Sumner might take the lead in a Senate witch hunt, immediately — and disarmingly — asked him to write a paper presenting the American case. Sumner replied that he was much too busy, and, besides, he had already made his statement. But he thought Caleb Cushing would be an excellent choice for the task, and Fish agreed to ask him.[40]

During the summer, Fish dealt with several attempts to settle the Alabama Claims by informal diplomacy. The most

37. Motley to Fish, July 30, 1869, Diplomatic Despatches.

38. Sumner to Longfellow, July 8, 1869, Sumner Papers. Sumner to Bemis, July 7, 1869, printed in Pierce, p. 410.

39. Sumner to Fish, July 11, 21, 1869, Fish Papers, L.C.

40. Sumner to Motley, Aug. 17, 1869, printed in Pierce, pp. 412-413; *ibid.*, p. 412.

important was an initiative made through Sir John Rose, the Canadian minister of finance who came to Washington in July 1869, ostensibly to discuss reciprocity, but with the understanding that the Alabama Claims would also be considered. Over dinner one night Rose suggested the possibility of a special mission. Fish was noncommittal, but a few days later the two had a longer talk. Calling to make his farewells, Rose said he was going to England soon and could he be of any service there? Outlining his views, Fish said that Sumner's speech was a fair statement of the American grievances, though all of them might not be "susceptible of indemnification." If Britain would accept that, he thought an expression of regret, an indemnity, and a retroactive amendment of the laws of neutrality (without Britain actually admitting any wrong) would form the elements of a settlement. The treaty would have to go much beyond the Johnson-Clarendon Convention, and the Alabama Claims would have to be treated separately from other commercial or even international claims. Fish was obviously thinking of the British property claims, which might be greater than the Alabama Claims and provoke a partisan storm. The two men then discussed the mechanics of a *rapprochement*. They agreed it would be best if Britain sent a special mission. Fish was all for the Duke of Argyll, but less keen on John Bright, whose reaction to Sumner's speech had been violent. Lord Granville and Sir Henry Bulwer were other names mentioned. Fish suggested that the best time would be early in the winter.[41] Fish was pleased with the meeting, though he had, of course, hedged on the consequential claims and had not said how large an indemnity he expected.

In late September, Caleb Cushing turned up at the State Department with the dispatch he had been asked to draft; Fish showed it at a cabinet meeting on the 24th and learned his

41. C. F. Adams, Jr., *Lee at Appomattox, and Other Papers* (Boston: Houghton Mifflin, 1902), p. 123. Bancroft Davis, p. 44. Fish Diary, July 11, 1869.

colleagues' views on the claims question.[42] Most of the discussion seems to have echoed Sumner's views: later the same day, Attorney-General Ebenezer R. Hoar wrote him that "I think matters with England are going to your mind — and that your speech and our acts will not trouble each other."[43] Next day Fish signed and sent the dispatch. At first glance it was disarmingly bland and, compared to Sumner's speech, moderate. But Cushing managed to work in most of Sumner's doctrines in short, key passages which said a little, but implied a great deal.[44]

Fish managed to have his cake and eat it, too, with this dispatch. It kept Congress quiet; many members were satisfied with just a glimpse of the manuscript, though Sumner demanded to see the whole correspondence in printed form.[45] Vice-President Schuyler Colfax told him that he was "intensely gratified"; the argument was "masterly and unanswerable ... able and convincing." "Commend us to Hamilton Fish," ran an editorial in the *Cincinnati Gazette,* "for such sturdy words. ... He has apparently forgotten to use the oil of diplomacy, but calls things by their right names." At the same time, he avoided offending the British. When Gladstone first saw the dispatch, he exploded that its "tone is Sumnerian: it is impossible to say anything worse about it," and declared that honor made any new British proposition impossible.[46] But Fish, after an attempt to defend

42. What was said is unknown — Fish did not record it in his diary — but George S. Boutwell scribbled the terms he would accept on a scrap of paper (this memorandum is in the Fish Papers, L.C.). He wanted a statement of the rights and duties of neutrals, set out in a treaty, and payment of the actual losses in ships sunk, to be ascertained by a commission. The consequential claims should be referred to the decision of a friendly power. Sumner would not have approved the last condition, for he regarded the claims as self-evident and unassailable.

43. Hoar to Sumner, Sept. 24, 1869, Sumner Papers. Hoar may have been thinking of the dispatch, for Fish would never have let anyone but Grant know that he was allowing Cushing and Sumner to usurp his office.

44. Fish to Motley, Sept. 25, 1869, Diplomatic Instructions.

45. Thornton to Clarendon, Dec. 21, 1869, FO 5/1330.

46. Schuyler Colfax to Fish, Dec. 24, 1869; *Cincinnati Gazette,* Dec.

every last word, in which he succeeded in sounding remarkably like Sumner justifying his speech, admitted confidentially to Thornton that he had wanted to prevent Congress passing resolutions that would make all negotiation impossible, or charging that the administration was neglecting the question. This satisfied the British government.[47]

Motley reported that Lord Clarendon was very anxious for a settlement, and during his interview with Fish on November 4, Thornton asked what kind of terms America could agree to. Fish said he would see how opinion in the Senate was tending, but he would have to wait until more members returned to Washington. A couple of days later he wrote to Sumner, who had been advising him to compose another strong statement and knock the American (i.e. Sumner's) principles into John Bull's head, to ask what the Senate and the country would accept. Sumner replied that it was not yet time to formulate any proposal to England. If Congress showed indifference, the way would be open for the secretary to act; if it expressed itself decisively, he would have a guide. But the people now had jurisdiction of the question. No administration could flout their requirements; it would be best to wait until England took the initiative. Sumner made two suggestions. First, the president should make a "careful, explicit and firm statement" of the American grievance in his message to Congress in order to satisfy America and wake up England. Second, a settlement could begin if England would show some good will and regret for what she had done.[48]

22, 1869, encl. in A. R. Corbin to Fish, Dec. 22, 1869; John H. Clifford to Fish, Dec. 24, 1869, Fish Papers, L.C. Gladstone to Clarendon, Oct. 23, 25, 1869, Gladstone Papers.

47. Fish Diary, Nov. 4, 1869. Thornton to Clarendon, Nov. 23, Dec. 21, 1869, FO 5/1330, 1331. Thornton to Clarendon, Nov. 9, 1869, Clarendon Papers, Bodleian. Gladstone to Clarendon, Nov. 22, 1869, Gladstone Papers.

48. Motley to Fish, Oct. 16, 1869; Fish Diary, Nov. 4, 1869; Sumner to Fish, Oct. 7, 11, 1869; Fish to Sumner, Nov. 6, 1869; Sumner to Fish, Nov. 9, 1869, Fish Papers, L.C.

Fish cannot have found this very helpful. The idea that England should inaugurate the process of reconciliation by expressing regret, "some kind word," was not new. Sumner had included it in his speech. Fish had mentioned it to John Rose, who had been busy spreading the idea in England.[49] As for leaving the matter to Congress, this was just what Fish had been desperately trying to avoid.

On the same day that Sumner replied, the claims question was discussed in the cabinet. Grant wanted to wait another year or so for a settlement; he thought England might soon withdraw from Canada, and he would be satisfied with the payment of actual losses in ships sunk and a settlement of maritime neutrality laws then. Fish said he was against making a definite proposal to delay negotiations. It was better to leave things as they were, with America maintaining her declaration of willingness to negotiate whenever England was ready.[50]

At the end of November, Fish told Rose that he did not think the time was ripe for the scheme of settlement they had discussed in July. He still hoped that negotiations would soon be renewed, and he would be able to tell what the chances were as soon as Congress assembled.[51] But in his heart of hearts, Fish must have known that Sumner still swayed the mind of the nation. When he came to prepare the part of Grant's message to Congress dealing with the claims question, he stated the grievances of America in squarely Sumnerian terms, prolongation of the war and all.[52] Fish had come a long way toward independence since May, but he could not yet make his own policy.

In the middle of November, Fish gave Thornton his private opinions on a settlement. He wanted Britain either to pay a

49. Sumner, *Works*, XII, 92. Fish to John C. Hamilton, June 12, 1869; Rose to Fish, Nov. 3, 1869, Fish Papers, L.C.
50. Fish Diary, Nov. 9, 1869.
51. Fish to Rose, Nov. 22, 1869, Fish Papers, L.C.
52. *Cong. Globe.*, 41 Cong., 2 sess., p. 6, Dec. 6, 1869. Fish Diary, Nov. 26, 29, 1869. Thornton to Clarendon, Oct. 12, 1869, Clarendon Papers, Bodleian.

gross sum in satisfaction of the claims or to allow a maritime commission to assess the damages. Both nations should agree on new rules of neutrality, and Britain should say "some kind words" of regret about the past. These were much the same terms that Fish had outlined to Rose in July, and once more he remained silent about the consequential claims. In a letter written nearly a year later he made it clear that when he spoke to Thornton he had been thinking only of payment of the actual losses in ships sunk. The gulf between Fish and Sumner was now immense.[53]

Thornton did not mention the consequential claims and presumably understood that Fish had abandoned them. He dug deeper into the terms than Rose had, though. Did Fish mean arbitration when he spoke of a "commission" to assess the damages, he asked? No, replied the secretary; the commission was only to decide the amount of the damages. Thornton said that the British could never admit so openly that they had been wrong; another sovereign authority would have to pronounce on this. Public men in England have admitted it, returned Fish; but Thornton said that opinion in the Commons largely sustained the government's course. To some more questions, about what rules of neutrality he had in mind, Fish replied that America wanted to outlaw the arming of a vessel at sea[54] and to state that the nationality of a ship could not be changed by sale or on the high seas. America might be willing to abolish privateering if Britain agreed to declare all private property on ships inviolable.[55]

53. And probably had been in July, when Fish told Rose that all the claims might not be capable of indemnification. Fish to Francis Lieber, Oct. 4, 1870, Fish Papers, L.C.

54. The *Alabama*, of course, had evaded neutrality laws by doing this.

55. Fish Diary, Nov. 15, 1869. Fish's first two conditions were designed to prevent future *Alabamas*. Privateering had been declared abolished by those countries — the major European sea powers — signing the Declaration of Paris in 1856. Secretary of State William Marcy

In London, Gladstone told Clarendon that he was all for giving Fish his kind words of regret; they were amply warranted by the admitted miscarriage of justice with the *Alabama*. But arbitration of the claims was essential.[56] Fish's abandonment of the consequential claims meant that the two sides were no further apart in the early winter of 1869 than Seward and Stanley had been in 1867-1868. Unfortunately, American public opinion was behind Sumner, and Fish could not move. All the same, the situation as 1869 drew to an end was much better than anyone would have dared to predict in April. The American drift to extremism had been checked; Fish could not make policy, but he could stop Sumner directing it. And he had managed to preserve a spirit of cordiality in Anglo-American exchanges; the rejection of the Johnson-Clarendon Convention and Sumner's inflammatory speech did not, thanks to Fish, embitter the personal relations between members of the two governments.[57]

---

had refused to sign the declaration unless Fish's last condition, the inviolability of private property at sea (that was not contraband of war; Fish presumably meant this) was added. The other powers would not allow this, and the United States did not become a signatory.

56. Gladstone to Clarendon, Nov. 29, 1869, Gladstone Papers.

57. Gladstone to Clarendon, Nov. 29, Dec. 25, 1869; Clarendon to Gladstone, Dec. 24, 1869, Gladstone Papers.

CHAPTER 6

The Critical Year

The scheme to exchange Canada for the Alabama Claims assumed a new importance under the stimulus of events in the winter of 1869-1870. Until then the Canadian Confederation had consisted of only four provinces: Ontario, Quebec, New Brunswick, and Nova Scotia. Both the Maritimes had been rail-roaded into the new Dominion by strong pressure from London, and both were disgruntled. In Nova Scotia, a majority opposed confederation and eyed the idea of annexation to the United States. Nevertheless, as the year drew to a close, the leaders of the two-year-old nation prepared to take over the vast tract of land between the Lake of the Woods and the Rockies. This area was inhabited only by Indians, a few thousand métis, hunters, and trappers, many of them half-breeds, and a handful of colonists settled there by Lord Selkirk years before. Both métis and colonists made their homes in the Red River district, around Fort Garry (present-day Winnipeg). Government, as far as it existed, meant vague supervision by the Hudson's Bay Company's agents. Alarmed by the prospect of a strong administrative authority from the Dominion, fearing for the continuance of their way of life, the métis rebelled in November 1869. There was no road connecting Red River and Ontario; Lake Superior was frozen over; until the spring the area could be reached only through the United States, and the rebels need have no fear of Canadian countermeasures. In Washington and St. Paul, in

Ottawa and London, the repercussions of the rising were soon felt.

Grant's cabinet discussed Canada's future and the Alabama Claims just a few days after the newly appointed Dominion officials of Red River took refuge in Minnesota. Grant remarked that he had heard rumors that John Bright was coming over to negotiate a settlement of the claims. He hoped they were untrue; he wanted to keep the question open until Britain was ready to give up Canada. George S. Boutwell, secretary of the treasury and the great pillar of the administration besides Fish, pointed out that Britain had guaranteed Canada's bonds and loans for railroads and other internal improvements. If she consented to negotiate the annexation of Canada before the claims were settled, the United States would have to assume the debt and offset the claims against part of it. But if the *Alabama* damages were already paid, the United States would have the money and the claims could not be bargained away. Grant replied that he thought keeping the claims open would make the British more eager to settle by the cession of Canada, and so it would come about sooner. Fish privately reflected that the two questions were most unlikely to influence each other. Britain, he knew, was not eager to keep Canada, but she would never part with it as an item in a negotiation or a bargain. Nor would she leave until the Canadians made it clear they wanted to cut the painter. But he spoke only to recall that Lord Carlisle had once told him that the British would be glad to get rid of Canada, which was nothing but an expense and a source of weakness. Hoar said Thornton had told him the same thing. "If that be so," said Grant, "I would be willing to settle at once," and every member of the Cabinet agreed.[1]

Fish was not an expansionist, and he did not care whether Canada was in the Union or out of it. Like nearly every Amer-

1. Fish Diary, Nov. 26, 1869. Once the British were out of Canada, Grant was willing to accept compensation for ships sunk and a statement of maritime neutrality law as a complete settlement. *Ibid.*, Nov. 9, 1869.

ican, he thought continental union inevitable eventually,[2] but he saw no reason to give destiny a shove. He was primarily interested in settlement of the Alabama Claims, and if this could be achieved through annexation, he would take that road. If it had been left to Fish alone, a treaty liquidating the dispute could probably have been signed in a matter of weeks; only the issue of arbitration separated the terms he had outlined to Thornton on November 15 from the British position. But, as he must have known, Sumner, Grant, and the country would not have accepted it. To get their support, he embarked on a policy which was fated to prove a year's aberration.

With the cabinet meeting in his mind, Fish decided just before Christmas to sound Thornton on the subject. Why, he suddenly demanded during an interview, should not Britain withdraw completely from Canada? When she did, the pretext for Fenian threats would be gone, and the Alabama Claims could be settled at the same time. "Oh," said Thornton, "you know that we cannot, the Canadians find great fault with me for saying so openly as I do that we are ready to let them go whenever they shall wish. But they do not desire it." Almost no one in Canada favored annexation. Fish replied that he had heard very different reports, that nearly everyone was for it, except the rich, the bankers, and the officials of the government.[3]

Thornton diligently reported this and other instances of American designs on Canada,[4] and Lord Clarendon, wrote acidly: "They are now *going in* for the British possessions and seem to think that we can transfer them as easily as a Virginia planter ten years ago might have conveyed his estates with the chattels on it to a neighbour."[5] Gladstone, hearing of the suggestions, snapped out the usual answer: Canada was free to go

2. *Ibid.*, Oct. 4, 1870.
3. *Ibid.*, Dec. 23, 1869.
4. Thornton to Clarendon, Jan. 3, 1870, FO 5/1191. Thornton to Clarendon, Jan. 4, 8, 11, 1870, Clarendon Papers, Bodleian.
5. Clarendon to Gladstone, Jan. 18, 1870, Gladstone Papers.

when she liked. But Britain would not be insulted by the manner of her going, and he resented Fish's tentatives.[6]

Early in the new year, Fish tried again. This time he did not mention annexation and modeled his policy much more obviously on the conditions that Grant had laid down for a settlement of the Alabama Claims in terms of actual losses alone.[7] He began by giving Thornton a copy of a petition from some inhabitants of British Columbia asking for annexation and inquired whether this, coupled with the troubles in Red River and the anticonfederation movement within the Dominion, did not show that the time had come for separation. Thornton had told him over and over, said Fish, that Britain was more than willing to withdraw; why not now, when there was nothing to affront the dignity of the country if it took up the policy? The Red River uprising was, he thought, more serious than the confederation government knew. Red River was linked geographically and commercially with the United States. It had no social or political intercourse with Canada proper;[8] the same was true of the Maritimes. And (the crux of the matter) "the removal of the British flag would render easy the settlement of all the questions between the two Governments." Thornton disobligingly replied that he thought the reverse was true. Fish closed the interview by suggesting that the minister write privately to Lord Clarendon on the subject; it might lead to results that would avoid future trouble and embarrassment.[9] A week later, on the 14th, he wrote to Motley to spread the idea of withdrawal from Canada among the members of the British government.[10] With this, Fish, thinking he had done all he could for the time being, dropped the subject for three months.

6. Gladstone to Clarendon, Jan. 14, 1870, Gladstone Papers.
7. Fish Diary, Nov. 9, 26, 1869.
8. That is, Ontario and Quebec.
9. Fish Diary, Jan. 6, 1870. Thornton to Clarendon, Jan. 8, 1870, Clarendon Papers, Bodleian.
10. Fish to Motley, Jan. 14, 1870, Diplomatic Instructions. Motley to Fish, Feb. 2, 1870, Confidential, Unofficial, Feb. 21, 1870, July 16,

Grant and Fish maintained a scrupulous neutrality toward the Red River uprising. Senator Alexander Ramsey of Minnesota, a leader in the movement to annex western Canada, came to the White House in mid-January saying that $100,000 was needed to make the rebellion a success, but Fish immediately replied that "we should not use money in that way," and Grant, too, condemned the idea.[11]

As soon as the trouble started, Fish realized that the British might ask for permission to march troops across American territory to suppress the rising, and he introduced the subject in the cabinet. Grant, with a soldier's veneration for authority, and possibly recalling that five years before he had been fighting rebels himself, was for letting them pass at first, but eventually yielded to the opposition of the two lawyers, Fish and Hoar.[12] As it happened, the British did not apply for permission during the winter; in April they asked whether boats carrying troops going to take part in Colonel Garnet Wolseley's expedition against the rebels might pass through the American-controlled Sault Ste. Marie Canal between Lakes Huron and Superior. Grant did not want to hinder the British in their attempt to end a rebellion that might lead to the annexation of all the north-west territories and was quite willing to let the boats through, if the British would only comply with the letter of the law of neutrality by disembarking the troops and marching them across the neck of Canadian land which divided the two lakes. William W. Belknap, the secretary of war, and Fish stood up for the spirit of the laws, and Grant yielded. Two weeks later Thornton asked if a supply vessel would be allowed through. He made a strong case for it, saying that the ship carried no munitions and pointing out that armed American craft had

1870, Diplomatic Despatches. Motley to Fish, June 1, 1870, Fish Papers, L.C. Donald Creighton, *John A. Macdonald: The Old Chieftain* (Toronto: Macmillan of Canada, 1955), p. 46.

11. Fish Diary, Jan. 15, 1870. Oscar Malmros to Ramsey, Jan. 14, 1870, Ramsey Papers.

12. Fish Diary, Nov. 23, 1869.

used the Canadian-controlled Welland Canal during the Civil War. Fish asked if an amnesty would be granted to the rebels and told Thornton to cable an inquiry about this to London. He made it clear that the promise of an amnesty would make it much easier for the United States to open the canal.

Next day the subject came up in the cabinet. Grant began by saying that he thought a refusal to let the vessel pass unfriendly to England, and added, in his slow way, "I guess we all feel so too." The members dissolved in laughter, and thinking that the Dominion authorities might retaliate by closing the Welland Canal, decided to let the ship pass.[13] At no time during the Red River rising did the American government try to force annexation by harrassing the British. Grant, who wanted to see Canada in the Union and was prejudiced against Britain, was actually more favorably inclined toward the imperial efforts to reassert control over Red River than Fish.

In dealing with the Fenians, who made their last attempt at direct action in America this year, the Grant administration showed the same spirit. In April, during a discussion about confiscating the Fenians' arms, the president grumbled that the British had not seized the *Alabama,* but in May he quickly ordered a proclamation issued against the Fenians, and their haphazard invading army was easily dispersed. When another Fenian raid on Canada from Pembina seemed likely, Fish asked Grant if he intended to issue special orders to the troops in Dakota. He replied he did not care to unless the general amnesty which the British had half-promised was proclaimed.[14] In fact, the proclamation already issued was quite sufficient, and the little band of Fenians that set out across the border were rounded up with the greatest of ease.

Ramsey did stir up a little noise in the Senate, but he met

13. *Ibid.,* April 7, 12, 28, May 14, 1870. J. C. Bancroft Davis to Fish, May 15, 16, 1870, Fish Papers, L.C. Fish did not attend the May 16 cabinet meeting, and he might have advocated waiting until the British gave a definite pledge of an amnesty.

14. Fish Diary, April 15, May 24, June 13, 1870.

with some unexpected opposition from Jacob Howard of Michigan. Howard was as zealous an annexationist as the Minnesotan, but he wanted to make Detroit, not St. Paul, the economic focus of the Northwest, and he may have feared that Ramsey would steal all the glory of annexation and all the power over the new territory. He spoke vigorously against a resolution of inquiry introduced by Ramsey early in December, declaring that the rising was a local affair, designed to secure representative government, and that it was none of America's business.[15] In January, Senator Henry Corbett of Oregon, quoting a petition sent by some British Columbia settlers to the Queen which declared that without financial aid from Britain the colony must join the United States, suggested that the territory might be taken in part exchange for the Alabama Claims. Howard, indulging in a few cross words with Ramsey during his speech, said that the whole tract of Rupert's Land from the Great Lakes to the Pacific might be transferred, but he would not consent to offset more than "a very small part" of the $200,000,000 Britain owed against it.[16] The next month Ramsey offered a resolution suggesting that the president should mediate between the government and the rebels and proposed that the people of Red River should vote for annexation either to Canada or the United States. On April 22, Zachariah Chandler moved that two commissioners should be sent to Winnipeg with powers to annex the country.[17]

All these resolutions broke down before the indifference of Grant and Fish and lack of interest in the country. The

15. *Cong. Globe,* 41 Cong., 2 sess., pp. 3, 29, Dec. 6, 8, 1869.

16. This may have been his way of hinting that he wanted the whole of Canada. *Ibid.,* pp. 324-325, Jan. 10, 1870. The resolution vanished into the graveyard of Sumner's Committee on Foreign Affairs.

17. *Ibid.,* pp. 933, 2808, 2888-2890, Feb. 1, 1870, April 19, 22, 1870. Thornton to Clarendon, April 25, 1870, FO 5/1192. On May 19, Senator Samuel C. Pomeroy of Kansas produced a Canadian petition asking for annexation and moved a resolution asking the president to open negotiations to this end. *Cong. Globe,* 41 Cong., 2 sess., p. 3606.

champagne mood of Grant's inauguration had passed away; the shortcomings of the administration, the eternal problem of the South, and the Cuban rebellion engaged popular attention.

In January, Grant revealed his half-baked scheme to annex Santo Domingo. Sumner soon decided he could not support this plan to "buy a civil war and a bloody *Cis pendens*."[18] Grant accused the senator of lying to him about his approval of the annexation scheme; Sumner discovered that Grant was using the Navy to prop up the insecure dictator who had signed away his country's independence; disagreement became a quarrel. In June, Sumner organized the opposition, led a bitter fight against ratification, and sent the treaty for the annexation of Santo Domingo down to defeat. Grant swore that no man who opposed him should influence the patronage or name ministers to England: "I will not allow Mr. Sumner to ride on me."[19] Motley was sent packing.[20] Simon Cameron and Ben Butler, two of the patronage lords so powerful with Grant, were nervous about trouble in the Senate and the reaction of Massachusetts to a clean sweep of her favorite sons;[21] they suggested sending Sumner to England as minister, arguing that a special envoy could always be appointed if negotiations were necessary. Grant grimly replied that he would do it to get Sumner out of the Senate, with the understanding that he would remove him as soon as the nomination was confirmed.[22] Fish tried to put a good face on the dismissal of Motley by claiming that the president had long been dissatisfied with the minister and that the death of Lord Clarendon made a change desirable; he tried to soothe

18. Sumner to Longfellow, March 21, 1870, Sumner Papers.
19. Fish Diary, June 14, July 1, 1870.
20. Fish to Motley, July 1, 12, 1870, Diplomatic Instructions.
21. Attorney-General Hoar had just left the cabinet because Grant considered that he was not giving whole-hearted support to the Santo Domingo adventure. Fish Diary, June 14, 17, 1870. C. F. Adams, Jr., *Lee at Appomattox, and Other Papers* (Boston: Houghton Mifflin, 1902), p. 142.
22. Fish Diary, July 27, 28, 1870.

Sumner.[23] But the rift between the two men became irreparable. Sumner called the Santo Domingo affair "worse than the treatment of Kansas";[24] Grant, walking round Lafayette Square, shook his fist at Sumner's house and growled, "That man who lives up there has abused me in a way which I never suffered from any other man living."[25]

With this, the control of American foreign policy finally passed to Fish. The ideas contained in Sumner's speech still moved in the popular mind; Grant was prejudiced against Britain. All the same, the secretary was master of the situation in a way he never had been before and was free to try to bring the president and the country over to his own moderate views on the Alabama Claims. But Fish, always inclined to shrink from risk or change, did not see things this way. At this moment he chose to resign.[26]

Grant managed to persuade him to stay on for a while. Fish, of course, had not wanted the secretaryship and had originally only intended to remain in the cabinet until December 1869.[27] But he probably would not have sent in his resignation at this time if he had seen any prospect of an Anglo-American accord. The truth was that the secretary was boxed in. His policies were having no effect, but he could not, it seemed, produce any satisfactory alternatives. During the late spring and early summer

23. Fish to Moran, Dec. 30, 1870, Diplomatic Instructions. Fish to J. S. Morrill, Aug. 26, 1870, printed in William Belmont Parker, *The Life and Public Services of Justin Smith Morrill* (Boston: Houghton Mifflin, 1924), pp. 234-235.

24. Sumner to Longfellow, Jan. 8, 1871, Sumner Papers. He told Boutwell that he should have resigned in protest. George S. Boutwell, *Reminiscences of Sixty Years in Public Affairs* (New York: McClure, Phillips, 1902), II, 216.

25. George F. Hoar, *Autobiography of Seventy Years* (New York: Scribner's, 1903), I, 211.

26. Fish Diary, March 22, 1870. Fish to Grant, July 7, 1870, Fish Papers, Columbia.

27. Sumner to Motley, Aug. 17, 1869, printed in Edward L. Pierce, *Memoir and Letters of Charles Sumner* (Boston: Robert Brothers, 1894), IV, 412-413.

of 1870, Fish continued to press for the withdrawal of Britain from Canada as a prelude to a settlement based on payment of the actual losses alone. On March 24 he warned Thornton that Europe was on the brink of war, and if England were to be drawn in the ocean would swarm with American *Alabamas.* The minister retorted that Britain would declare war at once. Then America would face it, said Fish. He was certain that raiders would be fitted out, in spite of all he and the administration would or could do to prevent it.[28] But such hints of trouble to come brought no response from England.

The only encouragement Fish received came from Thornton, who once or twice told him that he thought the new Dominion would not be economically viable without an American grant of reciprocal duties and that sentiment for independence was rising in Canada.[29] One of Motley's last official acts was to write a confidential letter saying that the British were adamant in keeping to their usual policy on independence or annexation; they would not detain Canada by force, but they would do nothing to drive her out.[30] Stalemated, Fish launched a trial balloon for a new policy at a cabinet meeting. He mentioned that Thornton was anxious to sign a treaty settling the Alabama Claims. The president answered, just as he had eight months before, that if Britain would evacuate Canada, the Alabama Claims could be settled in five minutes. George Robeson and Hoar both said, "Great Britain is ready to give up Canada, but Canada won't go," and Boutwell agreed. Fish then outlined a new policy, based on ideas that John Bright had proposed to a friend of his the previous August. Britain, thought Fish, would gladly pay the claims if she could do so upon the decision of some

28. Fish Diary, March 24, April 7, 1870. Thornton to Clarendon, June 14, 1870, Clarendon Papers, FO 361/1.
29. A curious way for a diplomat to talk. Fish Diary, April 1, June 23, 1870. Thornton may, of course, have been trying to persuade Fish to negotiate on the claims before the British abandoned Canada, as he did in January. *Ibid.,* Jan. 6, 1870.
30. Motley to Fish, June 1, 1870, Fish Papers, L.C.

third party, who would say that she was justly liable. She would willingly name three heads of state, including the Tsar, from whom the United States should pick one to be the judge (or vice versa), and would gladly settle new rules of maritime neutrality by treaty.[31] Fish recorded no reaction from his colleagues or from Grant in his diary; if there was any, it cannot have been favorable. Fish made no further attempts to break out of his policy straitjacket.

One or two events in this summer of 1870 showed that Anglo-American relations need not be all strife and woe. Thornton arbitrated in a dispute between the United States and Brazil.[32] The British neutrality law was altered to forbid assembling an expedition against a friendly power on British soil or knowingly supplying materials to one, and this stopped up the legal gap through which the *Alexandra* and the *Alabama* had escaped.[33] After months of delay while Parliament found time to pass legislation, Reverdy Johnson's naturalization protocol was converted into a treaty and ratified by the Senate. So was a treaty to abolish the mixed Anglo-American courts set up on the African coast by the 1862 agreement to put down the slave trade.[34] Against these achievements, earlier in the year Reverdy Johnson's San Juan arbitration treaty died unattended when the time allotted for its ratification ran out. A year earlier it had been stopped by a withering burst of rhetoric from Howard,

31. Fish Diary, June 3, 1870; John C. Hamilton to Fish, Aug. 28, 29, Sept. 17, 18, 1869; Bright to Hamilton, Aug. 12, 1869; Hamilton to Grant, Aug. 29, Sept. 11, 1869, Fish Papers, L.C.

32. Thornton to Fish, July 11, 1870, Caleb Cushing Papers.

33. Enclosure in Granville to Thornton (Draft), Aug. 12, 1870, FO 5/1189.

34. The protocol signed by Reverdy Johnson had been approved by the Senate on April 19, 1869. Thornton to Stanley, April 19, 1869; Motley to Clarendon, June 26, Sept. 10, 1869; Memorandum by C. S. Abbott, March 30, 1870; Telegram from Thornton to Edmund Hammond, July 9, 1870, FO 5/1357. Motley to Fish, May 12, 14, 1870, Diplomatic Despatches. Fish Diary, June 3, 1870. Fish to Motley, May 15, 1869, Diplomatic Instructions.

who saw it as a threat to his annexationist designs. He mustered enough votes to shelve it for the time being, and Fish never dared risk trying again.[35]

On July 15, Europe went to war. Six weeks more, and France was prostrate. On November 13, Prince Gortschakov announced that Russia would no longer be bound by the demilitarization of the Black Sea imposed on her after the Crimean War. British opinion threatened war. "What a time this would be," wrote Bancroft Davis to Fish, "to strike in London for the independence of Canada and the settlement of the Alabama Claims."[36]

Although not short of advice to take advantage of Britain's embarrassment,[37] Fish displayed his usual caution and did not try to force a settlement. He hoped that the European Götter-dämmerung would make Britain more inclined to compound her outstanding diplomatic debts, but still held to the policy of trying to consider Canadian annexation separate from the claims question. In the middle of August he advised Grant to postpone pardoning the leaders of the Fenian raid, for fear of irritating the Canadians.[38]

Already, however, a crisis was blowing up in the Atlantic that threatened grave consequences. With the end of reciprocity in 1866, American vessels lost the right to fish freely in Canadian

35. Sumner did all he could to get the treaty through. J. V. S. L. Pruyn to Fish, March 22, 1869; Thornton to Fish, July 9, 1870, Fish Papers, L.C. Caleb Cushing to William H. Seward, April 15, 1869, Seward Papers. Thornton to Clarendon, Jan. 11, 1870, Clarendon Papers, Bodleian. *Cong. Globe,* 41 Cong., 2 sess., Appendix, pp. 94-95, April 16, 1869.

36. Bancroft Davis to Fish, July 27, 1870, Fish Papers, L.C.

37. Carl Schurz to Fish, Aug 1, 1870; Matill to Fish, July 30, 1870, Fish Papers, L.C. Joseph Doutre to Schurz, Feb. 7, 1870; Schurz to Fish, Sept. 10, 1870, Schurz Papers. Also, Francis Lieber to Bancroft Davis, Aug. 27, 1870; Adam Badeau to Bancroft Davis, Aug. 16, 1870, Bancroft Davis Papers.

38. Fish to Trumbull, Aug. 5, 1870, printed in Horace White, *The Life of Lyman Trumbull* (Boston: Houghton Mifflin, 1913), p. 347. Grant to Fish, Aug. 18, 1870; Bancroft Davis to Fish, Aug. 17, 1870, Fish Papers, L.C.

inshore waters and to land for provisions, ice, and bait. The provinces set up a system of licenses, which granted these privileges for a fee. The cost of a license rose year by year, and the number of American fishermen bothering to buy them dropped. They had come to consider access to the inshore fisheries and landing rights their due, and the Royal Navy, under orders from London to avoid trouble, did little to dissuade them. In 1870 the exasperated Dominion government decided to build six schooners and enforce the licensing regulations themselves.[39]

Trouble began as soon as the 1870 season opened. "It looks blue here there is three cutters here and they mean work," wrote an American captain. "Sunday the commodore came here and sent a boat on board and ordered us off."[40] The fragile economy of the Massachusetts North Shore was almost completely dependent upon the Canadian inshore fisheries, and the issue was electric. In 1868, when the Royal Navy had showed signs of energy in dealing with unlicensed boats, Gloucester fishermen had armed themselves with the new Enfield rifles and prepared for a fight.[41] Even worse, the congressman for the North Shore was the redoubtable Ben Butler, who introduced a resolution just before the recess attacking the arrest of American ships.[42]

In late August things took a turn for the worse. American fishing boats were ordered out of the ports of Prince Edward Island, which was not a member of the Canadian Confederation and which had not, till then, systematically applied the stricter measures of enforcement. Fish was away on holiday, but Bancroft Davis sent for Thornton, who, by coincidence, was just

39. J. B. Brebner, *North Atlantic Triangle: The Interplay of Canada, the United States, and Great Britain* (New Haven: Yale University Press, for the Carnegie Endowment for International Peace; Division of Economics and History, 1945), p. 186.

40. Benjamin Bearse to B. F. Butler, June [n.d.], 1870; also, William Wilkeson to Butler, June 3, 1870, Butler Papers.

41. *New York Times,* Oct. 20, 1869, clipping in the Butler Papers, marked "This will interest you" in the writing of Butler's nephew George.

42. *Cong. Globe,* 41 Cong., 2 sess., p. 5055, July 1, 1870.

leaving for a vacation on the North Shore. He said nothing could be done except through London and added laughingly, "You had better leave it to arbitration." "The proceedings had better be abandoned," snapped back Davis, "You will have Ben Butler and all Essex County about your ears in Newburyport if you don't."[43]

Fish, getting worried, thought of stopping the shipment across American territory of Canadian goods in bond "to give the Canucks trouble in that way if they continue obstreperous." He threatened Thornton with this, but the minister retorted that the Canadians would then close their canals to American shipping.[44] During the next week Fish and Thornton met twice to discuss the fisheries and the claims. Fish was "extremely disturbed" about the Canadian action. Even though they said they were only acting to uphold their rights, their authorities were behaving in a way that was offensive and exasperating. New England was already dangerously excited about it and felt that the restrictions would make the fishing industry unprofitable. Fish feared a violent onslaught on the administration as soon as Congress met, guided by Butler, "who is but too ready to make himself the champion of those who imagine themselves aggrieved by England." The obvious solution, said Fish, was to give Canada her independence and then she would stop her annoyances.

In truth, assertive Canadian nationalism had sparked the action on the fisheries, and independence would probably have made things worse. But Fish was still applying the rigid formula he had derived from Grant's words the previous November. Thornton made the inevitable stock British answer to this that the British and American governments must settle the fisheries question. "How?" said Fish. By explicit definition of treaty rights and by explaining the limits within which Americans could fish, replied Thornton. The Alabama Claims could not be connected with

43. Bancroft Davis to Fish, Aug. 29, 1870, Fish Papers, L.C.
44. Bancroft Davis to Fish, Sept. 4, 1870; Fish Diary, Sept. 9, 1870, Fish Papers, L.C.

the question of Canadian independence, not even with a popular referendum on the subject. That could only be arranged by a spontaneous request from the regularly constituted authorities of the Dominion. As to the claims, Thornton said on September 15 that Britain would never agree to pay them without a decision by arbitration. Fish responded that the alteration of the British Foreign Enlistment Act was a practical admission of liability and guilt. In rejecting the Johnson-Clarendon Convention, the Senate had aso rejected arbitration, and without some other principle or concession there would be a deadlock on this point.

Conferring with Fish after church on Sunday, the 18th, Thornton repeated that Britain was ready to refer the question of her liability for the *Alabama*'s depredations (but only those of the *Alabama,* none of the other raiders) to arbitration, but the Canadians insisted that their claims for the damage and trouble and expense caused by the Fenian raids should be included in it as an offset. Britain could not admit that she had been wrong during the Civil War, but was willing to accept some other power's decision that she had been. Would Britain submit the question of Independence to Canada and open the fisheries, questioned Fish, if America agreed to take the Alabama Claims to arbitration? No, said Thornton for the hundredth time, independence, or a referendum on independence, could come only at a colony's own request. British Columbia was nearly unanimous for annexation to the Dominion, anticonfederation feeling in Nova Scotia was on the wane, and the feeling throughout Canada was utterly opposed to union with the United States. Independence meant annexation, they were one and the same thing, and it would not take. Fish vehemently contradicted this. He had received hundreds of letters from dissatisfied Canadians, expressing their wish for independence; some asked for annexation. He produced a bulky report from an agent of his in British Columbia estimating that four-fifths of the people wanted to join the Union. This was very different from what he heard, retorted

Thornton. If the Canadians really wanted separation from the mother country, why were they protesting so loudly about the recall of the imperial troops?[45]

When Thornton left, Fish was in a gloomy mood. "I do not find much in the tone and style of his conversation today," the secretary wrote glumly in his diary, "to encourage the idea either of a settlement of the Alabama question or of the Canadian or of the Fisheries question, except that as to the Fisheries question he said that the Home Government will take [it] up and must settle before another year." But the last question he had put to Thornton showed that the dead grip of the policy of abstracting Canada from the claims question and then settling on the basis of payment for actual losses was broken, shattered by his fear that the fisheries question might lead to a grave international quarrel and by his desire to see Grant re-elected.[46]

Later that day Fish wrote two letters that made it clear he had been doing some very hard thinking since Thornton left. One was to the eminent legal authority Francis Lieber. Fish outlined what the minister had said and asked if he thought a treaty conceding arbitration of the Alabama Claims and Fenian raid claims would pass the Senate. The other was to John Pruyn, an Albany Democrat who had won the respect of men in both parties during his service in the House of the Thirty-Eighth and Fortieth Congresses. Pruyn had written to Fish a few days before asking whether a prompt settlement of the claims was not desirable, and the secretary inquired how the Democrats felt about the question. The difficulty was, he said, that the same Senate that had killed Reverdy Johnson's treaty was forcefully committed against any other based on arbitration. Yet the British would take nothing else.[47]

45. Fish Diary, Sept. 15, 18, 1870. Thornton to Granville, Sept. 20, 1870, Granville Papers, FO 29/80.

46. Thornton to Granville, Sept. 20, 1870, Granville Papers, FO 29/80. Fish Diary, Sept. 18, 1870.

47. Fish to Lieber, Sept. 18, 1870; Fish to Pruyn, Sept. 18, 1870; Pruyn to Fish, Sept. 13, 1870, Fish Papers, L.C.

Neither of these letters did Fish much good; Lieber's answer was completely noncommittal,[48] and before Pruyn's arrived Fish had made his decision and thrown his old policy overboard. He met Thornton on the evening of September 26 and began with a long and sometimes bitter discussion of the fishery dispute. The imperial government, he charged, professed a willingness to be relieved of its colonies, and yet it always supported them in their irresponsible demands and petty complaints. These dependencies could annoy and harass while hiding behind the big brother whom they frequently moved to act against his will and without his consent. Thornton got up to go and had walked as far as the hall door when Fish said he hoped the minister had not lost sight of the claims question. There were persistent rumors about Russia's designs on Turkey, and if Britain were drawn into war all the good will in the world on his part would not stop Americans sending out raiders to prey on British commerce. Thornton replied he could see no hope of a settlement unless the United States underwent a change of heart. Suddenly, "disclaiming any official character or purport in the suggestion," Fish asked whether Great Britain would settle all the questions pending between the two countries at once. An equitable exchange of preconditions could be arranged. If America gave up her opposition to the arbitration of the Alabama Claims, Britain might abandon her claims to San Juan. All commercial claims could go to arbitration. If the inshore fisheries were opened to American boats, free trade in certain articles could be allowed between the United States and Canada. Thornton, thinking it over, said that Britain would come off worse in such an exchange. It was no concession for the Americans to agree to arbitrate the Alabama Claims; the British had said they were not liable for them, and they had made the concession in agreeing to submit to another authority's judgment. He also objected to the abandonment of arbitration on San Juan as "a point of honour." Fish reminded him that

48. Lieber to Fish, Sept. 22, 1870, Fish Papers, L.C.

he had said Great Britain attached no importance to the island and was quite willing to see it given to America. As the clocks struck midnight, the secretary told Thornton to "think seriously" about what he had said, and the interview ended.[49]

Fish had faced about and returned to the policy he had put forward a year earlier. For a time, he was a lonely, isolated figure, negotiating with the British on one hand and with Grant on the other. Gradually, cautiously, he began the work of persuading the president that a more moderate policy was needed. His impulse toward a settlement nearly came to grief in the first weeks of autumn. After a long and increasingly undignified search for a new minister to England,[50] the post was given to Oliver P. Morton, senator from Indiana. The president announced that he was to press for a settlement based on payment of the actual losses, amendment of the laws of neutrality, and the submission of Canadian independence to a popular referendum: "I think we want something more than a 'figurehead.'"[51] As Fish knew to his cost, the British would not hear of such terms, and Morton, though a man of great ability, did not know what compromise was: when war governor of Indiana, he had ruled the state as a military dictator for two years. Had he taken the post, negotiations would have come to a dead stop,[52] and since Morton was one of Grant's closest friends, Fish would have been helpless to change or ameliorate policy. Fortunately for the future of Anglo-American relations, the Democrats carried Indiana by a landslide in the autumn elections, and Morton, realizing that

49. Fish Diary, Sept. 26, 1870. Thornton to Granville, Sept. 27, 1870, Granville Papers, FO 29/80.

50. Fish Diary, June 25, Oct. 4, 1870; Grant to Fish, Aug. 18, 21, 1870; T. O. Howe to Fish, Sept. 3, 1870; Memorandum by Fish headed "Sumner," Sept. 10, 1870, Fish Papers, L.C. Bancroft Davis to Daniel E. Sickles, Aug. 19, 1870; Fish to Bancroft Davis, Sept. 5, 1870, Bancroft Davis Papers. White, p. 348.

51. Grant to Zachariah Chandler, Sept. 22, 1870, Chandler Papers, Fish Diary, Oct. 4, 1870.

52. Thornton to Granville, Oct. 4, 1870, Granville Papers, FO 29/80.

his resignation would leave his seat to one of the hated "Copper-heads" (perhaps Thomas A. Hendricks), declined the mission.[53]

During this time, Fish continued to protest bitterly about the fisheries situation. He tried to shame Thornton into using his influence for a cessation of Canadian activities by charging that Britain did not want a settlement and was encouraging Canada in her unfriendly course; now he threatened retaliation. His acerbity was the measure of his concern about the dispute. On October 16 he told Thornton that in six or eight months another fishing season would begin, and there was no sign of any settlement. The Canadian authorities were considering the subject in a better spirit now, protested Thornton. "Of course," retorted Fish acidly. "They have done us all the harm they can for this season, and now make-believe to be friendly."

Simultaneously, Fish returned to his arguments of September 26 about the claims and the grounds of a settlement. At one moment, Thornton's faulty memory nearly wrecked the chance of a settlement. He told Fish that the terms proposed on September 26 were, in his opinion, impossible. He began to list them and included a demand that Fish had not made, the abandoned proposal of September 20 for a Canadian plebiscite on the question of independence. What would the United States think, Thornton sarcastically asked, if Great Britain proposed that a vote on independence should be taken in Louisiana or any of the notoriously disaffected states of the South? Yet Fish asked for a poll in Canada, where the inhabitants gave abundant proof of their satisfaction with the imperial connection. These jeers stung the secretary into forgetting that the proposition was defunct. He began defending it vigorously, claiming that he had "multitudes of letters" proving that Canadians were tired of being linked to Britain and that only government officials, bankers, and smugglers opposed independence or annexation. Luckily, this part of the conversation did not stick in either man's mind, and the reawakened spirit of the policy Fish had

53. Fish Diary, Oct. 21, 1870.

abandoned soon slumbered again.[54] Early in November the minister suggested an accord on the fisheries question alone: the inshore fisheries might be opened to American vessels in return for the free introduction of a number of Canadian products. On November 11 the cabinet discussed the proposal. Columbus Delano of Ohio warned that the West would object strongly to free trade in grain, animals, and dairy products. No one seemed enthusiastic about a trade convention, and though Fish warned of "the excitement of the New England fishermen," Grant decided that the question had better be left open for settlement with the Alabama Claims.[55]

On November 20, Fish and Thornton had a "long and friendly conversation" about the claims, and the American gave the fullest details yet of the settlement he wanted. Britain must pay for the losses actually sustained and make some reparation for the national wrong. Fish was so sure a settlement was near that he felt obliged to reintroduce the consequential claims, which he had not mentioned openly since May 1869. He was not giving his own personal views now; these were the terms the nation wanted. Thornton, however, did not pick up the allusion. He was obsessed with the question of arbitration and saw that Fish did not admit the principle. No nation, he said, could admit that it had been wrong in such a way. Fish returned that he would not allow the matter of England's liability to go to arbitration, but he would submit the amount of damages to be paid. The Alabama Claims were national claims and could not be included with, or offset by, ordinary commercial claims. Once more Fish was showing that he had learned the lessons of the Johnson-Clarendon Convention and the threat that British property claims might outrun the Alabama Claims. Next he repeated that America must be given "some recognition of a wrong done, some

54. *Ibid.,* Sept. 29, Oct. 16, 20, Nov. 10, 17, 1870. Thornton to Granville, Oct. 4, 18, 1870, Granville Papers, FO 29/80.
55. Fish Diary, Nov. 11, 1870. Thornton to Granville, Nov. 15, 18, 22, 1870, Granville Papers, FO 29/80.

expression of regret, some kind word." The recent changes the British had made in their Foreign Enlistment Act were an admission that their wartime laws had not been good enough. It would be no humiliation to say that, under those laws, they had, by accident and carelessness, done America wrong, and wanted to make amends.

Finally, Thornton asked about changing the rules of neutrality. Fish gave him a rough memorandum which he had scribbled in pencil one evening when talking about a settlement. The first four points merely repeated the Declaration of Paris;[56] Fish added Marcy's fifth article, "All private property, not contraband, shall be protected from capture at sea, in time of war," and included some new rules of his own designed to deal with future *Alabamas*.[57] Subjects of Britain or the United States (or indeed, any other party who might assent to the new rule) found cruising as privateers against the other country, when the two nations were at peace, might be treated as pirates. The nationality of an armed ship might not be changed on the high seas. No unarmed vessel might be armed, manned, or fitted out as a vessel of war on the high seas. The public mails were to be inviolable.

As he was leaving, Thornton inquired whether the United States would purchase the right to use the inshore fisheries. Fish returned a blunt "No." About $200,000 a year would settle the question, said Thornton. "We may allow you something for it on account, when you pay the Alabama Claims," replied Fish jocularly. Except for some of the neutrality rules and the

56. (1) Privateering is, and remains, abolished. (2) The neutral flag covers enemy's goods, with the exception of contraband of war. (3) Neutral goods, with the exception of contraband of war, are not liable to capture under enemy's flag. (4) Blockades, to be binding, must be effective, that is to say, maintained by a force sufficient really to prevent access to the coast of the enemy.

57. Fish had mentioned most of these new rules to Thornton in Nov. 1869, Fish Diary, Nov. 15, 1869, see above, p. 117.

mechanics of submission to arbitration this conversation was almost a blueprint for the Treaty of Washington.[58]

During the last few days of November, Fish worked on the president's message to Congress and continued working on the president himself. On the 30th, Grant capitulated. "He thinks it advisable," Fish soberly wrote in his diary, "to have the Claims settled that they cannot properly be connected with the question of Canadian Independence and that it is important to have them settled before the next Presidential Election."[59] One can only guess at the hours of quiet, subtle persuasion that must have gone on to achieve this, arguably Fish's greatest diplomatic success. The last phrase of the diary entry shows that his trump card was the president's eager longing for re-election. Even Grant must have realized that he needed a triumph to bring that off, that he was halfway through his first term with nothing to show for it but scandal, muddle, corruption, and a quarrel with the leader of his own party in the Senate.

Others had been busy on the claims question that autumn besides Fish, but not Sumner, who had been visiting friends and making a lecture tour. He had confined his activities to urging George Bemis to write "one of your best articles" on the claims question and sending Fish a few articles and comments.[60] But the claimants themselves had begun to stir. Many of the claims had been taken over by insurance companies when they paid the shipowners compensation. One company that held $327,000 worth, the Great Western of New York, found itself in serious financial difficulties in early 1870, and its president, John A. Parker, decided that if he wanted to save it he must arrange for the payment of the claims. A New Yorker who had distinguished himself as a diplo-

58. Fish Diary, Nov. 20, 1870. Thornton to Granville, Nov. 22, Dec. 13, 1870, Granville Papers, FO 29/80.

59. Fish Diary, Nov. 30, 1870.

60. Pierce, pp. 449-450. Sumner to Bemis, July 22, Dec. 17, 31, 1870, Feb. 23, 1871, Bemis Papers. Sumner to Fish, Aug. 31, Sept. 12, 1870, Fish Papers, L.C.

mat, John Bigelow, was just going abroad, and Parker asked him if he could do anything toward getting the British to pay.[61] In London, Bigelow obtained an interview with Lord Clarendon through the good offices of Jacob Bright (John's brother) and presented his case. A few weeks later Thornton contacted Parker and told him that though the British government probably would not yield more than the terms Reverdy Johnson had gained, they had as good as admitted their liability for the Alabama Claims then. If the United States was willing, Britain would settle with each claimant fully and justly.

But Fish would not hear of it. He promised Parker that the government would assume the claims itself in the end, but the businessman replied that he wanted immediate action. Grant said he did not think the insurance companies were entitled to anything; they had been paid their premiums, and that was all they deserved. The outraged Parker responded that if it were known in New York that the government and Congress held such views, he could leave for London in a week with $5 million in claims for collection, permission or no permission, and Fish threatened him with the Logan Act.[62]

Parker continued to lobby for his scheme. When it seemed that Senator Frelinghuysen was going to London as minister, Parker wrote and asked his help;[63] he secured Reverdy Johnson's aid; and in October, he published the correspondence of the

61. Parker to Bigelow, April 23, 29, 1870, printed in John Bigelow, *Retrospections of an Active Life* (Garden City, N.Y.: Doubleday, Page, 1913), pp. 49-50, 52. *Cong. Globe*, 41 Cong., 2 sess., p. 2210.

62. Bigelow Diary, May 11, 16, 21, 1870, Bigelow Papers. Bigelow, *Retrospections*, pp. 53-64. Jacob Bright to Clarendon, May 17, 1870 (twice), Clarendon Papers, Bodleian. The Logan Act was the only one of John Adams' repressive laws of 1798-1799 remaining on the statute books. Dr. George Logan, a Philadelphia Quaker, went to Paris at that time to try to keep the peace. To stop his meddling, Congress passed a law declaring it a misdemeanor for any American to correspond with a foreign government on the subject of a dispute between it and the United States.

63. Parker to F. T. Frelinghuysen, Aug., n.d., 1870, encl. in Parker to C. F. Adams, Dec. 17, 1870, Adams Papers.

whole affair in the New York *Evening Post*.[64] Fish, a little worried at what Parker might do next, had a long answer to him printed in the *Washington Daily Chronicle*[65] and warned Thornton that the United States government would not recognize any settlement made with individual claimants as a satisfaction or diminution of its demands.[66] To keep Parker and his cohorts quiet, and to show the British that they had better advance toward a settlement rather more quickly than they had been, Fish decided to announce in the president's message that the government would shortly assume the claims.[67]

In the last weeks of November, aiming to stir up a storm just as Congress met, Ben Butler opened fire. Able, unscrupulous, theatrical, and overwhelmingly ambitious, the "Beast" had acquired a natural Anglophobia in his early days as a Massachusetts labor politician (perhaps the poverty of his childhood and his extreme ugliness also had an effect). England represented the apogee of that arrogant, entrenched aristocratic principle against which he was struggling in the Bay State. But Butler never did anything gratuitous: he made sure every one of his acts paid a handsome dividend. For this reason, he had not uttered a squeak about the Alabama Claims unil 1869 because the populace was not interested in them. Anglophobia in 1870 seemed a good investment; Massachusetts was aroused by the fisheries dispute, and Butler meant to run for governor in 1871. He would have blasted England in any case, for he always kept his political fences well mended, and the anger of his constituents left him little choice. But his gubernatorial ambitions led him to pitch his protests at a statewide audience rather than just at the fishermen of Cape Ann.

On November 23, he spoke in Boston on the Alabama Claims

64. Fish to the Rev. Thomas E. Vermilye, Dec. 5, 1870, Fish Papers, L.C. Johnson's letter to Parker, Nov. 28, 1870, is printed in Bigelow, *Retrospections,* Appendix B, pp. 423-430.

65. Fish to Vermilye, Oct. 31, 1870; Fish to John W. Forney, Nov. 1, 1870; Fish to John C. Hamilton, Jan. 10, 1871, Fish Papers, L.C.

66. Fish Diary, Nov. 28, 1870.

67. *Cong. Globe,* 41 Cong., 3 sess., p. 7, Dec. 5, 1870.

and the fisheries and demanded that Britain should instantly
cede Canada, pay the claims, or face a declaration of nonintercourse. "She shall have none of our cotton or breadstuffs until
this question is settled," threatened the general. "Such depriva-
tion to Manchester, Birmingham and Bradford might work a
revolution in her government in six months."[68] If Britain had
given up Canada, no one would have been more distressed than
Butler, for his constituents regarded the 20 percent tariff on
imported Canadian fish with the same veneration that they gave
to God, mother, and country. But they were not oversophisticated,
and Butler's adroit connection of their grievances with a program that pleased Boston manufacturers and merchants and
appealed to the huge Irish vote sent them into raptures.[69]

Fish, of course, had known for months that Butler intended
to make trouble. Late in September, the general had written
him a letter in which he demanded "a peremptory and not-to-
be-evaded" order to Britain to withdraw her claims and added
that he was inclined to think "that the Springfield rifle, loaded
at the breach, is the only negotiator, except it be a ten-pound
Parrott rifle, of this subject. We in the fishing districts are getting
to be a little warm upon this topic."[70] As in his action on the
claims, Fish decided to kill two birds with one stone. To silence
Butler and intimidate the Canadians, he included in the president's message a long denunciation of the Dominion's action
on the fisheries and its denial of American rights to the free
navigation of the St. Lawrence. The message recommended that
Congress pass an act giving the president power to forbid by
proclamation the transportation across American territory of
Canadian goods in bond, and "further, should such an extreme
measure become necessary," allow him to exclude Canadian
ships from American waters. With a fine capacity for setting a

68. New York *World*, Nov. 24, 1870.
69. Thomas Russell to Butler, Nov. 28, 1870, Butler Papers.
70. Butler to Fish, Sept. 25, 1870, Fish Papers, L.C.

thief to catch a thief, Fish got Zack Chandler to introduce the bill on December 12.[71]

By this brilliant stroke (which, of course, committed him to absolutely nothing), Fish stole Butler's thunder completely. The general told Fish he thought the country really supported his policy, but expressed "entire satisfaction" with the message, and confined himself to passing on complaints from various fishermen and presenting to Congress a petition which had been whipped up months before.[72]

When Morton refused the English mission in October, the interminable search for a suitable candidate began again. On November 10, Grant offered the post to Roscoe Conkling, but the New York senator refused —[73] another lucky escape for Fish, for Conkling would have been just like Morton. Finally, on December 4, Grant selected General Robert C. Schenck, an Ohio congressman who had recently lost his seat. Though neither outstanding nor brilliant, Schenck was an able enough man who had served fourteen years in Congress, on and off; he had been chairman of two House committees, Military Affairs and (very important) Ways and Means, and he had also been President Millard Fillmore's minister to Brazil. Thornton found him "quiet and unaffected, plain and straightforward"; "his manners are not of the most polished, but he is intelligent, though exceedingly obstinate and tenacious of any opinion he may have formed."[74] Most important from Fish's point of view, Schenck was not a crony of Grant's, nor so important a politician that he could not be controlled.

71. *Cong. Globe,* 41 Cong., 3 sess., pp. 14-15, 52, Dec. 5, 1870. Fish Diary, Dec. 10, 1870.

72. Fish Diary, Dec. 5, 1870. Fish to Butler, Dec. 19, 1870, Butler Papers (Series II). Fish to Butler, Jan. 13, 16, Feb. 13, 1871, Fish Papers, L.C. *Cong. Globe,* 41 Cong., 3 sess., p. 88, Dec. 13, 1870. F. J. Babson to Butler, Oct. 13, 1870, Butler Papers.

73. Roscoe Conkling to Fish, Nov. 11, 1870, Fish Papers, L.C.

74. Thornton to Granville, Dec. 13, 20, 1870, Granville Papers, FO 29/80.

Early in December, Fish received a letter from Sir John Rose saying that he had not written before because he knew that "the subject of our correspondence" could not be attained. But now things were different. He knew that Grant and Fish desired a settlement: *"a desire equally strong exists here."* Could it not be taken advantage of? As part of his campaign of education, Fish read the letter to the cabinet, saying that it seemed to show the British were willing to open a negotiation. He got some support from Boutwell, who remarked that he had seen a letter from Rose to his New York banking partner stating that the unsettled condition of the Alabama Claims interfered with the funding of the American debt in Europe. "President," records Fish's diary, "makes no comment."[75]

On December 20, Fish asked the president if he wanted the new minister to take up the Alabama Claims. Grant, demonstrating his usual grasp of the situation, replied that he was willing to give him the same instructions that had been given to Motley. Fish tactfully pointed out that Motley had been given none, except to suspend negotiations, and suggested trying for a settlement. Grant agreed, and said that Schenck should attempt this.[76] Meanwhile, the British were mulling over Fish's new proposals. "Thornton's letter," wrote Gladstone, "seems to point to important practical issues which if possible we should not forego on account of the great pressure of European cares."[77] The Russian crisis was at its height, and the desire which the members of Gladstone's cabinet already felt for an American settlement was considerably enhanced. Granville had asked for two memoranda on American policy: Lord Tenterden[78] was to range over the whole field of Anglo-American relations and

75. Rose to Fish, Nov. 26, 1870, Fish Papers, L.C. Fish Diary, Dec. 9, 1870.

76. Fish Diary, Dec. 4, 20, 1870.

77. Gladstone to Granville, Nov. 22, 1870, Gladstone Papers.

78. Who, as C. S. Abbott, had written the papers answering the American charges of Sept. 25, 1869, for Lord Clarendon.

recommend a course to follow, and Sir Frederick Rogers was to prepare a statement of the questions at issue between the United States and Canada.

Rogers made no suggestions about future policy, but Tenterden was full of ideas. He began by pointing out that Anglo-American questions called for "the gravest attention." England stood on the brink of a Russian war with all the transatlantic disputes unsettled. The difficulty was to find out exactly what the Americans wanted. The British Government could not possibly meet all the claims mentioned in the American dispatch of September 25, 1869. Unlike Thornton, Tenterden was alive to the threat of the consequential claims. On the other hand, as he noted, the picture was not all black. The principle of arbitration had been accepted, and some of the original heat of resentment had died away. How could Britain take advantage of this situation and achieve a settlement? Ordinary diplomatic channels were obviously useless. A special mission sent from Britain to negotiate in Washington would be looked upon as a surrender of the British case and an attempt to bribe America into neutrality during an Anglo-Russian war: American expectations would be inflated and impossible demands would be made.

Tenterden favored the reference of the disputes to a joint commission like the one that had ended the War of 1812. The commissioners would inquire into each question and recommend the best way of settling them, by arbitration, treaty, or any other means. The United States government would have to be persuaded to include the Alabama Claims in such a reference, and it would be best to confine the proposal in the first instance to a commission on Canadian affairs: the fisheries, the Fenian raids, San Juan, the survey of the boundary along the 49th Parallel, the free navigation of the St. Lawrence. Then it would be a matter of "leading the United States Government to make it a condition that the Commission should also take the 'Alabama' Claims into consideration." This could be allowed, and the United States government would have a concession to wave in front of public opinion.[79]

On November 22, Granville sent this paper, together with Rogers', to Gladstone. In his covering letter, he mentioned that he had had a long, confidential talk with Sir John Rose, who had now set up as a banker in London. Rose liked Tenterden's idea of a commission, and Granville remarked that if there was any chance of success it might be tried.[80] Four days later, Rose presented a memorandum of his own.[81] He emphasized that "it is not likely that in any future Secretary of State, so loyal a personal desire to bring about an agreement honourable to both countries will again be found, or that the qualities of frank and upright dealing, will be met with in a corresponding degree." He approved Tenterden's idea of a compromise, but thought that a formal British initiative would be much too dangerous. A secret intermediary was needed to set out a common basis of agreement beforehand. Another failure, he wrote, would be disastrous.[82]

On December 6, Tenterden composed a short paper on Grant's message. Very pertinently, he remarked that the president seemed to draw the same distinction between private and public claims that Fish had done in the dispatch of September 25, 1869. Both countenanced the idea that there were some vague, undefined public claims which Britain had to make good, and how much these might amount to no one could tell.[83]

Two days later he dealt with Thorntons' report of the November 20 interview.[84] He thought Fish's proposals more definite than anything that had come before, but warned that they were

79. Memorandum, Lord Tenterden, Nov. 19, 1870, Memorandum, Sir F. Rogers, Nov. 19, 1870, FO 5/1331.
80. Granville to Gladstone, Nov. 22, 1870, Gladstone Papers.
81. That same day, he sent off his letter to Fish appealing for action to take advantage of the favorable atmosphere for a settlement.
82. Memorandum, Sir John Rose, Nov. 26, 1870, FO 5/1331.
83. Memorandum, Lord Tenterden, Dec. 6, 1870, FO 5/1331.
84. Thornton to Granville, Nov. 22, 1870, FO 5/1331.

still vague. In particular, there was the worrying division of the claims into private and national categories. What the national claims were, Fish did not specify beyond the suggestion that the British should express regret for the depredations of the *Alabama*. But, "on the whole," wrote Tenterden, "I think the Despatch is not unpromising." Fish's statement showed that he was "not unwilling to contemplate" a settlement of the dispute, providing compensation only for the damage done by the Confederate raiders and abandoning the consequential claims. The idea that Britain should acknowledge liability without arbitration seemed so untenable to Tenterden that he thought it could not be maintained as a ground of quarrel. The difficulty might be got around by taking the revision of international law first. If the rules were laid down that it was illegal to supply vessels adapted for war to a belligerent or to recognize ships of war commissioned on the high seas, then America and Britain could probably strike hands on a compromise involving compensation for the ravages of the Confederate cruisers that sailed from England, "and even so much of the national claims as relate to the injury to American commerce from their escape."[85] Later, during the meeting of the High Commission, Tenterden must have felt that he had been an uncannily accurate prophet.

Rose was going to New York on business, and it was decided to use him as the secret intermediary he had himself suggested. His instructions were vague and tenuous: he was to investigate public feeling about an Alabama Claims settlement, both in official circles and among men who were likely to be influential behind the scenes. He was given authority to propose a discussion of all the disputes by a commission.[86] As the new year 1871 came in, he was halfway across the Atlantic.

85. Memorandum, Lord Tenterden, Dec. 8, 1870, FO 5/1331.
86. Granville to Rose (Draft), Dec. 19, 1870, FO 5/1298.

CHAPTER 7

The Last Quarter of an Hour

Fish and Rose met for the first time on January 9, 1871, for a working dinner with Bancroft Davis. Other meetings followed. Rose remarked about the strong British sentiment in favor of a settlement and offered the London government's proposal of a joint commission, like the one that had concluded the Treaty of Ghent in 1815, to discuss an arrangement of all the disputes between the two countries. Fish responded that success must be certain before a commission was set up; like Tenterden, he felt that another failure would worsen the situation. Would the British admit their liability for the Alabama Claims? No, said Rose. They were prepared to submit the question for arbitration, either to a panel of British and American jurists or to any other suitable tribunal, but public opinion would not allow them to go further. Fish replied that the Senate would not allow him to take less. After the rejection of the Johnson-Clarendon Convention, many senators were committed to regarding Britain as both guilty and liable. Even if they were inclined to retract, public opinion would be against them.

Nevertheless, he asked whether England would acknowledge her guilt over the *Alabama* alone, if the liability for the damages done by all the other vessels were submitted to arbitration. Rose again replied that this was impossible. Fish pointed out that he did not ask England to humiliate herself, to call her laws inefficient or her government unfaithful to its obligations. He thought Britain could easily say that, due to the incompetence or treachery of a local official, the *Alabama* had been allowed to escape from Liverpool, and the government had therefore become liable for it. This statement could be combined with an expression of regret for what had happened.[1]

When Grant heard what Rose had said, he was not at all pleased. He thought Schenck could extract more concessions in London.[2] Fish went to see the new minister and found him much more favorable than Grant to Rose's terms. He felt that an agreement was more likely if the commission sat at Washington. Schenck agreed, too, that there was grave doubt about Britain's liability for the damage done by any Confederate cruisers except the *Alabama*. If Britain would admit her guilt there, the country would be satisfied. The talk then turned to ratification. The first step would be to get a favorable report from the Senate Committee on Foreign Relations. Only three of its seven members — Morton, Simon Cameron, and James Harlan — could be counted upon to support anything the administration might do. With this in mind, Fish set out to sound senators on the conditions of a British treaty.

Not surprisingly, Fish received the most reassuring reception from the patronage barons.[3] Zachariah Chandler, the hammer of the British, who had advocated allowing American shipbuilders to construct and sell freely to friendly belligerents, the total repeal of all U.S. neutrality laws, and complete nonintercourse with England until she paid the Alabama Claims,[4] meekly replied to the secretary's questions that he favored a settlement. He thought that the terms offered by Rose, with

1. Memorandum in Fish Diary, Jan. 9, 1871. Thornton to Granville, Jan. 10, 1871, Granville Papers, FO 29/80. Rose to Granville, Jan. 10, 12, 1871, FO 5/1298.

2. Fish Diary, Jan. 9, 1871.

3. *Ibid.,* Jan. 11, 13, 1871.

4. *Cong. Globe,* 39 Cong., 1 sess., pp. 226-227, 4024; *ibid.,* 40 Cong., 1 sess., pp. 290-292, 329-330; *ibid.,* 40 Cong., 2 sess., pp. 83-84, Jan. 15, July 23, 1866, Dec. 9, 1867.

England's admission of liability for the *Alabama*'s depredations, would pass the Senate even over Sumner's opposition. Although amazing at first glance, this answer was quite characteristic. Chandler was always a good party man: though he had strong principles, he invariably abandoned every last one of them if they imperiled his Michigan machine and his political future. The most violent of radicals, he stood aloof from the John C. Frémont boom and nomination in 1864.[5] In Grant, he had a president after his own heart for once; for the first time in his career, he knew all the White House secrets and helped to make policy. He did not mean to fling all this away. The idea of helping the British must have been painful for Chandler. Ever afterward, he declared that America ought to have refused anything less than the annexation of Canada.[6] But only one thing could have made him deaf to the siren songs of the patronage. That was a threat to his personal ascendancy in Michigan, and when, in April, Fish proposed to admit Canadian salt and lumber free in return for the inshore fisheries, Chandler thought of the economy of his state and immediately said he would oppose it.[7]

Roscoe Conkling was also favorable to the proposal, but he thought that the public mind ought to be prepared before a treaty was made and suggested consultations with high-ranking Democrats. He reported that Horatio Seymour, the titular leader of the party, wanted to keep the dispute open and take revenge when Britain was drawn into war, but he thought that Senator Allen G. Thurman of Ohio would help.[8] Fish later followed this advice and secured pledges from some leading Democrats that they would treat a settlement on its own

5. Wilmer C. Harris, *The Public Life of Zachariah Chandler, 1851-1875* (Lansing, Mich.: Michigan Historical Commission, 1917), pp. 79-80.

6. Detroit *Post and Tribune, Zachariah Chandler: An Outline Sketch of His Life and Public Services* (Detroit: Post and Tribune, 1880), p. 256.

7. Fish Diary, April 8, 1871.

8. *Ibid.*, Jan. 13, 1871.

merits, not as a party affair.[9] Both Simon Cameron and Oliver P. Morton felt that the country would accept "Rose terms" with the addition of British liability for the *Alabama,* but Morton wanted Britain to pay the money the Union had spent trying to catch the ship: "This would be regarded as 'consequential' damages and would satisfy the public expectation on that point." Like Chandler, Morton was confident that a treaty of the kind Fish had outlined could pass the Senate despite Sumner's opposition.[10]

Fish was nearly as successful with senators who sometimes showed independence. James W. Patterson of New Hampshire, the key member of the Senate Committee on Foreign Relations, approved the proposals, giving Fish a majority of the committee. Later he won over John Sherman. With Lyman Trumbull, however, his progress was checked. Trumbull held that if Britain proposed a convention to settle all disputes, America could not refuse it, but he wanted hefty compensation — the cession of the territory west of Manitoba.[11]

Sumner's closest friend in the Senate was Carl Schurz of Missouri. At the State Department, Fish found him "guarded and reserved," saying nothing definite. But he offered Schurz a ride across to the Treasury in his carriage, and on the way the German unbent. He approved the Rose terms, with English liability for the *Alabama,* but asked if Sumner had been consulted.[12] On January 15, Fish set out to do this.

It was no easy matter, for Sumner had come to regard Fish as a malefactor second only to Grant, and hardly a week earlier the Motley correspondence had been published, carefully doctored to make the administration come out lily-white. In society, Sumner treated Fish and Bancroft Davis "with marked

9. Northcote to Granville, March 26, 1871, Iddesleigh Papers.
10. Fish Diary, Jan. 13, 15, 1871.
11. *Ibid.,* Jan. 11, 23, 26, 1871.
12. *Ibid.,* Jan. 13, 1871.

coldness, and declined even bowing to them."[13] The president, in turn, had come to hate Sumner with all the force of which his narrow but powerfully emotional nature was possible and opposed even consulting the senator. Eventually he yielded to Fish's arguments that Sumner would be exposed as extreme if he rejected or opposed the plan of settlement and trouble would be saved if he approved it. An interview was arranged through the good offices of Senator Patterson, and Fish ventured into the enemy's camp.[14]

The secretary outlined Rose's scheme; Sumner, in Fish's words, began to declaim. At this point, Boutwell called and was ushered into the room. Conversation continued, and Sumner declared that Great Britain's attitude on the various questions must be understood well in advance. Boutwell said that he had heard through the bankers that Great Britain intended to concede the inshore fisheries if the United States gave up its claim to San Juan. Fish, thinking of Howard's reaction to such a bargain, replied that it could never be allowed; the West would be a unit against it. The talk went on, and Fish tried to get a statement of opinion from Sumner, referring to "the danger of actual collision on the fishery grounds and the serious complications that would ensue." But Sumner would not commit himself. Finally, in exasperation, Fish announced that he was making an official call upon the chairman of the Senate Committee on Foreign Relations to ask his opinion and advice, and he was entitled to an answer. Sumner said the matter would need a good deal of thought, and Fish asked him to send his opinion within a day or two.[15]

On January 17, a full cabinet decided to accept Rose's proposition of a commission with the conditions that Britain should

13. Rose to Granville, Jan. 21, 1871, FO 5/1298.
14. Fish Diary, Jan. 11, 1871. James W. Patterson to Fish, Jan. 12, 1871, printed in J. C. Bancroft Davis, *Mr. Sumner, The Alabama Claims and Their Settlement* (New York: Douglas Taylor, 1878), pp. 14-15.
15. Fish Diary, Jan. 15, 1871.

admit her liability for the acts of the *Alabama* and (Morton's condition) should agree to reimburse the United States for the expenses incurred in hunting down the raider. The president, who had thought badly of Rose's terms at first, had been brought around to Fish's opinions again, probably by the sounding of Schenck and the senators. There was some discussion about stipulating that there should be no British claims for Confederate bonds, which were still quoted, though at rock-bottom prices, on the London Stock Exchange; the possibility of such claims had been one of the arguments used against the Johnson-Clarendon Convention. Grant was strongly against making any such condition, arguing that raising the objection would be evidence of doubt and conscious weakness. His views prevailed. Thornton and Rose were contacted and given the American answer with only the *Alabama* conditions.[16]

That same day Sumner sent Fish his answer. He began by saying that nothing could be better than the idea that Britain and America should be always at peace. The greatest source of trouble, anxiety, and unrest was Fenianism, which was excited by the presence of the British flag in Canada. The withdrawal of Britain from the Dominion was an essential preliminary of any settlement. "To make the settlement complete the withdrawal should be from this hemisphere, including provinces and islands." As for Fish's formula of a British admission of liability for the *Alabama*, "a discrimination in favor of claims arising from the depredations of any particular ship will dishonor the claims arising from the depredations of other ships, which the American Government cannot afford to do, — nor should the English Government expect it, if they would sincerely remove all occasions of difference."[17]

Sumner had already broached the subject of Canadian in-

16. *Ibid.*, Jan. 17, 1871. Thornton to Granville, Jan. 17, 1871, Granville Papers, FO 29/80.
17. Memorandum for Mr. Fish in reply to his inquiries, encl. in Fish Diary, Jan. 17, 1871.

dependence to Rose,[18] and on the days after he sent his memorandum he vigorously followed up the subject. "Haul down that flag," he told Rose, "and all will be right." He asserted that he knew English statesmen were really in favor of evacuating Canada. If he could only have a few minutes with Granville and Gladstone, he would soon convince them that there was only one course to be taken. At a dinner party with Rose, Schenck, John Sherman, Howe, Ben Butler, and N. P. Banks, Sumner warned Schenck — jocularly enough, but with undertones of menace — of "the hazards to *him* of favoring a policy of concession on his mission."[19]

Fish received the memorandum with a rare and vicious fury. He scrawled caustic comments and little legal points all over it ridiculing Sumner's argument. "If as Mr. S. proposes the British are to withdraw from this Hemisphere 'including the Provinces and Islands' we shall no longer be 'neighbours.' . . . Islands-Trinidad Barbados Antigua Falkland Islands? *but not Santo Domingo.*"[20] He need not have been so violent. Sumner, being Sumner, had to express his ideas in pompous and arrogant language, and his natural tendency to *hauteur* was heightened in dealing with two men who had done almost everything they could to discredit and insult him, who were even then vilifying him in society and in their correspondence. Part of the force of his words, and part of the rationale of his bearding of Rose and Schenck proceeded from a misunderstanding. Fish, perhaps a little unnerved at the occasion of the interview (as well he might have been) left Sumner with the impression that he proposed "to require from England the payment of losses by the Alabama, leaving the losses by other ships unmentioned."[21] Again

18. Rose to Granville, Jan. 16, 1871, FO 5/1298.

19. Rose to Granville, Jan. 19, 1871, FO 5/1298.

20. Memorandum for Mr. Fish in response to his inquiries, encl. in Fish Diary, Jan. 17, 1871. By "Provinces and Islands," Sumner probably meant just Newfoundland and Prince Edward Island, which had not joined the new Dominion.

21. Sumner to Fish, Jan. 22, 1871; also Sumner to Fish, Jan. 19, 1871, Fish Papers, L.C.

Sumner must have been thunderstruck when he heard how little the administration was prepared to accept. The last time he had been privy to negotiations, Grant had been talking in terms of making Canadian independence a condition of a settlement, and Fish had been supporting him. It was to this policy that Sumner now clung.

The letters he wrote after making his speech on the Johnson-Clarendon Convention and his vote for the Treaty of Washington[22] furnish good ground for thinking that Sumner did not mean to say that the memorandum contained the *only* terms he would accept. That winter he had told Thornton repeatedly that, though he wanted to see Canada a part of the Union, he acquiesced "in the impossibility of making this a condition of the settlement of the Alabama Claims."[23] Sumner did not, of course, ask for cession in the memorandum: he asked for Canadian independence. But everyone knew that the two were almost synonymous, and in the context of these remarks to Thornton the memorandum can be interpreted, at least in part, as an attempt to put some backbone into an administration that Sumner thought jellyfish-weak, and as an endeavor to push as hard as possible for a settlement favorable to America. In this light, the memorandum appears as a proposal for a hard-line policy (with the possibility of other expedients if it did not work), not as an ultimatum, which Fish took it to be. He told Thornton that he feared Sumner might take some rash or mischievous step, even make a public announcement of the negotiations and set himself up before the nation as the champion of extremism.[24] The secretary described Sumner as "bitterly vindictive and hostile." There was nothing he would not do to defeat anything the president proposed. "He is irrational and illogical, and raves and rants. No wild bull ever dashed more violently at a red rag than he does at anything that he thinks the President

22. Sumner believed the treaty sent the whole enormous mass of consequential claims for arbitration.
23. Thornton to Granville, Jan. 10, 1871, Granville Papers, FO 29/80.
24. Rose to Granville, Jan. 21, 1871, FO 5/1298.

is interested in."[25] Fish did not reach such conclusions lightly. He thought slowly, even painfully, but when he did make up his mind on a subject, nothing could shake him. During the autumn of 1870 he came to regard Sumner's opposition to the president whom he idolized as nothing short of criminal. In August 1870, Fish told Justin S. Morrill that he could not view Sumner as either a reasonable or a reasoning man. By the end of the year his attitude had hardened, and he seriously believed the senator partially insane, a monomaniac who lost the power of logical reasoning and became contradictory and violent on any matter relating to his own importance, ambitions, or relations with the president.[26]

But for Sumner's almost saintly restraint, Fish's attitude might have wrecked all hopes of an Anglo-American accord. The secretary did nothing to mitigate the bitterness of Grant's vendetta against the senator: indeed, he expressed opinions quite as violent as the president's. Fortunately, Sumner was not personally vindictive and never confused principles with personalities. Had he returned evil for evil, the Treaty of Washington would never have passed the Senate.

It was equally good for the future of Anglo-American relations that Sumner and Fish did not come to a modus vivendi. Had they set Santo Domingo aside and worked together in negotiating a British settlement, Sumner would have driven a far harder bargain than Fish, in fact, did. He would certainly not have been content with the treaty's ambiguous silences on the consequential claims; under such circumstances, the two sides probably would not have reached a settlement. Luck and chance were the two forces that made an Anglo-American accord possible in 1871-1872.

Fish kept the Sumner memorandum quiet for a couple of

25. Fish to Elihu B. Washburne, Feb. 20, 1871, Fish Papers, L.C.
26. Fish to Morrill, Aug. 26, 1870, printed in William B. Parker, *The Life and Public Services of Justin Smith Morrill* (Boston: Houghton Mifflin, 1924), p. 234. Fish Diary, Dec. 25, 1870, Jan. 8, 1871; also, Fish to John Jay, Feb. 25, 1871, Fish Papers, L.C. Thornton to Granville, Sept. 27, Jan. 17, 24, 1871, Granville Papers, FO 29/80.

days, probably to give himself time to think, and it was not until the evening of Friday, January 20, that he told Rose about it. He added that the administration must have a little more time to consider whether this "rather unexpected" development would force Grant and himself to change their terms.[27] The British spent a gloomy weekend. Thornton felt that there would be a good chance of success if only Fish and the other members of the administration would overcome their mortal fear of Sumner.[28] Rose was more inclined to be pessimistic and expected Fish to make the extreme conditions required by Sumner. He wondered if it might not be better to continue the negotiations with Schenck in London and even suggested that Fish might give the minister confidential instructions to yield in London the conditions that could not be dispensed with in Washington.[29]

Both Rose and Thornton were reckoning without their host. When Grant heard of Sumner's memorandum, his anger blazed up again. Forgetting all his original reservations and misgivings, he ordered Fish to accept Rose's proposals and avowed he was determined to secure the settlement which the secretary had designed.[30] Something besides his hatred of Sumner may have impelled Grant to take this course. He dearly wanted to reduce the heavy national debt and hoped to convert the interest rate from 6 percent to 4½ percent that year. But Boutwell found European bankers very reluctant to risk their money with the Alabama Claims outstanding: the Rothschilds gave him a flat refusal and stated their reasons explicitly. While Fish was busy polling senators, Rose and his partner Levi P. Morton were telling Boutwell and Grant how difficult it would be to carry through a successful scheme of conversion without a settlement.[31]

27. Rose to Granville, Jan. 21, 1871, FO 5/1298.
28. Thornton to Granville, Jan. 24, 1871, FO 29/80.
29. Rose to Granville, Jan. 21–24, 1871, FO 5/1298.
30. Fish Diary, Jan. 23, 1871. Thornton to Granville, Jan. 24, 1871, FO 29/80. Rose to Granville, Jan. 21–24, 1871, FO 5/1298.
31. Thornton to Granville, Jan. 10, 1871, Granville Papers, FO 29/80. Fish Diary, Dec. 9, 1870. Granville to Gladstone, Nov. 22, 1870, Gladstone Papers.

Fish and Rose met again on Tuesday, the 24th, and the secretary of state spoke of the administration's determination to secure a settlement, even if it meant conflict with Sumner. He did, however, take up the last suggestion made in the senator's memorandum and dropped the demand for a specific admission of British liability for the acts of the *Alabama*,[32] saying that the claimants for losses by other raiders might raise a storm against it. Instead he emphasized that in dealing with the whole corpus of Alabama Claims, it would be essential that the commissioners should make some important concession on the abstract question of liability. As for the *Alabama* proper, the claims would be the value of the property destroyed and (Morton's condition) the costs incurred by the United States government in tracking her down. Rose said this involved a very extended field of inquiry and might even involve compensation in the form of pensions. Fish replied that he did not want anything as remote as that and hinted that the difficulty might be got around by empowering the commissioners to award a lump sum which would cover everything. As for the inshore fisheries, he was willing to pay $500,000 or $750,000 a year for them.[33]

Next day Thornton received a cable from London stating that the British government stood firm on the principle of arbitration. But they were willing to express regret for the escape and depredations of the *Alabama* and would consider the suggestion of a commission of jurists which Rose had included in his first report. Rose took the telegram to Fish and told him he thought it a favorable sign. The secretary did not agree and grumbled that the British had not budged an inch from the Johnson-Clarendon Convention. Afterward, Rose spoke to Schenck and

32. John M. Forbes had also advised Fish to drop this demand, and his representations may well have had more effect than Sumner's. Forbes to Fish, Jan. 25, 1871, Fish Papers, L.C.

33. Fish Diary, Jan. 24, 1871. Rose to Granville, Jan. 21–24, 1871, FO 5/1298. Thornton to Granville, Jan. 24, 1871, Granville Papers, FO 29/80.

discovered that both he and Fish wanted to go ahead with the negotiations, even on the British terms, but that the secretary hardly saw enough arguments to justify such a course.

Rose hurried back to the legation and conferred with Thornton. They agreed upon a two-pronged attack. Rose was to write a memorandum for Fish, "which it would be rather for *him* to use towards others whose support was required," and they would ask him, after allowing some time for thought, to let the commissioners go on under British terms. But they expected him to refuse, and Rose also wrote a letter to Granville recounting their plans and asking him if he could not accept Fish's proposal of Tuesday the 24th. If neither side would give way, Schenck would be in England within a month, and he might offer a chance of settlement. Rose felt — it was only an impression — that Fish might allow the minister to accept full arbitration.[34]

With all his writing complete, Rose took the train for New York to attend the St. George's Society dinner. Thornton also turned to thoughts of dining and invited Fish to his house. During the evening he took the occasion to regret that the Americans were being so stern and exacting. If he hoped to find his guest mellowed by the atmosphere and the meal, he was sadly disappointed. Fish replied that he thought he was being very yielding and moderate. Great Britain was displaying intransigence. If she would say to America what had been said in Parliament in the debate on the Foreign Enlistment Act, there would be no problem. But she refused to make any concessions.[35]

In New York, Rose had already received another cable declaring that the British could not accept any foregone conclusions as to the payment of money. Returning to Washington, he confronted Fish; the negotiations stood on the very brink of failure.

34. Rose to Granville, Jan. 27, 1871, FO 5/1298. Telegram of Granville to Thornton, Jan. 24, 1871, FO 5/1296. Fish Diary, Jan. 25, 1871. Rose's memorandum is enclosed in Fish Diary, Jan. 26, 1871.
35. Fish Diary, Jan. 28, 1871.

But Fish admitted that if they did fail there could be no settlement for years. Finally, after a long discussion in which he made it clear that he expected weighty concessions, Fish said that he would not refuse a British proposal of a commission.[36]

With this the painful process of preliminary negotiations ended. To keep Sumner quiet and make him think the *pourparlers* had failed, Fish told him to go ahead with the bill for the government's assumption of the claims, which he had held up in mid-January. For the same reason, he allowed Zack Chandler to bring up the bill allowing the President to proclaim nonintercourse with Canada.[37] But two days later London cabled assent, and the Joint High Commission was announced.[38]

36. *Ibid.,* Jan. 30, 1871. Rose to Granville, Jan. 31, 1871, FO 5/1298.

37. O. P. Morton to Fish, Jan. 15, 1871; Fish to Sumner, Jan. 16, 1870 [error for 1871], Fish Papers, L.C. Fish Diary, Jan. 31, 1871. *Cong. Globe,* 41 Cong., 3 sess., p. 980, Feb. 6, 1871.

38. Telegram from Granville to Thornton, Feb. 1, 1871, FO 5/1296. Fish Diary, Feb. 1, 1871. Rose said that the British could not take the initiative on the Alabama Claims publicly after the rejection of the Johnson-Clarendon Convention, so it was arranged that the British should propose a commission to settle the Canadian disputes, and the United States should agree, provided the claims were included. Memorandum in Fish Diary, Jan. 9, 1871, *ibid.,* Jan. 11, 1871. Rose to Granville, Jan. 31, 1871, FO 5/1298. To make them more convincing the dates of the letters were altered. Rose to Granville, Feb. 2, 1871, FO 5/1298.

CHAPTER 8

The Treaty of Washington

The announcement of a Joint High Commission to settle all the disputes between the United States, Britain, and Canada was warmly welcomed by American public opinion. "I congratulate you most heartily on the way in which the public of all shades of party opinion have received the announcement of the negotiations," Rose told Fish.[1] The president's message about the commission met with a "triumphant reception" in the Senate,[2] and a correspondent told the secretary of state that it had "created a thrill of satisfaction (as far as I can learn) from one end of the country to the other."[3]

Before the announcement of the commission, Thurlow Weed had told Fish that he detected a general desire in the country for a settlement with England.[4] When Thomas Hughes, M.P., had delivered a lecture on the claims in Boston the previous autumn, several newspapers had noticed his arguments and called for an end to the dispute.[5] Ben Butler's Anglophobe tub-thumping had brought him little success in the national forum. The New York *Journal of Commerce* ridiculed his plan of non-intercourse and remarked that the press of all parties was kicking

1. Rose to Fish, Feb. 13, 1871, Fish Papers, L.C.
2. Timothy O. Howe to Fish, Feb. 10, 1871, Fish Papers, L.C.
3. Royal Phelps to Fish, Feb. 12, 1871, Fish Papers, L.C.
4. Thurlow Weed to Fish, Jan. 21, 1871, Fish Papers, L.C.
5. Thornton to Granville, Oct. 18, 1870, Granville Papers, FO 29/80.

it about like a football, amidst shouts of laughter.[6] *The Nation* denounced Butler's "rascality" and "gross and wild ignorance" and declared that his scheme might have issued "from the brain of a fuddled bar-keeper."[7]

The country was still sunk in torpor and lethargy, tired of excitement, and indifferent to all forms of agitation. The words "Let us have peace," with which Grant had ended his letter accepting the Republican nomination in 1868, expressed that national mood to perfection. Sumner had been able to attract attention and generate excitement for a while with his glittering vision of a horn of plenty pouring out dollars to pay the consequential claims, but after the early summer of 1869 nothing, not even Santo Domingo, caused a storm. "If General Grant were to go to sleep in his bed," wrote Charles Francis Adams, "and not wake up until the second Thursday in November, 1872, he would probably be elected by acclamation for a succeeding term."[8] Reformers like Henry Adams wanted no foreign difficulties or distractions,[9] so Fish was able to enter the high commission with public opinion well in hand. In March, Rutherford B. Hayes, then governor of Ohio, testified that the great majority of Republicans supported the administration in its treatment of the claims question.[10] But this tide of approval only extended to the principle of a settlement. Fish still had to deliver satisfactory terms, as John M. Forbes reminded him when he wrote

6. Encl. in E. M. Archibald to Granville, Dec. 2, 1870, FO 5/1331.

7. Dec. 1, 1870, encl. in Thornton to Granville, Dec. 5, 1870, FO 5/1331. Also condemning Butler were the *Chicago Tribune,* Jan. 4, 1871; Worcester, Mass., *Evening Gazette,* Dec. 7, 1870, clipping in Butler Papers.

8. C. F. Adams to Henry Adams, May 11, 1870, Adams Papers.

9. Henry Adams to David A. Wells, Jan. 17, 1871, Wells Correspondence, Springfield City Library, Springfield, Mass., transcript in Adams Papers.

10. Hayes to Charles Nordhoff, March 13, 1871, printed in Charles R. Williams, ed., *Diary and Letters of Rutherford Birchard Hayes, Nineteenth President of the United States* (Columbus: Ohio State Archaeological and Historical Society, 1924), V, 133-134.

that there was some concern lest American claims should be offset against British and their owners left to lobby Congress.[11]

While waiting for the commissioners to begin their work, both sides tried to smooth out some obstacles to conciliation. A couple of American fishing boats were under arrest in Canadian harbors, and Fish asked Rose to use his influence with the Dominion government to secure their release. "General Butler," he warned, "is very eager for a condemnation, and has recommended the owners to abandon their vessels as he is advised the offense is not one within the terms of the Treaty [of 1818], and he thinks his grievance will be strengthened if he can make out a case of illegal action by the Canadian authorities." Rose was successful, and there was no condemnation.[12]

In mid-January, to dramatize their willingness to be conciliatory, the British released the last three Fenian prisoners, and these men reached New York just as the Fish-Rose negotiations came to their successful end. Inevitably, the ward heelers of Manhattan fell over themselves to flatter the Irish vote and fete the former prisoners, and Ben Butler pushed a resolution through the House welcoming them "in the name and on behalf of the people of the United States."[13] But the public at large remained profoundly unimpressed, and the pro-Irish congressmen had lost their favorite cause of complaint against England due to the release.

On February 27 the hastily selected members of the Joint High Commission met in the library of the State Department. The precipitateness of the whole affair, which created distrust in the mind of a careful lawyer like George Bemis,[14] sprang from Fish's desire to reach a settlement before Congress adjourned for the summer vacation. The new House of Representatives

11. Forbes to Fish, Feb. 17, 1871, Fish Papers, L.C.
12. Rose to Granville, Feb. 2, 9, 1871, FO 5/1298.
13. *Chicago Tribune,* Feb. 1, 1871. *Cong. Globe,* 41 Cong., 3 sess., p. 838, Jan. 30, 1871.
14. Bemis to Sumner, Feb. 10, 1871, Sumner Papers.

which was due to assemble on March 4 was much more Democratic than the old, and so, by party tradition, much more Anglophobe. If a treaty was not presented to Congress until December, it would have to pass a Senate increasingly influenced by House policy and already thinking of the coming presidential elections.[15]

On the American side, the commissioners included Fish, Schenck, former Attorney-General Ebenezer Rockwood Hoar, Senator George H. Williams of Oregon, and senior Associate Justice Samuel Nelson of the Supreme Court.[16] Bancroft Davis was named secretary; there was some talk of making George Bemis his assistant, but he was eventually excluded (to Thornton's delight) as Sumner's tool. Fish, who still regarded the senator as the administration's foremost enemy, momentarily overcame his nervousness and submitted the nominations without a qualm. For, as he told Thornton, Sumner had just been badly defeated in his attempt to block the confirmation of Grant's brother-in-law William Cramer as minister to Denmark, and his colleagues were a good deal irritated with him.[17] In fact, there is no reason to think that Sumner would have opposed the commission.

The British choice comprised Earl de Grey and Ripon, Lord President of the Council; Thornton, and Montague Bernard, Chichele Professor of International Law at Oxford, who had written a book defending the British course during the war. Sir John MacDonald, the Dominion prime minister, represented Canada, and Sir Stafford Northcote, who had held the India office and the governorship of the Hudson's Bay Company and who was to be chancellor of the exchequer in 1874-1880, represented the British opposition party as Nelson represented the American.[18]

Unfortunately, Sir John Rose refused a place on the com-

15. Thornton to Granville, Jan. 10, 1871, Granville Papers, FO 29/80.
16. Fish Diary, Feb. 3, 13, 16, 1871. Adams Diary, Feb. 24, 1871.
17. Thornton to Granville, Feb. 7, 1871, Granville Papers, FO 29/80.
18. Granville to Thornton, Draft, Feb. 9, 14, 1871, FO 5/1296. Granville to Bright, Feb. 16, 1871, Bright Papers. Granville to Gladstone, Jan. 27, Feb. 5, 13, 1871, Gladstone Papers.

mission. His action was understandable; he wanted the negotiators to kill all Anglo-American difficulties and felt that his close links with the United States through his wife, friends, and business would invite charges of partiality and diminish a settlement's chances of acceptance.[19] Had Rose joined the commission, he might well have held Fish to a strict maintenance of the principles he had set out in the January preliminaries. At the time Fish bitterly regretted Rose's refusal and wrote that it lessened his confidence of a successful result. The secretary of state had come to regard Rose as a reasonable and conciliatory man and was gravely worried that Tenterden, the British secretary, and Bernard would refuse to budge from the positions they had taken, the one in the British reply to Fish's dispatch of September 25, 1869, and the other in his book.[20]

The commission sat for nine weeks; by the first days of May a treaty was ready. Most of the trouble during the negotiations came over Canadian matters, especially the fisheries. MacDonald fought the Americans and (in private) the British every inch of the way, threatening resignation from the commission or refusal to sign the treaty. Fish first offered the Canadians the free entry of fish, salt, coal, and firewood in return for access to the inshore fisheries. Canada demanded free trade in a longer list of products, and Fish suggested a money payment instead. For a time the Dominion government would not have this, and when they gave in they still haggled over the amount. On March 20, Fish offered a million dollars for perpetual access and was rebuffed.

Two days later he produced narrower terms: the fisheries in return for free admission of Canadian salt, mackerel, herring, cod, and after 1876, lumber. The four British commissioners

19. Rose to Fish, Feb. 13, 1871, Fish Papers, L.C.
20. Thornton to Granville, Feb. 14, 1871, Granville Papers, FO 29/80. Telegram from Thornton to Granville, Feb. 13, 1871, FO 5/1296. Fish Diary, Feb. 9, 16, 1871. Fish to Rose, Feb. 16, 1871, Fish Papers, L.C. Rose had met with opposition from the Canadian government, partly for these reasons. Rose to Granville, Jan. 26, 1871, FO 5/1298.

urged MacDonald and his government to yield the fisheries in return for the free entry of coal, fish, salt, and lumber, and actually tendered this proposal to the secretary of state on March 25. Fish went to see Zachariah Chandler, found him strongly opposed to the idea, and promptly withdrew all tariff concessions from discussion. De Grey brought up the suggestion of a payment again, Fish said each side placed such a different value on the concession there was no hope of agreement; but a sudden thought occurred to him, and he proposed arbitration of the amount to be paid by America. Grant agreed, provided the free navigation of the St. Lawrence was also conceded, and Fish offered the British arbitration, plus the free entry of Canadian fish into the United States. The British commissioners cabled London for approval, then agreed and forced this solution upon the unwilling MacDonald.[21] The arrangement was for ten years. De Grey told Granville that arbitration would greatly strengthen the treaty, especially regarding San Juan. If arbitration formed the basis of the settlement in all three major questions, fisheries, claims, and San Juan, the Senate would find it hard to reject, though referring the ownership of the island to an umpire's decision was "very distasteful" to them.[22]

'Mr. Secretary," scrawled Michigan Senator Jacob Howard in huge red letters after the commission was announced, "I enclose you my speech on *San Juan Island*. Please read it. Now is the time to acquire all British America West of Hudson's Bay,

21. Fish Diary, March 4, 5, 6, 17, April 12, 19, 21, 22, 1871. Northcote Diary, March 6, 18, 20, 22, 27, April 12, 16, 17, 18, 22, Iddesleigh Papers. Granville to the High Commissioners, March 8, 1871, FO 5/1299. High Commissioners to Granville, Secret, March 4, 6, 20, 1871; Telegrams from De Grey to Granville, March 6, 1871; High Commissioners to Granville, March 7, 1871, FO 5/1300. High Commissioners to Granville, Secret, March 22, 25, 27, 28, 1871, April 2, 15, 16, 1871; Telegrams from De Grey to Granville, April 12, 15, 1871, FO 5/1301. Goldwin Smith, *The Treaty of Washington, 1871: A Study in Imperial History* (Ithaca, N.Y.: Cornell University Press, 1941), pp. 46–90.

22. Telegram from De Grey to Granville, April 16, 1871, FO 5/1302.

and the Sault Ste. Marie to the *Pacific Ocean*. I believe it can be had almost for the asking, and I trust the High Commission will not neglect this great opportunity."[23] Five days later he brought up a resolution in the Senate welcoming the Joint High Commission, but declaring that Canada was by its very nature an obstacle to the permanent harmony of Britain and America and a standing invitation to people who wanted to involve the two in war. He therefore "earnestly recommended" that any settlement should, at the very least, include the cession of the Canadian West to the United States.[24] Fish was probably not too worried about Howard, who had failed to win re-election and occupied the politically unenviable situation of a lame-duck senator, but he had to remember the votes that Howard had marshaled to bury Reverdy Johnson's treaty sending San Juan to arbitration.

When the subject came up on March 15, the Americans argued that details of the 1846 negotiations proved the island should have gone to the United States. Two stormy sessions ensued, and when the Americans began to hint that Peel and Lord Aberdeen had deliberately tried to cheat by making the treaty of 1846 ambiguous, Northcote wanted to break up the negotiations.[25] De Grey, however, held on, hoping that when all the other questions were settled, Fish would give in rather

23. Howard to Fish, Feb. 13, 1871, Fish Papers, L.C.
24. *Cong. Globe,* 41 Cong., 3 sess., p. 1382, Feb. 18, 1871. "I was dining in his [Fish's] company last night. Allusion was made to Mr. Howard's resolution, as proposed in the Senate. I told him jokingly that a common burglar might as well say that in order that there might be no disturbance of friendly relations between us, I ought to hand over my Plate to him." Thornton to Granville, Feb. 21, 1871, Granville Papers, FO 29/80.
25. Fish Diary, March 16, 18, 20, 28, April 12, 13, 21, 1871. Northcote Diary, March 15, 16, 20, 1871, Iddesleigh Papers. Northcote to Gladstone, March 17, 1871, Gladstone Papers. Granville to the High Commissioners, April 1, 1871, FO 5/1299. High Commissioners to Granville, Secret, March 15, 16, 1871, FO 5/1300. Telegrams from De Grey to Granville, March 19, April 14, 1871, FO 5/1301. High Commissioners to Granville, Secret, March 20, 1871, FO 5/1301.

than lose the whole treaty for a tiny island. And this was what eventually happened. Late on the 16th, the Americans proposed that, as there seemed to be a misunderstanding about the 1846 treaty, the whole question of a boundary west of the Rockies should be renegotiated: an obvious bid for the cession of British Columbia. Privately Fish offered De Grey compensation in money or trade concessions for all or part of the colony. The British, however, replied that they were not empowered to suggest such a thing, and the Americans retired, as Schenck said, to chew the question.

On March 20, Fish offered neutralization of the whole area in return for the island, but London would go no further than suggesting the Douglas Channel, an intermediate strait which divided the archipelago in two, as the boundary. On April 12, when De Grey urged that all the Canadian questions ought to be settled together, Fish answered that if the Alabama Claims, the fisheries, and the St. Lawrence navigation could be settled on reasonable terms, he would let San Juan go to arbitration. De Grey asked him to explore this idea further; Fish went to Grant, who reluctantly gave his approval. But, nervous that the concession might drag the whole settlement down in defeat at the hands of annexationist senators, he stipulated that San Juan arbitration must go in a separate treaty. Fish replied that the British would not have this, and Grant told him to consult the other commissioners and some influential senators on the question. Applying the acid test, Fish presented the project to Zachariah Chandler. Chandler was not enthusiastic, but hesitated to take the responsibility of torpedoing the treaty, which might well end his influence with Grant. If nothing better could be obtained, he said, arbitration would have to do. This clinched the matter, and San Juan's future ownership was referred to the decision of the German emperor.

At their third sitting, on March 8, the commissioners attacked the Alabama Claims. That day and the next, both sides made long statements, and arguments raged back and forth on points of international law and the extent of British neutral obligations, in which Justice Nelson, according to Northcote, displayed "great power of twaddling."[26] As to a settlement, Fish said that the United States thought "the readiest and best way" would be for Britain to pay a gross sum and satisfy all the claims at once; the amount could be set then and there. But if this was impossible they would agree to refer the question of British liability to a tribunal or arbitration which could also assess the damages. In any case, they insisted that a decision upon the questions of British liability and the validity of the claims should be governed by certain principles of international law, which they presented forthwith:

(1) Any great maritime power with a strong government, possessed of the material resources requisite to enable it to perform its duties, is bound to use active diligence in order to prevent the construction, fitting out, arming, equipping, or augmenting the force, within its jurisdiction, of any vessel whereby war is intended to be carried on upon the ocean against a Power with which it is at peace, during hostilities between that power and its insurgent citizens who have been recognized as belligerents by such great maritime power.

(2) When such a vessel shall have escaped, such Power is bound to use like diligence to arrest and detain her when she comes again within its jurisdiction.

(3) Such power is further bound to instruct its naval forces in all parts of the globe to arrest and detain vessels so escaping, wherever found on the high seas.

(4) Any power failing to observe either of the rules of international law above described is justly to be held responsible for the injuries and depredations committed and damages occasioned by such vessel.[27]

At every point these rules denied the British doctrines of

26. Northcote Diary, March 8, 9, 1871, Iddesleigh Papers.
27. High Commissioners to Granville, Secret, March 8, 1871, FO 5/1300.

neutrality and belligerency and upheld the American view. In other words, the Americans demanded that the game should be played according to rules which made it certain they would win; this was Fish's substitute for what he had tried to get from Rose in January, a prior admission of British liability.

The British Joint Highs would not hear of paying a gross sum. They wanted arbitration unrestricted by any previous commitments.[28] De Grey urged the idea in strong terms, but Fish only replied that the Senate would never swallow it. A treaty based on such a principle would not get ten votes. As Thornton reflected, Fish so strongly opposed unrestricted arbitration partly because there was a good chance that the arbitrators would decide in Britain's favor if they were left to choose between the British statement of the nature of international law in 1861-1865 and the American. At the same time, the minister had to admit that a treaty couched in such terms would be too much like the Johnson-Clarendon Convention to save the Senate's face.[29]

The British soon saw that the United States would not give way. An open reference was impossible, De Grey cabled Granville on the 13th; if the American proposals were not accepted, all idea of arbitration must be abandoned. "I have again made a very strong effort to get unrestricted arbitration," he wired on March 19. "We are all convinced that no more can be done and that it is absolutely unattainable."[30] In London a battle royal was going on, and De Grey made an attempt to turn this to his advantage in the negotiations. After the meeting of the commission on March 18, he told Fish privately that there was great difficulty about yielding to the American terms.

28. High Commissioners to Granville, Secret, March 14, 1871, FO 5/1300.
29. Thornton to Granville, March 21, 1871, Granville Papers, FO 29/80.
30. Telegram from De Grey to Granville, Secret, March 13, 1971, FO 5/1300. Telegram from De Grey to Granville, March 19, 1871, FO 5/1301.

Two cabinet meeings had been held on the subject. If Fish would agree to a compromise on San Juan, either arbitration or agreement that the Douglas Channel should be the boundary, Gladstone and his colleagues might be persuaded to accept the American views on the Alabama Claims. Fish, however, was not so easily beguiled and categorically rejected the idea.[31] The British gave in, but Granville sent word that he wanted some changes in the proposed rules of international law before he would accept them.[32]

Although Fish had had ample opportunity to draw up his proposed rules, they were crudely and badly drafted. They looked too little like general legal principles which could be applied to any nation's acts and too much like a kangaroo court attempt to convict Britain for her specific violations of international law during the Civil War. The British Joint Highs justifiably called them "too broad and too loose" and objected particularly to the provision about preventing the construction of a hostile ship. As they pointed out, such a rule was entirely new; it was not even in American municipal law.[33] De Grey and his fellow commissioners made it quite clear that they were authorized to accept nothing but unrestricted arbitration, but agreed to discuss a statement of principles in order to clarify the American arguments.[34]

Next day the British presented a counterstatement:

[1] A neutral government is bound to take reasonable care that no ship in the service of either belligerent, or intended to be employed in such service, be equipped for war, or suffered to augment her armament, within the neutral territory.

31. Fish Diary, March 18, 1871.
32. Granville to the High Commissioners (Draft), Feb. 12, 1871, FO 5/1299.
33. High Commissioners to Granville, Secret, March 8, 1871, FO 5/1300.
34. High Commissioners to Granville, Secret, March 14, 1871, FO 5/1300.

[2] A ship which has been equipped for war in violation of the neutrality of a neutral state ought, if afterwards found within the jurisdiction of that state, to be detained, unless she have in the interval been commissioned as a public ship of war or have been deprived of all military equipment and bona fide converted into a ship of commerce.[35]

Perhaps not wanting to give up too much at first, the British held back many of the ideas Granville had set in their instructions:

That no vessel employed in the military or naval service of any belligerent which shall have been equipped, fitted out, armed or dispatched contrary to the neutrality of a neutral state should be admitted into any port of that state.

That prizes captured by such vessels, or otherwise captured in violation of the neutrality of any state should, if brought within the jurisdiction of that state, be restored.

That in time of war, no vessel should be recognized as a ship of war, nor received in any port of a neutral state as a ship of war, which has not been commissioned in some port in the actual occupation of the Government by whom her commission is issued.

The Americans retired to their own room for consultations and emerged with a modified set of rules which were much more professional:

(1) A Neutral Government is bound to use active diligence to prevent the construction, fitting out, arming, equipping or augmenting the force within its jurisdiction of any vessel whereby war is intended to be carried on against a Power with which it is at Peace.

(2) When a vessel thus constructed, armed, equipped, or fitted out shall have escaped, such Government is bound to use like diligence to arrest and detain her when she comes again within its jurisdiction, and is further bound to instruct its naval forces, in all parts of the globe, to arrest and detain vessels so escaping

35. High Commissioners to Granville, Secret, March 9, 1871, FO 5/1300.

wherever found upon the High Seas; but such liability to arrest or detention will cease upon the termination of the cruise in the preparation for which her offence against the neutral was committed.

(3) Any power failing to observe either of the rules of international law above described is justly to be held responsible for the injuries and depredations committed and damages occasioned by such vessel.[36]

Nevertheless, the British had a field day attacking them. Their opponents gave way on only one point: the substitution of "due and reasonable diligence" for "active diligence" in the first rule. This was not too far from the "reasonable care" of their own draft, but otherwise they made no progress. As before, they singled out the word "construction" in the first rule and argued that no neutral could be responsible for the building of a perfectly ordinary commercial vessel, which might be converted into a warship later. They suggested adding the words "for war" to "equipped" and objected that the provision for pursuit would inevitably lead to serious difficulties and collisions with other powers. Finally, they complained about the omission of their words dealing with commissioned vessels and contended that the third rule "would in a multitude of cases be unreasonable and unjust," as well as unnecessary, or "the two previous paragraphs had already laid down the responsibilities which it was sought to enforce."[37]

De Grey cabled Granville that he and the other British representatives thought that "construction" might be allowed if the expression about diligence and care was properly worded. They wished to hold out on the question of raiders regularly commissioned as public ships of war and thought that the Americans would probably yield as far as ships commissioned in the ports of the belligerent power were concerned; they would not agree to recognize ships commissioned on the high seas. The

36. *Ibid.*
37. *Ibid.* Northcote Diary, March 9, 13, 1871, Iddesleigh Papers.

home government, still undecided about accepting conditional arbitration, resolved to maintain the status quo for the time being and replied that, in their opinion, the reference should be unrestricted. They did not mind instructing the arbitrator about the principles of international law which should guide him, if Britain and America could agree what those principles were in 1861-1865. Fish, of course, was not concerned with that; he wanted his statement of the principles which he thought should have been followed made retrospective. Granville concluded with an objection to the term "construction."[38]

Though he held firm on that point, Fish did, as the British Joint Highs had prophesied, give way on the question of ships commissioned by a recognized sovereign power,[39] and on the 13th he presented a revised set of rules:

(1) A neutral government is bound to use due diligence to prevent the fitting out, arming, or equipping within its jurisdiction of any vessel intended to cruise or to carry on war against a power with which it is at peace; and also to prevent the departure from its jurisdiction of any vessel constructed, fitted out or equipped therein, intended thus to cruise or carry on war.

(2) Such neutral is bound not to permit or suffer either belligerent to make use of its ports or waters as the base of naval operations, or as the place for the renewal or augmentation of military supplies, or arms, or the recruitment of men.

(3) Such neutral is further bound to exercise due watchfulness over its ports and waters, and over all persons within its jurisdiction, to prevent any violation of the foregoing obligations and duties, the neglect of which renders it responsible nationally for the injuries and losses occasioned by such neglect to the aggrieved Belligerent.

(4) A vessel which has departed from the jurisdiction of a

38. Telegram from De Grey to Granville, March 10, 1871, FO 5/1300. Granville to the High Commissioners, March 11, 1871, FO 5/1299.
39. High Commissioners to Granville, Secret, March 10, 1871, FO 5/1300. Telegram from Granville to the High Commissioners, March 13, 1871, FO 5/1300.

neutral government in violation of the neutrality thereof, if afterwards found within the jurisdiction of that government, ought to be detained, unless she have, in the interval, been duly and lawfully commissioned as a public vessel of war; but if she have been thus commissioned as a public vessel of war, and be permitted to depart, the national responsibility of the Government from whose jurisdiction she originally departed in violation of its neutrality, continues for injuries and losses occasioned to the aggrieved belligerent, subsequent to such departure, and until she be purged of the original offence.[40]

Once more the British arrayed objections, especially to the word "constructed." Their protests of March 10 had borne fruit in one respect, though: the pursuit clause had vanished.[41] Next day there was even more gratifying news. Fish abandoned the liability provision in the third rule, replaced "constructed" by "specially adapted, in whole or in part, within such jurisdiction, to warlike use," and altered the fourth rule, which now read:

A vessel which has departed from the jurisdiction of a neutral government in violation of the neutrality thereof if afterwards found within the jurisdiction of that government ought to be detained, unless she have, in the interval, been duly and lawfully commissioned as a public vessel of war; but if she have been thus commissioned as a public vessel of war and be not detained, the national responsibility of such neutral Government continues in respect of injuries and losses occasioned to the aggrieved belligerent subsequent to such departure and until the original offence be terminated by the bona fide termination of the cruise.[42]

Three days later the stormy deliberations of the British cabinet ended, and Granville relayed the results to the commissioners. The British government, he said, could not agree

40. High Commissioners to Granville, Secret, March 13, 1871, FO 5/1300.

41. *Ibid.* Northcote Diary, March 13, 1871, Iddesleigh Papers.

42. High Commissioners to Granville, Secret, March 14, 1871, FO 5/1300. Northcote Diary, March 14, 1871, Iddesleigh Papers.

to regard the rules as actually in existence in 1861-1865 (this would impugn the honor and good faith of the Palmerston government), but, providing everything else could be satisfactorily settled, they would agree that the arbitrator should assume that Britain had undertaken to act on such principles. This only applied to the first three articles; the fourth was not clear, and clarification was required. On the 22nd, five days later, Granville proposed an amended Article Four, which read:

"Also, that if a vessel has departed from its jurisdiction in violation of the obligation under Articles One, Two, and Three, a neutral government is bound to detain such vessel if afterwards found within any port or place within its jurisdiction if the local authority of such port or place has, upon representation made, reasonable and probable grounds for believing that such vessel has so departed as aforesaid, unless such vessel has in the interval been commissioned as a ship of war."[43]

De Grey took the new article to Fish, declared that it was designed solely to cut off opposition in Parliament, and begged him to make as few alterations as possible. But the secretary of state refused to change the essentials of his article, and the harried De Grey realized that the negotiations had reached an impasse. He sent Granville two cables saying that he would try to secure a fourth article based upon Fish's last draft, but with the last phrase changed to read: "any liability attaching to such neutral on account of such vessels shall not be in any way affected by the fact of the vessel having entered and quitted in the manner aforesaid a port of the neutral state."

This was merely a roundabout way of giving in to the American contention that an illegally launched warship could not be rendered respectable by a commission until she reached the end of her cruise in a port belonging to her own government. It would have been simpler to keep the ban on warships being commissioned on the high seas, as the Joint Highs had agreed on March 10. But De Grey was quite convinced that if the

43. Granville to the High Commissioners, March 17, 22, 23, 1871, FO 5/1299.

Americans would not accept this revised article, their proposals should be accepted. If not, the commission would break up.[44]

Although impressed by the desperation of the cables, Granville decided to fight a rear-guard action. Fish had offered the words "armed, fitted out and equipped" as a substitute for "specially adapted" in the first article, and the foreign secretary said he would prefer this form. He also drafted a new Article Four, very much like the one De Grey had offered, which abandoned the British attempt to purge themselves of liability for a commissioned raider calling at a port.[45]

Granville had now come down to evading double jeopardy. Some of the Confederate raiders had been welcomed and provisioned at British colonial ports, like the *Alabama* at Cape Town, and an arbitrator might hold that Britain had compounded her original liability each time this was done. The British Joint Highs used their utmost arts of persuasion upon Fish, and after long consultations with his colleagues, he agreed to the change in Article One and more or less accepted Granville's ideas in Article Four.[46]

44. Fish Diary, March 24, 1871. Telegrams of De Grey to Granville, n.d., March 24, 1871, FO 5/1301.

45. "The local authority should use his utmost endeavors to detain a vessel which has departed from the jurisdiction of a neutral in violation of the obligation of Articles I, II, III, if afterwards found within any port or place within the jurisdiction of the neutral if such local authority should have reasonable grounds for believing that such vessel had so departed as aforesaid; unless such local authority has no reasonable grounds for believing that such vessel has in the interval been duly and lawfully commissioned as a ship of war; but if such vessel be not detained, any ground of complaint that might be made against the neutral nation shall not be affected by the fact of the vessel having entered and quitted the port of the neutral state." Granville to the High Commissioners, March 27, 1871, FO 5/1299.

46. So that it read: "A vessel which has departed from the jurisdiction of a neutral Government, after having been specially adapted, in whole or in part, within such jurisdiction to warlike use, with intent to cruise or carry on war against a Power with which such neutral is at peace, ought (if) afterwards found in any port or place within such jurisdiction, to be detained, if the local authority of such port or place have reasonable grounds for believing that she has so departed and

London, remembering that the rules would in future bind the two countries with the force of international law, wanted to keep the escape hatch contained in the words "utmost endeavours." What, asked Granville, if a local authority found itself without a strong enough force to prevent a ship leaving port? But if the American Joint Highs would not agree to his version, he would be perfectly content to scrap the article altogether.[47] Fish, perhaps thinking that he would do just as well, if not better, at the tribunal if the arbitrators were left to apply the first three rules to a raider's whole cruise, and certainly worried about the reaction of the Senate, agreed, on condition that the words "specially adapted" should go back into Article One.[48] A majority of the British cabinet were in favor,[49] and on April 4 the articles stood complete at last.[50]

---

unless she have in the interval been duly and lawfully commissioned as a public ship of war, but if she have been thus commissioned as a ship of war and not be detained, any liability attaching to such neutrality on account of such vessel shall not be in any way affected by the fact of the vessel having entered and quitted in the manner aforesaid a port of the Neutral State." Telegram from the High Commissioners to Granville, March 30, 1871, FO 5/1301.

47. Granville to the High Commissioners, April 1, 1871, (two), FO 5/1299.

48. Telegram of the High Commissioners to Granville, March 30, 1871; High Commissioners to Granville, April 3, 1871, FO 5/1301.

49. Granville to the High Commissioners, April 4, 1871; Telegram from Hammond to Granville, April 4, 1871, FO 5/1299. De Grey to Fish, April 4, 1871, Fish Papers, L.C.

50. A neutral government was bound: "(1) To use diligence to prevent the fitting out, arming, or equipping, within its jurisdiction, of any vessel which it has reasonable ground to believe is intended to cruise or carry on war against a power with which it is at peace; and also to use like diligence to prevent the departure from its jurisdiction of any vessel intended to cruise or carry on war as above, such vessel having been specially adapted, in whole or in part, within such jurisdiction, to warlike use, (2) Not to permit or suffer either belligerent to make use of its ports or waters as the base of naval operations against the other, or for the purpose of the renewal or augmentation of military supplies or arms, or the recruitment of men. (3) To exercise due diligence in its own ports and waters, and, as to all persons within its jurisdiction, to prevent any violation of the foregoing obligations and duties."

Only details remained to be settled. The British claims were sent for arbitration to a three-man tribunal to be appointed by Britain, America, and Spain. The British had already conceded the "kind words," an expression of regret for the escape of the Confederate cruisers "under whatever circumstances."[51] Between April 5 and 10, the manner of arbitration was settled. The British wanted a sovereign head of state, but the Americans pressed for a commission of jurists, and they got their way.[52] Britain, America, the emperor of Brazil, the king of Italy, and the president of the Swiss Confederation were to appoint one arbitrator each, and they were to meet at Geneva in December.[53] Only one matter was neglected: the consequential claims.

Fish, delighted at the way the negotiation was going, told the leading Maine Republican Israel Washburn that he hoped the treaty would turn out well. "It looks promising at present," he summed up, "but some cow always kicks over the pail when nearly full."[54] His misgivings were justified; before the treaty was complete there was a ferocious melee over the wording of the preamble[55] and the Alabama Claims articles, and at one point Fish warned De Grey that if the British government wanted to break up the treaty, it was going the right way. Eventually the differences were patched up, and the Treaty of Washington was signed on the 8th of May amidst the greatest good humor and jollity.[56] "If we have not built a castle," wrote Northcote

51. Treaty of Washington, FO 5/1301.
52. High Commissioners to Granville, Secret, April 5, 10, 1871, FO 5/1301. Granville to the High Commissioners, April 10, 1871, FO 5/1299. De Grey to Fish, April 9, 1871, Fish Papers, L.C.
53. Treaty of Washington, FO 5/1301.
54. Fish to Israel Washburn, Jr., April 6, 1871, Fish Papers, L.C.
55. High Commissioners to Granville, Secret, April 6, 8, 10, 12, 1871; Telegrams from the High Commissioners to Granville, April 10, 1871; Telegram from De Grey to Granville, April 14, 1871; High Commissioners to Granville, April 15, 1871, FO 5/1302. Granville to the High Commissioners, April 13, 1871; Telegram from Granville to the High Commissioners, May 1, 1871, FO 5/1299. Northcote Diary, April 25, 1871, Iddesleigh Papers.
56. Fish Diary, April 25, May 8, 1871. Northcote Diary, May 8, 1871, Iddesleigh Papers.

of the Joint High Commission's work in Anglo-American relations, "we have laid the foundations of a very nice cottage, which may be turned into a castle at some future day."[57]

In the light of what was to come, the festivities seem hollow and unreal, and the sunlight scene shadowed. A few more months were to disclose the gravest defects in the treaty, and the brilliant ceremony of the signing was like a Hallowe'en charade in which the innocents were using real skulls painted to look like pumpkins.

57. Northcote to Gladstone, April 18, 1871, Iddesleigh Papers.

CHAPTER 9

Ratification

On the whole, the country received the treaty very well. "Public opinion here," Rockwood Hoar wrote from Boston, "I find as generally favourable as could be expected." Jacob D. Cox, the former secretary of the interior, thought it the best practicable settlement.[1] From his Cornell University lecture room high above Lake Cayuga, Goldwin Smith told Gladstone that the popular reaction in Ithaca, a typical American small town, was as good as possible.[2] "Henceforth," said William Lloyd Garrison, "may perpetual peace and amity exist between the two nations."[3] Surveying the national press, the Montgomery *Alabama State Journal* found the drift of public sentiment almost unanimous in favor of the treaty.[4]

During the January *pourparlers,* Schenck had told Rose that it would be very important to overcome latent prejudice against England by placing "judicious articles" in the press as soon as an understanding was reached,[5] and Fish was not behind in his propaganda efforts now. A State Department clerk was detailed to supply information to the newspapers, and Caleb Cushing was

1. E. R. Hoar to Bancroft Davis, June 1, 1871; J. D. Cox to Bancroft Davis, May 10, 1871, Bancroft Davis Papers.
2. Goldwin Smith to W. E. Gladstone, May 14, 1871, Gladstone Papers.
3. William Lloyd Garrison to Charles Sumner, May 10, 1871, Sumner Papers.
4. May 20, 1871.
5. Rose to Granville, Jan. 19, 1871, FO 5/1298.

set writing articles in favor of the treaty for the Washington press.[6] Some time before, Fish had fallen out with the editors of the *Evening Post,* and he had no great New York daily to take his part. But this problem was solved by his wife, who appealed to their son-in-law Sidney Webster to use his influence with the New York *World.* Webster rose to the occasion and composed several articles for the *World,* which were "much talked of."[7] In this way the nation's leading Democratic paper came out for the Republicans' treaty.

The oddest enemy of the treaty was not American at all; he was the Russian minister, Constantin de Catacazy. When he first arrived in Washington in 1869, Thornton had described him as "a restless, intriguing Greek, belonging to the jeune Russie party. . . . very ambitious and anxious to distinguish himself here, and wishes to strengthen the alliance with the United States, and in case of need to make it offensive."[8] "It is a pity," commented Fish, "that one can never trust Catacazy or believe a word he says." During the crisis when Russia abrogated demilitarization of the Black Sea, he had urged Fish to press for the payment of the Alabama Claims, alleging that during the Civil War, Napoleon III, with Palmerston's knowledge, had offered the abrogation of the 1856 peace treaty ending the Crimean War in return for moral support of Anglo-French intervention on the Confederate side. When the appointment of the Joint High Commission seemed to presage an Anglo-American entente, Catacazy began to spread this and other anti-British stories all over Washington. His favorite ploy was to declare that Britain had come prepared to yield all. "Oh, you will have everything you want," he told Fish; "Lord de Grey comes out with Canada in his pocket to ask you to accept it." By raising expectations to the highest peak, Catacazy hoped to create

6. R. S. Chew to Fish, July 4, 1871, Fish Papers, L.C. Fish Diary, May 5, 1871. D. C. Forney to Caleb Cushing, May 9, 12, 19, 1871; W. J. Murtagh to Cushing, May 20, 1871; William Hayes Ward to Cushing, May 4, 9, 1871; Cushing to Ward, May 12, 1871, Cushing Papers.

7. Julia Kean Fish to Webster, May 5, 11, 14, 1871, Fish Papers, L.C.

8. Thornton to Clarendon, Nov. 9, 1869, Clarendon Papers, Bodleian.

enough bitterness and disappointment when the terms came out to defeat ratification. When Sumner was deposed as chairman of the Senate Committee on Foreign Relations, "the Cat" spread reports that Grant and Fish had acted at Thornton's command. He also paid "extreme court" to the press, but had no luck until late May, when the *New York Herald* took up some of his rumors. When the British commissioners were leaving for home, Catacazy sent them a message: "Blessed are the peacemakers." "Query," wrote Northcote in his diary, "Blessed are the humbugs?"[9]

The fisheries settlement naturally evoked strenuous opposition from the coastal districts of Massachusetts. "The producing interests in the fisheries is being sacrificed by giving Canada free markets for their fish," the president of the Gloucester Board of Trade telegraphed the two Bay State senators. "Can it be stricken from the Treaty — Help or we perish."[10] Ben Butler, never slow to look for votes, issued a hastily written pamphlet denouncing the treaty.[11] He must have known the fight was hopeless: no one would repudiate a generally popular treaty for the sake of a few Massachusetts fishermen. All the same, he kept up his drum roll of attacks,[12] even after a "stop Butler" coalition of all the other candidates deprived him of the Massachusetts Republican gubernatorial nomination in September. The general never neglected his political base. But by the end of the year, even he was advising the fishermen to concentrate on lobbying Congress for a tonnage bounty upon their boats.[13] A correspondent of N. P. Banks, who was in charge of the legis-

9. Fish Diary, Nov. 17, 19, 1870, Feb. 20, May 25, 1871. Thornton to Granville, Feb. 21, 28, March 14, 1871, Granville Papers, FO 29/80. Northcote Diary, May 7, 9, 23, 1871, Iddesleigh Papers.

10. Telegram from Joseph O. Procter to Charles Sumner and Henry Wilson, May 12, 1871, Carl Schurz Papers.

11. Benjamin F. Butler, *The Treaty of Washington. An Examination of Its Provisions, Showing the Advantages Thereby Gained to England over America. Letter by Benj. F. Butler to Hon. A. Ames, U.S. Senator* (Lowell: Mardon & Rowell, 1871).

12. New York *Sun*, Oct. 17, 26, 1871.

13. S. B. Phinney to Butler, Dec. 9, 1871, Jan. 9, 1872, Butler Papers.

lation to carry the treaty's fisheries provisions into effect, wrote that the intelligent part of Cape Ann now realized that free fish would not hurt them.[14] It might have been a different story if Fish had not asked the British to admit American boats to Canadian waters that summer without waiting for Canada to ratify the treaty;[15] more seizures might have led to violence which Butler could have exploited. But Fish's adroit action effectively disarmed the only organized pressure group opposed to the treaty.

Even before the High Commission assembled, Fish sent some information about the Alabama Claims to Oliver P. Morton, the leading administration senator, and at critical moments during the negotiations he consulted men like Simon Cameron and Zack Chandler whom he counted upon to secure ratification.[16] At the same time, the British Joint Highs were indulging in a different kind of persuasion. Doubtless recollecting that Lord Elgin had floated the 1854 Reciprocity Treaty through the U.S. Senate on a sea of champagne and remembering Seward's "Alaska dinners," the British stopped at nothing in their quest for popularity; even Northcote did not blench when, on a trip down the Potomac to Mount Vernon, "old Chandler" bored him by insisting on sitting below and playing euchre with a filthy old pack of cards, when he would rather have been on deck enjoying the view.[17] "We send the cook up to Washington to-night with the Legation Messenger to get his battery (probably such artillery may be a useful support) in good order," reported Tenterden as soon as he arrived in New York.[18] A useful point

14. William Stowe to N. P. Banks, Dec. 18, 1871, Banks Papers, I.S.H.L.

15. Fish to Thornton, May 10, 1871, Fish Papers, L.C.

16. Fish to Morton, Feb. 9, 1871, Fish Papers, L.C. Fish Diary, April 5, 8, 13, 26, 1871.

17. Northcote Diary, March 28, April 1, May 8, 1871, Iddesleigh Papers.

18. Tenterden to Granville, Feb. 21–22, 1871, Granville Papers, FO 29/106. Evidence of the wining and dining: Thornton to Granville, March 7, 1871, Granville Papers, FO 29/80. Northcote Diary, March

of contact was that both De Grey and Tenterden were Free-masons — De Grey was Grand Master of England — and the American lodges gave them a banquet which thirty congressmen and senators attended.[19]

How much Fish relied upon the flattering attentions of the British commissioners to swing votes was seen when Gladstone, nervous lest the Senate should realize that they were still on the spot and open new negotiations in its own right by passing amendments to the treaty, cabled them to come home as soon as they had signed. "Grand consternation" ensued at 1311 K Street, the British headquarters. Grant and Fish were definite that the Joint Highs should pay the Senate the compliment of awaiting its discussion of the treaty and hoped they might be able to influence individual senators, especially among the Democrats and dissidents like Sumner. Gladstone relented and the commissioners stayed, though they did heed his advice enough to split up and make it plain that the High Commission had ceased to exist as a negotiating body. The big guns, De Grey, Northcote, Thornton, and MacDonald, stayed in Washington, while Tenterden and Bernard went north to Boston and New York to lobby jurists like Richard H. Dana, Bemis, and Woolsey and to try and secure support from Empire State Democrats.[20]

4, 8, 14, 20, 22, 24, 25, 28, 29, April 15, 22, May 10, 12, 1871, Iddesleigh Papers. G. F. Edmunds to De Grey, April 3, 1871; T. F. Bayard to De Grey, April 21, 1871; De Grey to Schurz, March 3, 1871; De Grey to Blaine, March 13, 1871, Ripon Papers. Grey to Zachariah Chandler, n.d., 1871; Bancroft Davis to Chandler, March 4, 1871, Chandler Papers. Mrs. John A. Logan, *Reminiscences of a Soldier's Wife: An Autobiography* (New York: Scribner's, 1913, p. 261.

19. Tenterden to Meade, with enclosure, April 11, 1871, Granville Papers, FO 29/106. John T. Heard to De Grey, Feb. 27, 1871, Ripon Papers.

20. Gladstone to Granville, May 2, 1871, Gladstone Papers. Northcote Diary, May 2, 3, 1871; Northcote to Disraeli, May 9, 1871, Iddesleigh Papers. Telegrams from Granville to the High Commissioners, May 2, 3, 1871, FO 5/1299. Tenterden to Granville, May 2, 8, 1871, Granville Papers, FO 29/106. Memorandum by Lord Tenterden, May 8, 1871, sent to Bancroft Davis, May 11, 1871, Ripon Papers.

The British cultivated no one more assiduously than Sumner.[21] By the time the High Commission opened, Fish had managed to work himself into an almost pathological state of fear and dread about what the senator might do. He saw Sumner's hand everywhere, collected every piece of gossip about his intentions, and effusively thanked such honest plain dealers as Ben Butler for defending him to the senator.[22] Fish thought it certain that Sumner would oppose any treaty he might make; sitting with the British commissioners one afternoon when Sumner was announced, he sprang up, faded into the background, and slipped out behind De Grey's back,[23] lest Sumner should see him, think that the two delegations were on cordial terms, and become immune to the British arguments in favor of the treaty.

Convinced of the senator's enmity, Fish committed a staggering blunder that, but for Sumner's restraint and intellectual integrity, would have ended all hope for the treaty's ratification. In March, when the new Congress assembled, the Republican caucus, controlled by administration senators, stripped Sumner of his chairmanship of the Committee on Foreign Relations. This was not merely Grant's doing; Fish was just as implacable and rejected all talk of olive branches or a compromise plan proposed by Senator Howe that would have added two members to the Committee and assured the administration of control, whatever the chairman might do.[24] Thornton was understandably uneasy about the deposition, fearing a reaction in favor of Sumner, who, though not much liked, was esteemed and re-

21. Samuel Hooper to Sumner, May 5, 1871, Sumner Papers. Also, Northcote Diary, March 5, 20, April 17, 18, 24, 25, May 6, 8, 13, 21, 1871; Northcote to Disraeli, May 9, 1871, Iddesleigh Papers. Charles Sumner to Ripon, April 26, 1871, Ripon Papers. Charles Sumner to Caleb Cushing, n.d., 1871, Cushing Papers.

22. Thornton to Granville, March 14, 1871, Granville Papers, FO 29/80. Fish Diary, April 9, 18, 19, 21, May 14, 1871.

23. Northcote to Granville, March 26, 1871; Northcote Diary, March 5, 1871, Iddesleigh Papers.

24. Fish Diary, March 6, 8, 1871.

spected for his ability, long service, and complete honesty —
something of which his successor, the Pennsylvania boss Simon
Cameron, was never accused.[25]

And, indeed, if Sumner had shown himself as vindictive as
Fish and Grant, the British commissioners might as well have
packed their bags immediately. The last occasion when a prominent senator was deposed from his committee chairmanship had
been Stephen Douglas' removal by Buchanan. Sumner could
not have defeated the treaty merely by action on Capitol Hill;
he had no personal following of any size, and before the Joint
High Commission was agreed upon, Fish had secured pledges
from leading Democrats that they would treat the question on
its merits.[26] But if Sumner had gone to the country and proclaimed an anti-British crusade, paying special attention to the
Irish vote, he might very well have given quite a few Republican
senators pause and the Democrats reason to think again. There
is some evidence that not all the Republicans voted according
to their convictions on ratification, and it only took twenty-four
senators to defeat a treaty.[27]

Sumner unquestionably regarded Fish as a turncoat and a
traitor to his principles. In April he delivered a philippic against
the Santo Domingo scheme and prepared a speech denouncing
Fish for his part in the removal of Motley, which, for some
reason, he never delivered.[28] But he approached the treaty with
an open mind and even the British Joint Highs, unfamiliar with
the situation[29] and relying mostly on Fish for information, could

25. Thornton to Granville, March 14, 1871, Granville Papers, FO
29/80.
26. Northcote to Granville, March 26, 1871, Iddlesleigh Papers.
27. See below, p. 198. George Smalley to *The Times*, Feb. 14, 1872,
published Feb. 15, 1872. Schurz to C. F. Adams, Jr., Feb. 3, 1902,
printed in Frederic Bancroft, ed., *Speeches, Correspondence and Political
Papers of Carl Schurz* (New York: Putnam, 1913), VI, 281-283.
28. Probably because his attention was taken up by the treaty. See also
Fish Diary, April 18, 19, 1871.
29. Except for Thornton, and even he had not been given the full

see that the secretary of state's attitude was unjustified.[30]

At first Sumner obviously feared that the administration intended to railroad the treaty through the Senate by fair means or foul, and he threatened opposition if it was not given full and careful attention. He was agreeably surprised to hear from Senator Patterson that the Committee on Foreign Relations planned to keep it at least seven days.[31] The day after the signing Sumner telegraphed George Bemis for advice and asked Caleb Cushing round to his house for consultations.[32] He had already promised De Grey that he would not attack any part of the treaty without giving him a chance to defend and explain it, but the next time he and Thornton met it became clear there would be no need for that. The more he read the treaty, said Sumner, the better he liked it.[33]

Northcote was delighted, not realizing that Sumner believed the consequential claims were included in the arbitration.[34] Just how many senators' votes were gained for the treaty by this belief is problematic. Carl Schurz, Sumner's closest friend on Capitol Hill, must certainly have thought they were comprehended in the treaty. James W. Patterson, another senator on good terms with him, probably thought so, and judging by his reply to Fish's inquiries in January,[35] Lyman Trumbull must be counted in this group too. The extent of this opinion in the country is equally uncertain. The New York *Evening Post* thought that Sumner's speech could be presented to the arbitrators in its entirety as the measure of the American demands. As it pointed out, the treaty set no restriction whatever upon the evidence or argu-

---

inside story before the Joint High Commission was set up.

30. Northcote Diary, April 18, 1871, Iddesleigh Papers. Thornton to Granville, Feb. 28, March 14, 1871, Granville Papers, FO 29/80.

31. Northcote Diary, May 8, 1871, Iddesleigh Papers.

32. George Bemis to Sumner, May 9, 1871; Caleb Cushing to Sumner, May 9, 1871, Sumner Papers.

33. Northcote Diary, May 6, 13, 1871, Iddesleigh Papers.

34. George Smalley to *The Times,* Feb. 14, 1872, published Feb. 15, 1872.

35. See above, p. 155.

ments that either side could present at Geneva.[36] The Montgomery *Alabama State Journal* estimated the private claims
at $13,662,560.35, and assured its readers that Fish meant to
claim for "the outlay caused by the increased premium and
enhanced freights resulting from the special risk growing out
of the operations of the rebel cruisers fitted out in English ports."[37]
But the *New York Herald* held that only compensation for the
actual damages suffered by American commerce could be expected; Sumner's arguments about the Neutrality Proclamation
and complaints about Lord Russell's policy were abandoned.[38]
And the *Sacramento Daily Union* declared that "the moral
damages for the Alabama spoliations, so forcibly urged by Sumner in his speech, have been waived by the American Commissioners."[39] The overwhelming majority of the commentators
upon the treaty simply did not think of the consequential claims.
Even in 1869 many people had been confused about what Sumner
had actually asked for,[40] and time had not made the question any
plainer.

Those who opposed the treaty, men like Ben Butler, George
B. Upton, or Samuel Hooper, must have believed that the consequential claims were included in it. They would never have
wasted their breath complaining that Britain might press claims
for Confederate bonds or alleging that the American coasting
trade would be destroyed by cheaply built Canadian ships,[41]
when so obvious and important a matter lay neglected. The one
person who seems to have had some inkling that the consequential claims might not be comprised in the reference was George
Bemis. Dispatching a white-hot protest to Sumner, Bemis remarked that he felt inclined to come to Washington and lobby

36. May 11, 1869.
37. May 30, 1871.
38. May 10, 12, 1871.
39. May 10, 1871.
40. See above, pp. 76-77.
41. George B. Upton to Sumner, May 12, 15, 1871; Samuel Hooper
to Sumner, May 9, 26, 1871, Sumner Papers. Upton to Butler, Dec.
12, 1871, Butler Papers.

against the treaty. "Perhaps if I could reach or appear before a conference of Senators," he wrote, "it might be worthwhile.[42] But Sumner did not encourage him nor take any notice of his views, probably because Bemis admitted that he was only going upon telegrams of the terms published in the *Boston Daily Advertiser,* not the full text of the treaty. If Bemis had come to Washington and stuck to his interpretation of the terms, the whole negotiation might have blown sky high.

Instead Sumner, fully satisfied with the treaty, turned to placing his ideal principles of international law in it as amendments. On Sunday, May 14, he went to see Schurz, who was in bed with a bad cold and a sore throat. Schurz was still a member of the Committee on Foreign Relations, and together they discussed what could be done.[43] Schurz agreed to try to present some amendments to the committee the next day.

As usual, the administration did almost everything possible to drive honest disagreement into factional opposition. Fish decided that any amendments proposed by Sumner or Schurz would be designed to kill the treaty and sent word to Simon Cameron and his administration stalwarts on the committee, Hannibal Hamlin, Morton, and Harlan, that no changes could be allowed. To ram home his point, he dispatched Bancroft Davis to read the protocols of the High Commission to the committee. As soon as Davis had finished, Schurz got ready to move his amendments; Hamlin cut him off with a motion to lay every one on the table. Schurz angrily demanded to know the reason why. The evidence they had just heard, said Hamlin, showed that any amendment would be fatal to the treaty, and he added his personal opinion that any amendment likely to be proposed would be picayune. The question was put: Patterson, who suffered from a constitutional inability to make up his mind and was generally at the mercy of the last piece of advice, joined with the administration forces to vote down Schurz and

42. Bemis to Sumner, May 17, 1871, Sumner Papers.
43. Schurz to Sumner [May 14], 1871, Schurz Papers.

Eugene Casserly. Disgusted, Schurz slammed down his papers and stalked out.[44]

There was still a chance to add amendments, however, when the whole Senate considered the treaty in executive session, and Sumner presented three. They were all concerned with the rules of neutrality. The first one replaced the abandoned Article Four; the second (read with the last part of the first) reinstated the pursuit clause which the British had knocked out of Fish's draft articles on March 13.[45] The third, and most important, amendment was Marcy's old proposal, with some new refinements. Private property was to be inviolable at sea, and blockades were abolished except against vessels carrying contraband of war and against all national vessels, whether armed or unarmed.

Although Fish had thought of including this principle in a settlement himself, he persisted in thinking it and the other amendments part of Sumner's plot to kill the treaty. Orders went out for their defeat, and they died the death. Thornton called the presentation of the amendments "wicked of Sumner . . . [it] looks as if he still meant to give trouble."[46] In fact, the senator had promised De Grey that he would not press the amendments to a division.[47] Some of his closest friends were in

44. C. E. Hamlin, *Life and Times of Hannibal Hamlin* (Cambridge, Mass.: Privately published, 1899) pp. 530-532. Hamlin's account is based upon evidence given him by Samuel F. Barr, the clerk of the committee.

45. A neutral government was bound, ran the amendments: (4) "To exclude from its ports in time of war any armed vessel engaged in hostilities which does not hold a commission delivered to it at some port of military or naval equipment in the actual occupation of the commissioning government; and no such armed vessel is entitled to any protection on the high seas from seizure by the nation in violation of whose neutrality it was fitted out, armed or equipped," and (5) "To treat as a pirate any armed vessel which plunders and burns prizes at sea, without taking them into a home port for adjudication." *Journal of the Executive Proceedings of the Senate of the United States of America* (Washington: Government Printing Office, 1901), XXIII, 106-107 (hereafter, *Executive Journal*).

46. Thornton to De Grey, May 23, 1871, Ripon Papers.

47. Sumner to De Grey, May 23, 1871, Ripon Papers.

favor of the treaty; the closest of all, Edward L. Pierce, told him that the people supported it and urged him to vote for it.[48]

Looking back, Sumner was inclined to be bitter about the loss of the amendments. "We have lost what we should not," he told George Bemis, and blamed him for not writing more and making the subject well known.[49] International law, he wrote to George Smalley, had been sold short. For the sake of the amendments, which he regarded as safeguards to civilization, he would have been willing to give up much of the American case. "Such a Treaty I could not have opposed, even if it gave us nothing."[50] But, at the time, he yielded to the arguments of his friends. Could he, who had always advocated peaceful arbitration of international disputes, vote against the first great treaty to incorporate the principle?[51] So, when the British Joint Highs went to see Bancroft Davis on May 19, they heard that Sumner had been making an enormous speech "over four hours, of which the first three and a half were spent in giving a history of the World and showing how much more he knew than anybody else, and the last half hour in discussing the three rules in the Treaty, which he approved and then sat down without moving any amendment."[52]

Meanwhile, Fish had other worries. Throughout the negotiations, he had been desperately anxious to sign a treaty in time to send it to the Senate before the end of the session. If it was not ratified then, it would have to wait all the summer and autumn, while "outside intriguers and politicians could bring evil influence to bear" upon the senators.[53] Late in April, Fish

48. Francis W. Bird to Sumner, May 11, 1871 (two); John M. Forbes to Sumner, Feb. 10, 1871; Pierce to Sumner, May 8, 1871, Sumner Papers.

49. Sumner to Bemis, June 5, 1871, Bemis Papers.

50. Sumner to Smalley, June 18, 1871, quoted in Smalley to *The Times*, Feb. 14, 1872, published Feb. 15, 1872.

51. E. P. Whipple, *Recollections of Eminent Men, with Other Papers* (Boston: Ticknor, 1887), pp. 208-209.

52. Northcote Diary, May 19, 1871, Iddesleigh Papers.

53. Thornton to Granville, Feb. 28, 1871. Granville Papers, FO 29/80.

had two more factors to consider: the effect upon senators' tempers of being kept waiting for the treaty, and the fact that the Ku Klux Klan hearings were scheduled to start in the last week of May. Once they began, all hope of a bipartisan foreign policy would vanish.[54] Both Fish and Grant were anxious to get a vote on the treaty as soon as possible.[55]

Meanwhile, Fish continued to woo senators. The day after the signing, Hamlin, Patterson, and Frelinghuysen spent several hours at the State Department, examining the Treaty and listening to portions of Fish's diary being read. "Poor Patterson," noted Fish later, "belongs to somebody. Yesterday, he was in favour of the Treaty. He passed some time last evening with Sumner; today, he didn't know where he is. As to whom he belongs, he higgles, he wants to support it [the Treaty] but does not know whether he will be allowed to."[56] The secretary's persuasions were sweetened by a little patronage.[57]

As it happened, Fish had most trouble with a reliable party regular, Timothy O. Howe of Wisconsin. The country, he told Fish, would not be satisfied with arbitration of the San Juan boundary, though, personally, he had no objections to it. His real worries were two. First, regarding the fisheries, he feared that when Congress had to appropriate money to pay the Canadians their award, there would be disagreement which might cripple the Republican party in the presidential elections. Fish pointed out that the commission to make the award would not meet until both the United States and Canada incorporated the fishery clauses of the treaty into legislation. Congress could pass nothing until next winter, and the Dominion Parliament was not due to meet until February 1872. The commission would take months to set up, and the award would almost certainly

54. Tenterden to Granville, April 21, 1871, Granville Papers, FO 29/106.

55. Fish Diary, May 10, 1871.

56. *Ibid.*, May 8, 9, 1871. Fish to Carl Schurz, May 8, 1871, Schurz Papers.

57. Fish to Grant, May 22, 1871, Fish Papers, L.C.

be made after the American elections. Reassured, Howe brought up his second concern, which he said embarrassed him most and would trouble the public least. He had some bizarre ideas on neutrality; he wanted to abolish all neutrality laws and allow neutral states to trade freely in whatever they liked, even arms or ships. Fish expounded international law for a couple of hours and left the impression that Howe's vote was safe.[58]

Another man with a rather different problem was Adelbert Ames. A distinguished Civil War officer, Ames became involved in Southern politics afterwards, and in 1871 was carpetbag senator from Mississippi. He was married to none other than Ben Butler's daughter, and, though Blanche Butler Ames was, unlike her father, a noted beauty, she inherited her parent's spirit. "Is it not a pity the Treaty has proved so unsatisfactory?" she demanded. "No doubt that old English High Comm. feel they have fixed things nicely. This to me is the aggravating point. Everyone must feel that we have been a little out-witted. No amount of money can salve the wound given our pride. We are rich enough. It is not possible we are to be satisfied with a few English sops. We might have taken Canada with some degree of good will, although that would not have amounted to much, as we shall have it ere long, anyway. You hear enough of this twaddle, Dearie, without having any from me, so we will change the subject."

During the early days of the debate Ames sought out other Republicans and reported their reactions to Butler. Henry Wilson and Hannibal Hamlin were strongly for the treaty; Hamlin said it was much better than anything he had expected. George F. Edmunds, though, remarked that it was not the treaty he would have made. Roscoe Conkling was not happy with the neutrality rules. As Ames and Conkling were talking on a street corner Chandler came along. Questioned, he said, "We will ratify it as it is." Ames raised the fisheries question. "Well,"

58. Fish Diary, May 7, 1871; Howe to Fish, May 3, 1871, Fish Papers, L.C.

replied Conkling, "it is but for ten years, anyhow." Chandler thought that the fishermen would be in the same position as they had been under the Reciprocity Treaty.

As a carpetbagger, Ames did not want to break party ranks, and the day before the vote was taken on the treaty, he wrote to his wife telling her that his friend, Lot M. Morrill of Maine, had pointed out a way to save the fisheries. The relevant articles of the treaty would not go into effect until Congress and the parliaments of Britain, Canada, and Prince Edward Island passed the necessary legislation. "So you see," he concluded, "Congress has this subject under its own control, and need not act on these articles; in the meantime, the other parts of the treaty will go into effect." (In fact, Congress was bound to pass the required legislation.) Next day Ames cast his vote for the treaty.[59]

In New York, Tenterden and Bernard found the merchants universally favorable to the treaty. Several told them they had written or would write to senators about it; A. T. Stewart, the dry goods king, said he had been in touch with both Reuben E. Fenton and Patterson.[60] News came from England that Lord Russell intended to attack the treaty; as Northcote noted, this made all the Americans think better of the settlement, but it also meant that speedy ratification was more desirable than ever.[61]

Meanwhile, the Senate had dissolved into a mass of quarrels, accusations, and recriminations over the illegal publication of the treaty in the *New York Tribune*. Senators saw chances of gratifying personal vendettas and paying off old scores by fasten-

59. Mrs. Ames's reaction is not recorded. Blanche Butler Ames to Adelbert Ames, May 15, 1871; Adelbert Ames to B. B. Ames, May 23, 1871, printed in B. A. Ames, ed., *Chronicles from the Nineteenth Century: Family Letters of Blanche Butler and Adelbert Ames, Married July 21, 1870* (n.p.: Privately published, 1957), I, 278, 284-285. Ames to Butler, May 13, 14, 15, 1871, Butler Papers.

60. Tenterden to De Grey, May 14, 1871, Ripon Papers.

61. Northcote Diary, May 19, 1871, Iddesleigh Papers. De Grey to Fish, May 15, 1871, Fish Papers, L.C.

ing guilt on a colleague: Sumner, Fenton, and Morton were variously suspected and denounced, and tempers grew higher hour by hour. Grant summoned Cameron and Conkling on the afternoon of the 16th and told them he wanted ratification at once, with no amendments; next day he sent for Matt Carpenter, a leader in the publication witch hunt, and ordered him to suspend the investigation.[62] Tenterden advised De Grey to announce that the British commissioners would leave for home on the 24th, ratification or no ratification, in the hope of hurrying things up.[63]

No sooner was the publication inquiry smothered than Lyman Trumbull brought up an objection to the second neutrality rule. Could it not be construed, he asked, so as to prohibit a neutral selling arms in the ordinary course of commerce? Thornton told Fish that the same question had been raised in Parliament by Sir Roundell Palmer and suggested that they should sign an agreement explaining the rule and denying Trumbull's interpretation. Fish, however, said he preferred that the Senate should adopt a declaratory resolution setting out their construction of the rule, together with another motion asking the president to obtain the concurrence of the British government. Calling at Trumbull's house, Fish showed him a draft resolution explaining that the rule did not apply to "military supplies or arms purchased, sold and shipped in the ordinary course of regular commercial transactions." The Illinois senator objected to the words "military supplies." He thought coal might be refused to a belligerent on such terms and wanted it made quite clear that the resolution referred only to supplies that could be used for nothing but war.

That evening Fish dined at the White House, with Rockwood Hoar, Vice-President Colfax, Boutwell, Matt Carpenter, and Belknap. Carpenter raised the same objection to the second rule that Trumbull had originally put forward and warmly

62. Thornton to Granville, May 30, 1871, Granville Papers, FO 29/80. Fish Diary, May 16, 1871.
63. Tenterden to De Grey, May 17, 1871, Ripon Papers.

approved the idea of a declaratory resolution. But Hoar had seen Sumner about the matter and agreed to an amendment of the rule.[64]

Fish, as usual, declared he would have no amendments, but Hoar said he had committed himself to this course. Worried, Fish sped round to the British legation, with Hoar in tow, and arrived just in time to catch the end of an argument between De Grey and Thornton, on the one side, and Northcote, on the other. Like Hoar, Northcote had seen Sumner and had agreed to an amendment. Thornton again proposed a joint declaration, which Fish again refused. Taking the minister's sketch for a declaration, he sat down and drafted a resolution on the spot.[65]

Unfortunately, the Senate refused to pass the resolution, and Fish did not want to press them too hard for fear of giving the impression that the treaty required amendment in any way. Once one was passed, an avalanche might begin. Early in June, London ordered Thornton to carry out an exchange of declaratory notes. Fish refused. He felt that he had no right to construe a treaty and bind his government. The Treaty of Washington, by then, was the supreme law of the land, and the courts should interpret it.[66] There the matter was dropped.

64. It would then read: "Secondly, not to permit or suffer either belligerent to make use of its ports or waters as the base of naval operations against the other, or for the purpose of the renewal or augmentation of the *warlike force of any ship or the recruitment of men by/for any ship.*" Fish Diary, May 21, 1871.

65. "Resolved, that the understanding of the Senate and of the Government of the United States is that the acts mentioned in the second Rule contained in Article VI of the Treaty signed on the 8th instant are prohibited only when done for the service of a vessel carrying on war or intending to cruise or carry on war against either of the Belligerents, and that the provisions of that rule do not extend to any exportation from the neutral country of arms or other military supplies in the ordinary course of commerce." Fish Diary, May 21, 1871.

66. Fish Diary, May 21, 22, 1871. Northcote Diary, May 21, 1871, Iddesleigh Papers. Thornton to Granville, May 23, 30, 1871, Granville Papers, FO 29/80. Thornton to Granville, June 4–5, 1871, FO 5/1297. *Executive Journal,* pp. 109-114.

On May 24, the Senate again took up the treaty. Henry B. Anthony, asked to dinner at the Fish home that night, scribbled a hasty note to say that he could not come; a vote was imminent.[67] Sumner's amendments were smothered without a division, and a couple of attempts to change the second rule to meet Trumbull's objections were defeated.[68] A Democratic motion to strike out the three new rules of neutrality altogether was lost by 45 votes to 18; all the Democrats and four Republicans, Howe, Matt Carpenter, William Sprague, and J. Rodman West, voted for it. Casserly, the treaty's deadliest enemy, then tried to add a provision allowing either country to terminate its agreement to observe the rules in future on twelve months' notice. Eleven senators voted for this amendment; ten Democrats, including Thomas Bayard of Delaware and William Hamilton of Maryland, and one Republican, Thomas Tipton of Nebraska. Forty-six voted against it. Finally Cameron rose and moved that the Senate advise and consent to the Treaty of Washington. It passed, 50 to 12,[69] "a very good majority," noted Thornton.[70]

Sumner voted for the treaty, and so did Schurz, Patterson, and Trumbull. Only two Republicans voted against ratification, J. Rodman West, a Louisiana carpetbagger, and William Sprague of Rhode Island. West's vote was probably motivated by the complex factional politics of his home state, where the Republican party had split wide open; Grant's brother-in-law was collector of the Port of New Orleans and a leader of the spoils faction. Sprague, a millionaire textile manufacturer, had earned himself a well-deserved reputation as the Walter Mitty of American public life by 1871, and his vote was very likely just another fantastic posture.[71]

67. Anthony to Mrs. Fish, May 24, 1871, Fish Papers, L.C.
68. One, Sumner's amendment, nearly passed. The vote was 32 to 25.
69. *Executive Journal,* pp. 105-109.
70. Thornton to De Grey, May 30, 1871, Ripon Papers.
71. See Thomas Graham Belden and Marva Robins Belden, *So Fell the Angels* (Boston: Little, Brown, 1956). Henry Howard to De Grey, May 30, 1871, Ripon Papers.

It is doubtful, to say the least, if Anglophobes like William Stewart and Nye of Nevada or Tipton of Nebraska voted their convictions on the treaty; party regularity and the patronage were probably the most eloquent arguments to them in its favor. When Cornelius Cole of California came to write his memoirs, he abused the treaty up hill and down; if he had had his way, he wrote, America would have demanded a hundred million dollars cash or gone to war. Yet Cole voted for the treaty.[72]

Two Democrats, Bayard of Delaware and Hamilton of Maryland, voted for the treaty; ten voted against it.[73] Many prominent Democrats had come out in favor of it. Reverdy Johnson published an open letter calling for ratification.[74] "I am sure our people with all their past resentment against England for her conduct towards us during the war, prefer an honourable settlement of the Alabama Claims to the risk of a war with England," wrote August Belmont, the Democratic national chairman. "The Radicals have tried to fasten upon us the charge of factious opposition and revolutionary tendencies and we must not allow them to have substantial excuses for this calumny which hurt us both in 1864 and '68. In my opinion, not only the best interests of the country but the welfare of the Democratic party call for its support by the Senators on our side of the House."[75] If the provisions of the settlement were as published, the semiretired but still influential Montgomery Blair told Manton Marble, editor of the New York *World,* he would accept them. But he would not vote against the treaty, even if it were

72. *Memoirs of Cornelius Cole, Ex-Senator of the United States from California* (New York: McLoughlin Brothers, 1908), pp. 343, 345-347.

73. Casserly, Henry Cooper, Garret Davis of Kentucky, Henry Gassaway Davis of West Virginia, James Kelly, Willard Saulsbury, John Stevenson, Stockton, Thurman, and George Vickers. Frank Blair of Missouri, who would have voted against the treaty, paired off with two Republicans in favor, Howe and Orris Ferry of Connecticut.

74. Frederick *Maryland Union,* May 25, 1871. *Wilmington Daily Commercial,* May 24, 1871.

75. August Belmont to Frank P. Blair, Jr., May 11, 1871, Blair Family Papers.

far less favorable. It was not part of Democratic policy to humiliate England or force a war with her. Peace was the interest of the Democracy: peace, to encourage the reviving interest of the South, the spread of free trade ideas, and to help the reform movement in England.[76]

A number of the Democratic senators declared their unqualified support of the treaty in the days just after the signing, and two or three of those who subsequently voted against it said they would vote in favor. Though some opposed it, Thornton wrote home, they would all take care that it was not defeated. To try and hold the Democratic leaders to the promise they had given him in January of an impartial consideration of the settlement, not a partisan attack, Fish brought John Pruyn down from Albany. But by the day before the vote was taken, it was certain that the treaty would be ratified, and caucusing, the Democrats decided that their best policy as a party was to vote against it; if nothing else, they would please the Irish vote. Bayard and Hamilton, though, held out against all persuasion and cast their votes in favor.[77]

A few weeks later Parliament, too, approved the treaty, and ratifications were exchanged on June 17, the anniversary of the battle of Bunker Hill.[78]

76. Montgomery Blair to Manton Marble, May 11, 1871, Blair Family Papers.
77. Northcote to Granville, March 26, 1871; Northcote Diary, May 14, 1871, Iddesleigh Papers. Thornton to Granville, May 23, 30, 1871, Granville Papers, FO 29/80. Thornton to De Grey, May 30, 1871, Ripon Papers. Thornton to Granville, May 29, 1871, FO 5/1297.
78. Fish to Schenck, June 17, 1871, Fish Papers, L.C.

CHAPTER 10

The Indirect Claims

From June till December 1871 the work of preparation for
the arbitration at Geneva went on busily. Bancroft Davis was
appointed agent, Caleb Cushing, William M. Evarts, and Morri-
son R. Waite counsel, and Charles Francis Adams was named
the American arbitrator. Late in November they set out for
Geneva and the world's first great tribunal of arbitration. En
route they met the British, led by Chief Justice Sir Alexander
Cockburn, genial and agreeable then, though he was to show a
different temper before things were all over. On December 15
the tribunal opened. Besides Adams and Cockburn, the arbitrators were Jacob Staempfli, a lumbering, beetle-browed Swiss;
Baron D'Itajuba, Brazilian minister in Paris, who had been
thirty years in Europe, had married a German, and had practically ceased to be a Brazilian; and Count de Sclopis, a tall,
aristocratic, and voluble Italian.[1] The two sides presented their
cases, and the tribunal adjourned to consider them.

Tenterden, the British agent, was given a copy of the Ameri-
can case on the 15th; Schenck, who had taken up his post in
London during the summer, left a dozen copies at the Foreign
Office on December 20 and some more a couple of days later.
No one seems to have found time to read the case. Perhaps it was
just as well for their enjoyment of the Christmas holiday, for the

1. Adams Diary, Dec. 10, 13, 15, 16, 1871. Tenterden to De Grey,
Dec. 17, 1871, Ripon Papers. Bancroft Davis to Fish, Dec. 17, 1871, Fish
Papers, L.C.

indirect claims, the huge demands originated by Sumner which the British had thought abandoned, were included in the American case.

The wording of the treaty itself was so vague that it would justify either interpretation: the American, broad reading, including the claims, or the narrow British construction, excluding them. Fish always swore that both sides had acted in good faith; the British thought the indirect claims were abandoned, the Americans believed they were included in the arbitration. He found the root of the trouble in the first meeting of the High Commission to discuss the Alabama Claims, held on March 8, 1871. Opening the discussion, Fish had delivered a long speech about the grievances of the American nation and then moved on to the matter of compensation. The claims for ships destroyed, he said, came to about $14 million, though many other claims would probably be presented once a settlement was arranged, and this would probably raise the amount. Then, according to the protocol of the meeting, he said "that in the hope of an amicable settlement no estimate was made of the indirect losses, without prejudice, however, to the right to indemnification on their account in the event of no such settlement being made."[2] The Americans asked for an admission of liability and payment of a gross sum as compensation, the amount to be settled at once. The British refused and demanded arbitration of their liability, which the treaty finally provided. The British thought this was the "amicable settlement" Fish had mentioned, but it was not; by "amicable settlement" the secretary of state had meant admission of liability and payment of a gross sum. When the British refused this, he considered himself at liberty to present the indirect claims for indemnification, just as he had warned them he would.[3]

2. Protocols, FO 5/1301.
3. Remarks upon the Memorandum accompanying Lord Granville's note to General Schenck of March 20, 1872, n.d. [April 19, 1872 ?], Fish Papers, L.C.

So Fish's story ran; but it is not quite as easy as that. The protocols of the Joint High Commission were not made after each meeting, but at the end of the negotiations. At the very beginning Fish and Davis had openly admitted to the British Joint Highs that if the proceedings were formally recorded day by day, "they would be obliged to put in statements and make 'bunkum' speeches to please the American public, as the protocols must be laid before the Senate"; the British therefore agreed to wait and see if the deliberations could come to a successful end before any official minutes were made, but they sent home reports of their doings after each session, and their account of what Fish said on March 8 is slightly, but vitally, different: "the claims on account of the losses of private citizens alone amounted to $14,000,000, to these must be added the cost incurred in the pursuit of the cruisers and it was believed by the United States Government that they had also a good and equitable claim for indirect or constructive losses: these latter, however, they did not prefer and their not doing so must, they considered, be regarded as a great concession. The readiest and best way to meet these claims would be for Great Britain to pay a gross sum."[4]

Closer consideration of the negotiations raises other disturbing questions about the secretary of state's actions. Why did Fish never mention the indirect claims after March 8? In his interview with Thornton on November 20, 1870, he had demanded a measure of compensation for the wrong done the United States as a nation. Talking to Sir John Rose on January 12, 1871, though, he had taken a different tack and "enlarged again" upon the great concessions made by America in throwing aside Sumner's extravagant ideas about England's responsibility for prolonging the Civil War by the premature recognition of Confederate belligerency. This, he emphasized, was a large and

4. High Commissioners to Granville, Secret, March 8, 1871, FO 5/1300. Tenterden to Granville, March 24, 1871, Granville Papers, FO 29/106.

perilous step, and the administration still had to persuade the people and many influential members of Congress that it was justified.[5]

One point emerges clearly from these interviews. Before the commission met, Fish was aware of the importance of the indirect claims and concerned to express his opinion about them. Why, then, was he so silent about them in the commission? They did not go unnoticed: the British categorically refused to agree to include those claims in the arbitration. On April 6 the commission considered the mechanics of the arbitration tribunal, and the Americans proposed that the arbitrators should be empowered to award a gross sum, once British liability had been established. De Grey responded that he would first want to know the terms of the reference: what yardstick would be provided with which to measure the amount of compensation? The reference would be difficult to define, said the American commissioners. They thought the arbitrators should be given the whole of the diplomatic correspondence and whatever documents, evidence, or verbal argument either government wanted to present. To this they should apply the three rules agreed upon in the conference and other relevant principles of international law. De Grey, alarmed, said this would be far too vague. "It might permit the introduction of such extravagant claims as had sometimes been put forward as for instance for expenses arising from the prolongation of the war." He wanted a definite statement of the American view in writing.[6]

In the meantime, the Americans presented a draft of the Alabama Claims articles. It began: "The High Contracting Parties agree that all the differences between the governments which arose during the recent rebellion in the United States, growing out of the acts committed by the several cruisers which have given rise to the claims generally known as the Alabama Claims, and all such claims shall be referred to five commis-

5. Rose to Granville, Jan. 12, 1871, FO 5/1298.
6. High Commissioners to Granville, Secret, April 6, 1871, FO 5/1302.

sioners." The British attacked at once: the word "differences," they contended, read with "all such claims," implied that all the differences treated in the official correspondence between the two governments were to go before the tribunal. Later on it was openly revealed that they were all to form part of the American case. Such a reference was much, much too wide. A tremendous range of subjects had been discussed in that correspondence and questions raised which included claims and demands of huge proportions. The British had already clearly opposed a reference like this; now, here it was, face to face with them. Nothing in their instructions would allow them to accept such wording. Fish argued that his letter of January 30 to Thornton justified the phrasing of the draft; the British shot back that Thornton's reply removed any such possibility.

He and his colleagues, remarked De Grey, were happy to believe that the American commissioners did not intend to introduce ambiguities which might later be taken to mean more than Britain had agreed to, but the importance of the negotiations meant they had to be careful and to remember that the end of the arbitration might find the United States government in different hands. Another administration might not feel itself bound to respect doubtful stipulations and might attempt, under this wording, to introduce claims not contemplated by either side in the commission.

Fish grumbled that he wanted a "conclusive settlement" of everything at issue between the two countries. He doubted whether the mere reference of one part of the differences to arbitration would satisfy the American populace. De Grey replied that discussion of these differences in the commission was wholly different from sending them to arbitration. And these vague terms were wholly unnecessary. Justice Nelson said he understood that the Americans meant to confine the claims to the acts of the vessels. To this, Fish made a notably equivocal reply: the draft, he said, was meant to refer to the breaches of neutrality growing out of the acts of the ships. Nelson impatiently returned that this was a mere matter of words. That was no doubt so, said De Grey, but the British wanted those words exact. They must guard against the charge that they had no assurance that the "wide claims" would not be presented. Fish warned that too strict a definition would threaten the success of the treaty in the United States, but De Grey snapped back that people in England were fully determined not to truckle to unreasonable demands, and their feelings on the subject were just as strong as any American's could be. The American commissioners agreed to reconsider their draft, and some alterations were made that satisfied the British.[7]

The general impression given by the British report of this meeting is that Fish was cautiously probing his opponents to find out just how sensitive they were on the indirect claims. Two days later the Americans produced a new version of their "gross sum" article; De Grey again attacked its phrasing as vague and insisted upon a change.[8] On April 12 there was a melee over the tenth article. The Americans wanted to state openly that their claims for the expense of tracking down the Confederate cruisers should go to arbitration. De Grey announced flatly that the British would agree to no such thing, for it would mean enlarging the terms of the first article. After consultations, the Americans yielded, as far as the wording of the article was concerned, though they added that they were not agreeing to exclude their claims. They agreed to the language used because they thought it "sufficient" to include all claims of the government which the arbitrators might find just.[9] The shadow of the indirect claims fell across the negotiations just once more, when, on May 1, the British gave up their demand for arbitration of the Canadian claims for annoyance and damage caused by the Fenian raids which the United States had failed to pre-

7. High Commissioners to Granville, Secret, April 8, 1871, FO 5/1302.
8. High Commissioners to Granville, Secret, April 10, 1871, FO 5/1302.
9. Protocols, FO 5/1301. High Commissioners to Granville, Secret, April 12, 1871, FO 5/1302.

vent. In doing so, they added that the concession was made all the more readily, as part of these claims were "of a constructive and inferential character."[10] The inference was obvious that the British regarded all indirect claims unfavorably. Yet there was no response from the American side of the table.

De Grey and his colleagues were well aware that the American commissioners were trying to bring up the "wide claims," but by the middle of April the British were convinced that they had been completely scotched.[11] There was solid foundation for this belief: indirect claims were totally ignored in the treaty, and as Fish had ruled them out as grounds of damages in his talk with Rose, the onus of putting them back in the discussions rested with the Americans. The British had several times said outright that they would not and could not agree to submit any remote or consequential claims to arbitration; the Americans had never replied that they would sign no treaty that did not concede this.

Fish skirted the subject, made the vaguest of proposals, and used the most ambiguous language, but he never said the one thing that, given his knowledge of the subject and the amount of British resistance he was encountering, he should have said: that he wanted the inclusion in the settlement of every American claim, in height and breadth, just as Sumner had stated them on April 15, 1869. Fish had been in office when Sumner made his speech and had read the reports of the British reaction. It is beyond the bounds of possibility that he should have believed that the British commissioners would tacitly accept in 1871 what had roused national frenzy among their people two short years before.

Quite apart from the weakness of Fish's justification by interpretation of the protocols (in February 1872 he told L. P. Morton that he would accept £10 million as a gross sum in settle-

10. Protocols, FO 5/1301.
11. Telegram from Fish to Granville, April 14, 1871; High Commissioners to Granville, April 15, 1871, FO 5/1302.

ment of all claims,[12] which put him in the position of arguing that America was entitled to $48 million if Britain paid her debts on the nail, but to $2,500,000,000 if she went to arbitration), an item in the secretary of state's diary casts an unfavorable light on his doings. Just as he was leaving Senator Howe's house on May 7, his hours of persuasion and blandishment in favor of the treaty over, Fish veered to a different topic. On what grounds, he inquired, would Howe ask Britain to make compensation for the *Alabama* depredations? Britain's early recognition of the Confederates gave them a status they did not deserve and would not otherwise have had, replied the senator, and it showed Britain's unfriendly spirit. But he would admit the absolute right of a sovereign power to decide, subject to its own responsibility, when to concede belligerent rights. Fish probed deeper. Was that responsibility financial? And would it befit the dignity and honor of the American government to ask money damages on those grounds? Howe hesitated and would not say yes.[13]

Thus the day before the treaty's signing, Fish showed just that sharp awareness of the indirect claims and concern about their presentation to the tribunal so conspicuously missing in his performance at the Joint High Commission. It is not easy to believe that suddenly, on May 7, he woke to the importance of the indirect claims for the first time since January. The conversation clearly implies that Fish was still undecided whether or not to press the indirect claims and was interested in learning the opinion of a senator who was both a party regular and a good friend of Sumner's.

An interpretation of events capable of reconciling all these contradictions of the official story would run as follows. Fish did not believe in the justice of the indirect claims and did not want to present them. But, knowing the power of Sumner's views over the popular mind, he felt obliged to include them

12. Fish Diary, Feb. 4, 1872.
13. *Ibid.*, May 7, 1871.

in the terms he outlined to Thornton on November 20, 1870. Buoyed up by the favorable aspect of the negotiations and by the encouragement he received from members of Congress, Fish gave his own inclinations free rein when talking to Rose and abandoned the indirect claims. Later, with Sumner's hostility made overt and his fears rising, the old doubts returned, and Fish decided to hedge upon this point during the High Commission.

He found this all the easier since none of his colleagues in the American delegation, not even Hoar, were really familiar with the complex details of the disputes.[14] Moreover, as the High Commission wore on, it became customary for the British and American members to sit in separate rooms. Fish and De Grey would parley; each then returned to his own men, asked for advice and guidance, and went back to meet the other chief. "When a settlement has been pretty well arrived at, we all meet, read protocol, formally open the points which have been already decided, let off a proper amount of gas, which will have to be duly recorded by and by, and come to the foregone conclusion."[15]

Several times during the negotiations Fish tried to insert the indirect claims into the arbitration. Each time the British made it clear that they would break off the talks rather than agree. So Fish drifted into accepting vague phrases capable of several interpretations and, to secure the passage of the treaty, he directed Bancroft Davis to make the slight change in the protocols to which he later pointed as justification for his interpretation of the treaty.

There is nothing in Fish's character to make such a course in-

14. Adams Diary, April 12, 1871.
15. Northcote Diary, April 25, 1871, Iddesleigh Papers. Fish Diary, April 24, 25, 28, 1871. Recollecting the affair in 1880, Fish wrote that "the presentation of the indirect claims was a necessity (forced upon the Department by Mr. Sumner's speech, and the Hurrahs on one side, and the denunciation on the other side, which that speech excited)." Fish to Boutwell, Feb. 10, 1880, Fish Papers, L.C.

herently impossible. Granted, he was an honest and principled man; yet he found no difficulty in publishing lies to excuse the dismissal of Motley, or in tolerating the idea of annexation of a foreign country whose population had not been consulted. Fish was devoted to Grant, and the Treaty of Washington was the administration's first success; he sincerely desired an Anglo-American *rapprochement*. Under such circumstances, it is not at all impossible to imagine Fish choosing to do a little evil to gain a great good.

The explosion of January 1871 was by no means inevitable. If the British had only had the wit to keep the American case out of the hands of the press (as Fish did), the crisis need never have arisen. When he first heard of the American demands, Granville was inclined to deal with them in the British countercase, and without the popular furore Whitehall might well have contented itself with a stinging demonstration of the indirect claims' absurdity (which would not have been hard) and a reflection that the country could always withdraw from the arbitration later if that did not take.

One thing is certain: the indirect claims affair reflects no credit upon Fish. He emerges from it as either a knave or a fool, and it is not easy to justify his reputation as a great secretary of state upon his conduct of the Alabama Claims negotiations.

CHAPTER 11

The Supplemental Article

The first British newspaper to sound the alarm over inclusion of the indirect claims in the American case was the *Morning Post,* which called attention to the danger on Thursday, December 28. Not until *The Times* took fright on the second of January did the matter cause any popular excitement. With the "Thunderer" aroused, the rest of the press began to sit up and take notice. Condemnation of the claims was universal.[1]

The government, its members scattered during the parliamentary vacation, was much slower to react. Early in January, Lord Westbury warned Granville of the gravity of the American declaration and urged him to send a protest to Washington. But Granville could not believe that the Americans were serious. Most of their case, he held, was intended for home consumption and could be dealt with in the British countercase. The attorney-general, Sir Roundell Palmer, shared Westbury's concern over the ambiguity of the treaty, but agreed with Granville,[2] and nothing was done until the popular outcry forced the government to act.

1. London *Morning Post,* Dec. 28, 1871; *The Times* (London), Jan. 2, 1872; London *Echo,* Jan. 4, 1872; London *Spectator,* Jan. 13, 1872; London *Morning Advertiser*, Jan. 4, 1872; London *Daily Telegraph,* Jan. 6, 1872. Clippings encl. in Schenck to Fish, Feb. 6, 1872, Diplomatic Despatches.
2. Westbury to Granville, Jan. n.d., 7, 1872; Granville to Westbury, Jan. 8, 1872; Roundell Palmer to Granville, Jan. 10, 12, 1872, Granville Papers. PRO 30/29.

The public alarm only grew as time went on. Schenck found the excitement "intense." "John Bull has just now one of his paroxysms of madness on him," wrote Bancroft Davis, "*The Times* alone has had thirteen articles on our Case, and the cry is still they come."[3] It began to appear that the ministry's hold on power, already precarious, might be lost unless action was taken upon the indirect claims.[4] On February 3, Granville sent Schenck a note stating that the British could not agree that such claims came within the terms of arbitration. Privately the American minister commented that the note was "involved, obscure and without logical sequence"; it only called America's attention to Britain's different interpretation of the treaty, leaving her government to ask the British, "Well, what are you going to do about it?"[5]

At first it seemed that the American government was not even going to do that. When Thornton called at Fish's house to give him the news, the secretary of state told him that the United States would never withdraw any part of her case. She would let the tribunal decide; she would be content to see the indirect claims rejected. But she would never allow any power to dictate to her what claims or complaints she should advance.[6] After church next day, Fish found Boutwell and Levi P. Morton waiting for him. Morton had a telegram from his partner, Rose, urging conciliation, but Fish gave him the same reply that he

3. Schenck to Bancroft Davis, Jan. 29, 1872, encl. in Bancroft Davis to Fish, Jan. 31, 1872, Fish Papers, L.C. Also, Bancroft Davis to Fish, Jan. 7, 1872; Schenck to Fish, Jan. 11, 1872; Badeau to Fish, Feb. 10, 1872, Fish Papers, L.C. W. H. Huntington to John Bigelow, Jan. 30, 1872, printed in John Bigelow, *Retrospections of an Active Life* (Garden City, N.Y.: Doubleday, Page, 1913), V, 14. Edmund Hammond to A. H. Layard, Feb. 2, 1872, Layard Papers. Adams Diary, Feb. 3, 1872.

4. Schenck to Bancroft Davis, Feb. 5, 1872, encl. in Schenck to Fish, Feb. 6, 1872; London *Pall Mall Gazette*, Jan. 26, 1872, clipping encl. in Schenck to Fish, Feb. 6, 1872, Diplomatic Despatches.

5. Schenck to Bancroft Davis, Feb. 5, 1872, encl. in Schenck to Fish, Feb. 6, 1872, Diplomatic Despatches.

6. Fish Diary, Feb. 3, 1872. Rose to Morton, Jan. 27, 1872, Levi P. Morton Papers.

had made Thornton. Boutwell thought the English should lodge a protest with the tribunal, arguing that the indirect claims were excluded by the treaty. Both he and Fish agreed that there was very little likelihood of an award for indirect claims, but the secretary of state maintained that they were included in the treaty.[7]

Later that Sunday, Morton called again and proposed a return to the idea of Britain paying a gross sum to settle the Alabama Claims at once. Now that arbitration seemed to have failed, many men turned back to the notion; Schenck, for instance, mentioned it to Fish and recommended it to Sir Stafford Northcote. Charles Francis Adams suggested it to Lord Ripon.[8] Fish asked what sum Morton had in mind. Twelve or fifteen million dollars, answered the banker. But this was not enough for Fish. If he had said ten million pounds, the secretary replied, he might have accepted. Morton, undeterred, went off to dine at the White House and returned once more to report that Grant had taken his suggestion well.

Fish would have been well content with payment of a gross sum provided the British would agree to make the formal proposal. America, he felt, could not take the initiative, for she had offered this type of settlement the previous year and had been rebuffed. At a cabinet meeting on February 6, Fish found Grant receptive to the idea, though less favorable than Morton had said. And all the members of the cabinet agreed that no part of the American claims could be withdrawn.[9] Three days later the President's attitude had hardened. He wanted messages sent to all the other powers who had appointed arbitrators urging them to continue the tribunal proceedings, no matter what Britain did. If necessary, he declared, Adams should sign the

7. Fish Diary, Feb. 4, 1872.

8. Schenck to Bancroft Davis, Feb. 5, 1872, encl. in Schenck to Fish, Feb. 6, 1872, Diplomatic Despatches. Northcote to Ripon, Feb. 4, 1872, Ripon Papers. Adams Diary, Feb. 7, 1872.

9. Fish Diary, Feb. 4, 6, 1872. Fish to Schenck, Feb. 5, 6, 1872, Fish Papers, L.C.

award alone. As so often happened, it was left to Fish to moderate his ardor by pointing out that the treaty required a majority of arbitrators to sign an award.[10]

Meanwhile, on the 7th, Parliament had opened with intransigent speeches from both Gladstone and Disraeli.[11] Fish became alarmed. "Is the Government sending troops to Canada?" he cabled Schenck on February 12.[12] Still no solution appeared.[13]

Since Granville was adamant in his refusal to admit the indirect claims, Fish decided to stonewall too. On February 27, he composed a long dispatch justifying the American case and urging the British to let the indirect claims go before the tribunal, just as the United States government had allowed claims for the Confederate cotton loan to go before the mixed claims commission in late 1871, even though the treaty specifically barred them.[14] As it was being copied, Schenck cabled a fresh proposal from Granville. The British, he said, would not press for the withdrawal of the American case if the United States government would inform the arbitrators that it neither desired any award for indirect claims nor wanted them considered in fixing a gross sum of compensation.[15]

Fish telegraphed back that this suggestion was "inadmissible," but Granville renewed it next day.[16] That was met by another refusal, although Fish sugared the pill with an expression of willingness to agree on "any honorable adjustment of the in-

10. Fish Diary, Feb. 9, 1872.
11. Telegram from Schenck to Fish, Feb. 7, 1872, Fish Papers, L.C.
12. Telegram from Fish to Schenck, Feb. 12, 1872, Diplomatic Instructions. In his private letters, Fish denounced the British bitterly. Fish to Levi P. Morton, Feb. 14, 1872; Fish to George Jones, Feb. 14, 1872, Fish Papers, L.C.
13. Adams Diary, Feb. 20, 1872.
14. Fish to Schenck, Feb. 27, 1872, Diplomatic Instructions.
15. Telegram from Schenck to Fish, Feb. 27, 1872, Diplomatic Despatches.
16. Telegram from Fish to Schenck, Feb. 27, 1872, Diplomatic Instructions. Telegram from Schenck to Fish, Feb. 28, 1872, Diplomatic Despatches.

cidental question which has arisen.''[17] Reports of a favorable British response gradually turned sour, and Granville's final reply to the formal American dispatch of February 27 settled nothing.[18] The foreign secretary again argued the correctness of the British view and repeated his demand for an American capitulation. Fish responded with a justification of his case and stood pat on his ground that the tribunal should be allowed to judge whether the indirect claims were just or unjust.[19] In this way, three months went by, with nothing to break the deadlock. By his unwise decision to press the indirect claims, Fish had painted himself into a corner. The British would not go on with the arbitration unless he withdrew; he could not withdraw without a catastrophic loss of prestige to a discredited administration that faced a struggle for re-election in six months' time.[20]

Behind the official facade, various solutions were canvassed. Speaking to Thornton on February 29, Fish almost begged the British to go on with the arbitration. The United States, he said, was quite content to have the indirect claims rejected. Confidentially, he did not think they stood a chance. America was almost never a belligerent, and her interest was obviously protection of neutral rights rather than neutral obligations. The finest thing imaginable for American interests would be to have the indirect claims thrown out and a ruling made that neutrals, even when derelict in their duty, were liable only for the direct losses springing immediately from the specific act of failure. Thornton was not so easily convinced. What about the possibility of huge damages? Fish suggested that the two governments should agree upon a limit to be set upon the award.[21]

Next day, the secretary took this idea to Grant. He did not

17. Telegram from Fish to Schenck, Feb. 29, 1872, Diplomatic Instructions.

18. Adams Diary, March 18, 20, 25, 29, 1872.

19. Fish to Schenck, April 16, 1872, Diplomatic Despatches.

20. Thornton to Edmund Hammond, March 12, 13, 1872, Hammond Papers, FO 391/18.

21. Fish to Schenck, Feb. 29, 1872, Fish Papers, L.C.

approve it, but he did look more favorably upon a scheme concocted by Schenck: America would agree to drop the indirect claims if Britain would abandon her claim to San Juan. The minister was ordered to sound Granville on the idea, but he received a flat "No."[22] The foreign secretary wanted the two governments to make a convention withdrawing the power to award a gross sum from the arbitrators. This would effectively cut off any compensation for indirect claims, but to be doubly certain the Americans should also agree not to present them to the assessors if the main tribunal found Britain liable.

Schenck responded that this was asking the United States to go further than she had ever gone before, but Granville would hear of nothing else, not even an agreement on maximum and minimum damages. Privately the minister reflected that Gladstone's vigorous denunciations of the indirect claims had left him no room for maneuver. He was convinced that the British meant to withdraw from any part of the arbitration in which the indirect claims were raised.[23]

Early in April affairs began to move at last, though whether toward disaster or settlement was unclear. But, for the moment, things got no worse. The treaty survived, and neither side made a move to break it. The British consented to file their counter-case, as provided by the treaty, though they insisted that this action would not prejudice any position they might take on the indirect claims.[24] Fish deliberately delayed replying to Granville's

22. Schenck to Fish, Feb. 14, March 18, 1872; Schenck to George Bancroft, March 2, 4, 8, 15, 16, 1872; Bancroft to Schenck, March 2, 6, 11, 1872, Diplomatic Despatches. Schenck to Fish, March 16, 1872, Fish Papers, L.C. Fish to Schenck, March 1, 1872, Diplomatic Instructions. Fish Diary, Feb. 29, March 1, 1872.

23. Schenck to Fish, Unofficial, March 20, 1872, encl. in Schenck to Fish, April 10, 1872, Diplomatic Despatches. Schenck to Fish, March 20, 1872, Fish Papers, L.C.

24. Telegram from Schenck to Fish, April 1, 1872, Diplomatic Despatches. Telegram from Fish to Schenck, April 2, 1872, Diplomatic Instructions. Granville to Fish, March 21, 1872; Schenck to Granville, March 22, 1872; Schenck to Fish, April 10, 15, 1872, Fish Papers, L.C. Adams to Schenck, April 15, 1872, Adams Papers.

formal note of March 20 until it was certain that the arbitration would not break on this rock,[25] but in the second part of April he launched a full-scale peace offensive.

His decision may well have been influenced by a threat of congressional intervention in the dispute; a Maine Republican, John W. Peters, brought in a resolution condemning the indirect claims, and he stood to get all the votes of the Democratic representatives and a good few of the Republican.[26] There was also reason to believe that the British might be more conciliatory. In the last week of April, it was touch and go whether Gladstone's shaky ministry would not fall on the Irish University Bill, and Lord Russell was pressing a motion to suspend arbitration until America abandoned the indirect claims.[27]

On April 19, Fish took the problem to the cabinet. Everyone agreed that there could be no backing down on the presentation of the indirect claims. At the same time, it was clearly in America's future interest to have them decided adversely. Postmaster-General John Creswell suggested that the United States might say she wanted the tribunal to decide whether Britain was liable for the indirect claims, but would agree to leave the matter of damages to be arranged between the two nations. Secretary of the Navy Robeson liked the idea; Attorney-General Williams, one of the Joint Highs, argued that no award would be made on the indirect claims and that nobody should wish for one. He advocated a package deal. If Britain would agree that in all future wars in which she was belligerent and the United States neutral, no demand for indirect damages would be made, then the present claims would be dropped. Fish was favorably impressed by the idea,[28] but contented himself with asking Adams

25. Fish to Schenck, April 11, 1872, Fish Papers, L.C.
26. Fish, of course, did not know that Thornton was behind this. Thornton to Hammond, March 19, April 9, 16, 22, 1872, Hammond Papers, FO 391/18. The resolution was considered in the cabinet, and Fish was dispatched to N. P. Banks with strict orders for him to kill or emasculate it. Fish Diary, April 19, 1872.
27. Telegram from Schenck to Fish, April 22, 1872; Schenck to Fish, April 18, 1872, Diplomatic Despatches.
28. Fish Diary, April 19, 1872.

to spread the word that he did not consider Britain liable for the indirect claims and would pronounce against them at the arbitration.[29]

On the evening of the 23rd, however, Granville warned Schenck that if America continued to maintain the indirect claims Britain would withdraw from the arbitration,[30] and the secretary realized that Gladstone required something more definite than Adams' promises. On the 24th, Fish prepared a draft dispatch based on Williams' suggestion, which he read to the cabinet on the 25th and again on the 26th. It was approved, but the president insisted that Britain should appear to take the initiative. Fish hurried off to see Thornton, who thought the idea promising, and then cabled Schenck.[31]

Granville, after grumbling a good deal about Britain making the first public move toward conciliation, finally gave in. But on another point he stood firm. Fish had written that the United States would not press for an award on the indirect claims; the British argued that they should not even be before the tribunal. Nevertheless, Granville assented to the American draft in all its essentials.[32]

Schenck himself remarked that he could see no good reason for leaving the indirect claims before the tribunal when the two nations had already settled their fate. But Fish insisted that under the Constitution, no part of the American case could be withdrawn by the president alone. He also objected that Granville had changed his proposals for the future. Where he had stipulated that "any indirect, remote or consequential" claim

29. Adams Diary, April 19, 24, 1872. Fish Diary, April 20, 1872.
30. Telegram from Schenck to Fish, April 24, 1872, Diplomatic Despatches. This ultimatum was, in fact, withdrawn in favor of a threat to take the matter into Parliament the next day. Telegram from Schenck to Fish, April 25, 1872, Diplomatic Despatches.
31. Fish Diary, April 26, 1872. Telegram from Fish to Schenck, April 26, 1872, encl. in Schenck to Fish, May 2, 1872, Diplomatic Despatches. Telegram from Fish to Schenck, April 27, 1872, Diplomatic Instructions.
32. Telegram from Schenck to Fish, April 30, 1872, Diplomatic Despatches.

should be barred, the British only bound themselves not to advance such claims in cases and circumstances similar to the American Civil War. No two cases, he wrote, were similar, and Britain would not be faced with civil war in the foreseeable future; the terms proposed guaranteed America nothing.[33]

In London the situation looked black. Russell was still threatening to bring up his motion interdicting arbitration until the indirect claims were abandoned, and he was unlikely to wait until after the Whitsun recess, which began on May 13. If the Gladstone government could not produce a satisfactory solution by then, Russell's motion stood every chance of passing both Lords and Commons almost unanimously, and the treaty would be at an end.[34] Schenck cabled back as soon as he received Fish's objections, warning that the British would never agree to leave the claims before the tribunal. Would Washington approve a note which was silent on that point, conceded that no award should be made for the claims, and made the future prohibition of them binding on both sides?[35]

Fish took this to a cabinet meeting on the 6th, where it was badly received. He himself thought it "evasive"; "it did not meet us in the spirit of fairness and of compromise."[36] At first Grant was for ignoring the proposal and sending no reply, but when Fish pointed out that this would throw the responsibility and odium of breaking the treaty upon America, he acquiesced in a proposal put forward by the secretary of state and drafted by Robeson. This cable, decidedly noncommittal and unenthusiastic in tone, reminded Schenck that any agreement binding the future action of the United States would have to receive Senate approval. A decision by the tribunal would settle the

33. Schenck to Fish, May 2, 1872, Diplomatic Despatches. Fish Diary, May 2, 1872. Telegram from Fish to Schenck, May 4, 1872, Diplomatic Instructions.
34. Schenck to Fish, May 2, 1872; Telegram from Schenck to Fish, May 5, 1872, Diplomatic Despatches. Adams Diary, May 7, 1872.
35. Telegram from Schenck to Fish, May 5, 1872, Diplomatic Despatches.
36. Fish to Schenck, May 7, 1872, Fish Papers, L.C.

affair and guide the future conduct of the two nations just as well, without the bother of congressional action, but if the British really wanted to open negotiations for a separate agreement the president would give their suggestions the most careful consideration.[37] But before the ink of the telegram was quite dry, Schenck was beginning a two-hour wrangle with Granville, and as the cabinet was meeting, he was sending off the result. It differed only in wording from the proposal he had cabled the day before.[38]

Negotiations were now at a critical stage. All the propositions made by the British involved, overtly or covertly, what the Americans could not, for reasons of prestige and constitutional law, agree to: the withdrawal from the tribunal of the right to pronounce upon the indirect claims. Though the United States stood ready to promise not to press the claims, the arbitrators could still award damages on their own initiative, and the British could not risk this. Since the trouble had sprung from an ambiguous treaty, neither side was willing to give way without a form of wording of whose meaning they were absolutely certain. While discussion raged, time was running out. On Monday, May 6, Granville won a week's respite from Russell's motion by giving a firm promise that by the 13th he would either produce the diplomatic correspondence or make a definite statement of the country's position. This was the very limit, only secured by a solemn assurance that he would not compromise or depart from his view that indirect claims were outside the scope and intention of the Treaty of Washington. Schenck glumly anticipated the foreign secretary's withdrawal from the arbitration.[39] "The thing," wrote Charles Francis Adams, "is more ticklish than I expected."[40]

37. Fish Diary, May 7, 1872. Draft telegram by Robeson, May 7, 1872, in Fish Papers, L.C.
38. Telegram from Schenck to Fish, May 6, 1872, Diplomatic Despatches.
39. Telegram from Schenck to Fish, May 7, 1872, Diplomatic Despatches.
40. Adams Diary, May 6, 1872.

Fish, obviously expecting a break, began to try to rally the Republican party around the administration. Before he sent off his reply to London on May 4, he summoned the G.O.P. members of the Senate and House Committees on Foreign Relations to the State Department, showed them the recent correspondence and his draft, and incorporated some of their criticisms into the dispatch.[41] Thornton had never known him so unpleasant or uncomfortable and divined that he was greatly perplexed. He was inordinately proud of his achievement in negotiating the treaty, yet dared not save it by withdrawing the indirect claims without a concession to brandish before the public.[42]

In London "the poor men at the Legation"[43] kept at it night and day, ciphering and deciphering by turns, while Schenck, with a splitting head, slaved over his dispatches and dreamed of a holiday at Torquay.[44] Adams, who was then passing through London on his way back to Geneva, offered to put before the arbitrators any proposal which Granville and Schenck agreed to, either to decline absolutely or to disapprove the indirect claims, once the two governments had settled their dispute. He would pronounce against national responsibility for indirect claims, and as he would be speaking against his own country, the three independent arbitrators were bound to agree with him.[45] But would the two governments settle?

Fish's reply to the formula produced by Granville and Schenck clung obstinately to the same old ground. The British offer, he wrote, carried with it the connotation that they had been right all the time, that the tribunal had no right to pass on the

41. Senators Harlan, Morton, Hamlin, and Patterson (Simon Cameron did not attend, and Schurz had bolted the party); Representatives Banks, Leonard Myers, Charles Willard, Jacob Ambler, Jasper Packard, and Holland Duell. See Fish Diary, May 4, 1872.

42. Thornton to Hammond, May 7, 1872, Hammond Papers, FO 391/18.

43. Charles Francis Adams to Henry Adams, May 22, 1872, Adams Papers.

44. Schenck to Fish, May 16, 1872, Fish Papers, L.C.

45. Adams Diary, May 7, 1872. Telegram from Schenck to Fish, May 7, 1872, Diplomatic Despatches.

indirect claims. America could not admit this, and the president could not withdraw any part of the American case. If the British persisted in their course, the responsibility of breaking the treaty would rest with them. Both Grant and Fish were reluctant to take such an embarrassing problem as the indirect claims to the Senate in an election year[46] (which was one of the reasons why they were so keen for the tribunal to pass upon them) but there seemed no alternative. The president hoped, wrote Fish, that the British would agree to prepare a new article supplementing the Treaty of Washington.[47]

The British cabinet ministers warred bitterly amongst themselves when they heard the news from America, with Robert Lowe, the chancellor of the exchequer, leading the opposition to any new article.[48] Finally, Granville informed Schenck that a new clause knocking out the indirect claims would have to be so broad in its language that it would commit both governments to more than they would wish. Indeed, it might well be construed to exclude many of the American direct claims. He preferred two interchanged notes, in which the problem could be stated exactly and narrowly. Schenck raised the constitutional problem, and Granville asked whether the president could not submit the notes to the Senate for advice. Schenck answered that he would cable to ask, but he did not expect the American government to go beyond the terms stated on April 27.[49]

In the mind of the American minister, the treaty was as good as lost.[50] He underestimated the British anxiety for a settlement with the United States; next morning a message came to say that the cabinet were holding another meeting, and, early

46. Thornton to Hammond, May 7, 1872, Hammond Papers, FO 391/18.

47. Telegram from Fish to Schenck, May 8, 1872, Diplomatic Instructions.

48. Adams Diary, May 9, 10, 1872.

49. Three telegrams from Schenck to Fish, May 9, 1872, Diplomatic Despatches.

50. Adams Diary, May 11, 1872.

in the evening, Granville himself brought a draft article to the legation. Schenck grinned from ear to ear: "I suppose you have now got what you want," snapped the foreign secretary.[51]

The article proved to be the note of May 6, drawn up as a contract. Both nations' arguments were stated, and it was made clear that neither was giving way. But, in future, neither power would urge indirect claims against the other, and the president of the United States would make no claim for them at Geneva. "I do not see why it would not answer," wrote Adams.[52]

It certainly saved the treaty in England. When Parliament met for the last time before the Whitsuntide recess on May 13, Gladstone and Granville were able to make satisfactory statements, and though Russell made a "scolding and offensive" speech, he withdrew his motion.[53] In Washington, Fish consulted his colleagues about the proposed article and set to work to line up a Senate majority. On the 11th he called twelve administration stalwarts to a White House conference and asked for their advice.[54] During the days that followed, he kept in close touch with congressional leaders. On Zack Chandler's advice, Fish sent off telegrams to influential men, such as Levi P. Morton, asking them to whip up support for the article in their communities.[55] The morning after the meeting, George F. Edmunds of Vermont wrote to Fish advising him to submit the article for the advice of the Senate, rather than for ratification. Advice only required a majority of votes; consent needed two-thirds. By asking only for advice, the administration could

51. Two telegrams from Schenck to Fish, May 10, 1872, Diplomatic Despatches. Granville to Gladstone, May 10, 1872, Gladstone Papers.

52. Adams Diary, May 11, 1872.

53. Telegrams from Schenck to Fish, May 13, 1872, Diplomatic Despatches.

54. Hamlin, Edmunds, Anthony, Frelinghuysen, Scott, John Pool, William D. Kellogg, Stewart, Harlan, Howe, John A. Logan, and Oliver P. Morton. Boutwell, Robeson, and Speaker James G. Blaine, who was running for the Senate, also attended. Fish Diary, May 11, 12, 1872. Draft by Robeson, May 12, 1872, Fish Papers, L.C.

55. Fish Diary, May 14, 1872.

test the strength of the article's support in the Senate without risking a public, and politically damaging, defeat. Fish at once saw the sense of this suggestion and adopted it.[56] On Simon Cameron's suggestion, the diplomatic correspondence was printed and distributed.[57]

Charles Sumner was, of course, violently opposed to the article.[58] During the first week of May, reported Thornton, when it seemed that all negotiations had failed, Sumner could not conceal his satisfaction.[59] But he was now a sick man; his power was sapped and gone. Younger, stronger men had to lead the Liberal Republican opposition to Grant. Sumner might prove troublesome, but he was no real threat to the article.

On May 18, the article came before the Senate Foreign Affairs Committee, with Fish present, as a witness, to grease the wheels. Schurz wanted to know whether an article similar to the proposition Schenck had outlined on May 5 could be obtained from the British; Fish replied that he doubted it. Hamlin and Harlan said they would vote for the article as it was; Simon Cameron and Morton both wanted amendments, but if that was impossible they would accept the article rather than lose the treaty. Patterson had changed sides and now joined Schurz. Casserly, the only Democrat on the committee, Fish thought "seemingly fair, but very guarded."

After several hours' discussion, Fish drew up an amendment that he hoped would satisfy Patterson and Schurz. In effect, the change softened the article to make it appear less of a submission by the United States. Fish included a few expendable words as a bait for Schurz, hoping that the German would knock them out as the price of his support.[60] Unfortunately, this

56. Edmunds to Fish, May 12, 1872; Fish to Edmunds, May 12, 1872, Fish Papers, L.C.

57. U. S. Grant to Fish, May 16, 1872, Fish Papers, L.C.

58. Sumner to Bemis, May 20, 1872, Bemis Papers. Thornton to Hammond, May 28, 1872, Hammond Papers, FO 391/18.

59. Thornton to Hammond, May 14, 1872, Hammond Papers, FO 391/18.

60. Fish Diary, May 18, 1872.

stratagem failed, and so did an appeal by General Horace Porter, Grant's private secretary, to Levi P. Morton, that he should bring his influence to bear upon those New York Democrats, like S. L. M. Barlow, who were close friends of Senator Casserly. Porter told Morton that a unanimous report in its favor from the committee would be half the battle gained.[61] But the amended article emerged from the committee with four in favor, two (Schurz and Casserly) against, and one (Patterson) in favor of modifying the proposition so that the indirect claims stayed before the tribunal with an understanding that the Americans would not press for money damages on their account.[62]

But when the article came to a vote on the Senate floor, Fish had better luck. Schurz voted for it, and so did Patterson; Lyman Trumbull, whose attitude had been doubtful, was won over.[63] A few minor changes satisfied Roscoe Conkling and George F. Edmunds. Though many Republicans, like John Sherman, did not like the article, they did not break party ranks. As for the Democrats, some had never believed in the indirect claims, some disliked Sumner, some were under the influence of Reverdy Johnson, who regarded the article as his justification. Thurman of Ohio took the opportunity to blast Fish's diplomacy, but the article passed, 43 to 8; five Democrats, Sumner, Tipton of Nebraska, and West of Louisiana, voted against it.[64]

All was well — except that the British would not swallow the amended article. They charged that the Senate's wording was so vague that it would justify almost anything; the article would condone willful misconduct by a neutral state as easily as a failure from lack of due diligence.[65] They demanded further revisions. Fish absolutely refused. Not only would the Senate

61. Porter to Morton, May 20, 1872, Morton Papers.

62. *New York Herald,* May 18, 20, 1872.

63. Porter to Morton, May 20, 1872, Morton Papers.

64. *New York Herald,* May 22, 25, 1872. Henry S. Northcote to Sir Stafford Northcote, June 14, 1872, Iddesleigh Papers.

65. Two telegrams from Schenck to Fish, May 28, 1872, Diplomatic Despatches.

reject the change, he said, but their draft protected America from Canadian claims for damage caused by the Fenian raids, while the British proposal excluded any claims rising out of the acts of vessels under circumstances which would probably never recur.[66] At a quarter to three in the morning on May 31, Granville sent Schenck a new British proposal which remedied the difficulties about the Senate article's ambiguity between willful misconduct and a lack of diligence. But by the time it reached Washington, only thirteen hours remained in which the Senate could consider and pass it. On June 15 the arbitrators were to meet, and the final arguments were to be handed in. Britain would never take this step with the indirect claims unresolved. Granville advocated signing a treaty to postpone the arbitrators' meeting, but this, too, had to go before the Senate and there was no time. Fish let it be known that the United States would agree to a motion for the tribunal's adjournment once the arguments were in, and this would give both sides a breathing space in which to reach agreement. But Granville made it clear that he intended to ask for an adjournment without presenting the British argument.[67] "I think that the Treaty is broken up," wrote Fish.[68]

66. Telegram from Fish to Schenck, May 28, 1872, Diplomatic Instructions. Fish Diary, May 27, 1872. Fish to Schenck, May 28, 1872, Caleb Cushing Papers. Thornton to Hammond, May 28, June 11, 1872, Hammond Papers FO 391/18.

67. Telegrams from Schenck to Fish, May 31, June 1, 2, 3, 6 (two), 7, 8, 11, 12, 1872; Schenck to Fish, June 8, 1872, Diplomatic Despatches. Telegrams from Fish to Schenck, May 31, June 1, 2, 4, 7, 8, 9, 1872, Diplomatic Instructions.

68. Fish to John C. Hamilton, May 30, 1872, Fish Papers, L.C.

CHAPTER 12

The End of the Battle

The Americans went to Geneva in a mood of grim pessimism, determined to do right and present their argument, even if the British did not.[1] In Washington, Grant was already planning a public statement justifying the administration's policy and promising government assumption of the individual claims.[2] At this moment when Fish's policy seemed to have come to an end, a new course suddenly opened.

The idea of the tribunal taking action, once unofficially assured that the two parties to the dispute would acquiesce, hovered over the negotiations all through the long, dreary months of proposal and counterproposal. Just after the crisis began, Schenck suggested to Bancroft Davis that the two nations should agree upon a gross sum. Charles Francis Adams and Chief Justice Cockburn should confidentially inform their fellow arbitrators what it was and should have the final award made accordingly. Adams, called back from his vacation in Egypt by the eruption of the British public, told Bancroft Davis that he saw no need for any reference to Washington or London to see if the indirect claims should be withdrawn; the question affected no one but the arbitrators. In mid-April, Bancroft Davis, talking to Tenterden about the treaty, suggested that the two counsels might itemize for the arbitrators the points of law that both sides

1. Telegram from Fish to Bancroft Davis, June [9?], 1872, encl. in Bancroft Davis to Fish, June 10, 1872, Adams Papers.
2. Grant to Fish, June 1, 1872, Fish Papers, L.C.

could agree upon. In this list might be included the rule for the measurement of damages. Tenterden reacted favorably, but Fish quashed the idea. A couple of days later the British counsel put forward a scheme. Why should not the arbitrators come together on their own initiative before June 15, for the avowed purpose of relieving the two governments of the responsibility for deciding the indirect claims question? Both sides could put in arguments, and the arbitrators would hand down a judgment.

At much the same time in Washington, Fish, thinking over the problem, realized that he would have to give the British something more definite than his own assurances that the United States desired no monetary award for the indirect claims. He remembered that Adams, when he attended the cabinet meeting on February 23, had said that he did not believe Britain was liable for the indirect claims. What if the British knew that? Cockburn obviously would not award huge damages against his own country, and the three other arbitrators would not go against the two most directly involved. This might be the way to a solution. He fired off a telegram to Adams and dispatched Boutwell to New York to meet him. The two conferred in a minute room in the Parker House on Fifth Avenue, and Adams promised to do all he could to relieve the British dread of an award of mllions against them. Fish himself told Thornton that the United States wanted nothing but a decision upon the issue of neutrality, hoping that word would go back to Count Sclopis, who he knew was in touch with the minister.

The supplementary article removed the necessity for this course, but it remained in Adams' mind; while in London he offered to put an Anglo-American gentleman's agreement before the tribunal on his own responsibility, avoiding the need for an official presentation. When Adams saw what state things were in during the first weeks of June, the idea of independent action by the tribunal loomed larger in his thoughts. In February he had written: "Thus I see that it seems the will of the

Deity to place me once more in the position of peacemaker." In
June he justified these words."

On June 15, Bancroft Davis put in the American argument,
and Tenterden read a statement announcing that the British
could not agree to present theirs while the indirect claims question remained unsettled. They therefore asked for nine months'
adjournment. After the session ended, Itajuba called on Adams
and said he feared that waiting so long would be fatal to the
arbitration. Adams agreed and went for a walk to think things
over; he became so preoccupied that he went too far. When
Adams finally returned, he asked Bancroft Davis to sound Tenterden on the possibility of going on with the arbitration of the direct
damages. The Englishman said this was impossible, and if Adams
meant business, he would have to go much farther than that.
What did this mean? said Bancroft Davis. Tenterden would not
say, but at half-past eleven he got Davis out of bed to hear a
proposition made by Sir Roundell Palmer, the leading British
counsel, after consultations with Cockburn. The British would
be satisfied with an opinion given extrajudicially by the arbitrators against the indirect claims. The British arbitrator could
not take an active part in this decision, and the two governments would have to give their approval.

This once more raised the specter which had bedeviled the
negotiations between Granville and Fish. The British argued
that the indirect claims were not comprised in the reference
to arbitration and could not be considered by the tribunal. The
Americans maintained that the treaty did cover such claims
and that the tribunal could consider them, although they were
quite content to see the decision go against them. After con-

3. Schenck to Bancroft Davis, Jan. 29, 1871, encl. in Schenck to
Fish, Feb. 6, 1872, Diplomatic Despatches. Fish to Schenck, April 23,
1872, Diplomatic Instructions. Bancroft Davis to Fish, Feb. 5, April
15, 17, 1872; Fish to Boutwell, Feb. 10, 1880; Fish to Schenck, April
23, 1872, Fish Papers, L.C. C. F. Adams to Fish, Sept. 20, 1872, Adams
Papers. Adams Diary, Feb. 8, April 19, 24, 1872. Fish Diary, April 15, 20,
1872.

sulting Evarts, who had been talking to Roundell Palmer about
the terms, Adams spent Sunday drafting a paper in which he
endeavored to reconcile the two positions. He began with the
rule that the tribunal would decline to pass upon any question
not fully laid before it by the free act of the two parties and
drew for the rest upon the draft statement agreed on by Granville and Schenck on May 5, which had formed the body of the
supplemental article.[4] His youngest son, Brooks, made a fair
copy of the proposal, and Adams hurried down into Geneva to
show the counsel, who approved it with some minor changes.

Early on the Monday morning Adams called on the three
independent arbitrators and found them all opposed to the
idea of adjournment for eight months. At the meeting of the
tribunal, Bancroft Davis said he had no instructions and could
do nothing, whereupon the session ended abruptly. The arbitrators were left alone in the empty chamber to discuss the difficulty.
Adams expressed himself strongly against an adjournment. A
presidential election was due in the United States, a general
election seemed likely in England, and the arbitration would
inevitably become an issue in both. The indirect claims were the
only obstacle, said Cockburn. Perhaps an extrajudicial opinion
would deal with them. Adams saw his chance. Would Britain
accept one? Yes, said Cockburn, he thought so. Then, said
Adams, he would take the responsibility of initiating it. He would
make a proposition, not for the United States, but for all nations.

Next morning the five men met at the house of the tribunal's
president, Count Sclopis. At his suggestion, the British had been
allowed to make a new draft. The Americans agreed to it, and
it was issued the following day, Wednesday June 19, as a declaration by the five arbitrators.[5] The statement rehearsed the British

4. Telegram from Schenck to Fish, May 6, 1872, Diplomatic Despatches.
5. Adams Diary, June 15, 16, 17, 18, 1872. Tentenden to Granville,
June 15, 16, (two), 19, 1872, Granville Papers, FO 29/106. Cockburn
to Granville, June 30, 1872, Gladstone Papers. Caleb Cushing to Sidney
Webster, June 30, 1872, Cushing Papers

request for an adjournment and the reason given for it, the dispute over the indirect claims. The arbitrators, it said, did not propose to express or imply any opinion upon the issue, but it was obvious that the adjournment was intended to give them time to work out an agreement. They might well not arrive at one, and after many months of suspense the arbitration would be broken up. So the arbitrators wished to state that after careful study of everything urged by the United States counsel, they had concluded, "individually and collectively," that the indirect claims were not a good foundation for an award and should be excluded from the tribunal's consideration. The arbitrators laid this statement before the parties so that the United States government might consider whether any course could be adopted on the indirect claims which would relieve the tribunal from action on the British motion.[6]

In plain language, would the United States withdraw the indirect claims? The arbitrators' declaration saved both sides' faces, for neither had given way. But, in reality, the British carried their point. Though the Americans got the decision they had wanted, it was an extrajudicial one, and the claims did not officially go before the tribunal. Though he knew there was no other way out, Adams was worried and nervous about the reaction from Washington. But Fish knew a good bargain when he saw one and cabled instructions to withdraw the offending claims.[7]

6. Telegram from Schenck to Fish, June 19, 1872, Diplomatic Despatches.

7. Adams Diary, June 19, 23, 1872. Fish did not give up the ship: his reply *acquiesced* in the tribunal's declaration and added that the president regarded the claims as "adjudicated and disposed of." Consequently, the United States would not *insist* upon them before the tribunal. Lest this touch off a storm, Bancroft Davis wisely suppressed all language implying that the declaration was a judicial act. When shown Adams' draft declaration, Fish had demanded "the further expression in some proper but sufficient form of the opinion that these claims although of a nature legally inadmissible as the foundation of an award in money against a neutral for failure to observe its obligations

The arbitration was saved, and the tribunal set about considering its verdict on the direct claims, though not without some trouble from Cockburn. The British chief justice had been so certain that the arbitration would end that he had not bothered to read any of the arguments, and he found himself quite unprepared to take part in the tribunal's deliberations. Roundell Palmer tried to save him by asking for further printed rebuttals and arguments, necessitating six weeks' adjournment. But neither Fish nor the other arbitrators would hear of this, and Cockburn had to face the music. Under the stress of long hours' work after the tribunal's sessions, his temper and his health suffered. He had conceived a profound contempt for all three of the independent arbitrators,[8] and came to trouble less and less about concealing it. Quarrels racked the tribunal, and the British arbitrator lost much of the influence he might have had with his colleagues.[9]

While the claimants waited and planned,[10] the tribunal made its decision in the greatest secrecy. On July 22, by a vote of 4

---

have nevertheless been properly submitted to the Tribunal well within its province. If thus accompanied it will place this Govt. right." Telegram from Bancroft Davis to Fish, June 17, 1872; Telegram from Fish to Bancroft Davis, June 18, 1872; Bancroft Davis to Cushing, Evarts, and Waite, June 26, 1872, Caleb Cushing Papers.

8. Adams seems to have been the only person in Geneva for whom he had any respect. Cockburn to C. F. Adams, Sept. 9, 1872, Adams Papers.

9. Adams Diary, Feb. 9, 1872. San Francisco *Daily Alta California,* Feb. 16, 1872. Thornton to Hammond, July 16, 28, 1872, Hammond Papers, FO 391/18. Tenterden to Granville, July 18, 24, 26, Aug. 28, Sept. 16, 1872, Granville Papers, FO 29/106. Adams to Fish, Sept. 20, 1872; Henry Adams to C. M. Gaskell, Aug. 29, 1872, Adams Papers. Bancroft Davis to George Bancroft, Oct. 10, 1872, Bancroft Papers. Bancroft Davis to Fish, Sept. 25, Oct. 11, 1872, Fish Papers, L.C. Fish to Bancroft Davis, July 19, 1872; Adam Badeau to Bancroft Davis, Feb. 6, 1873; George Bancroft to Bancroft Davis, Oct. 6, 1872; John Jay to Bancroft Davis, Feb. 15, 1872, Bancroft Davis Papers.

10. John A. Parker to William M. Evarts, Aug. 20, 1872, Evarts Papers.

to 1, Britain was judged responsible for the damage done by the *Florida,* while Cockburn raged. In mid-August, to Fish's disgust,[11] claims for the *Georgia*'s depredations were unanimously thrown out. Britain was held responsible for the *Alabama* and for the *Shenandoah* after she left Melbourne. The British began to wonder if adjudication of each separate claim by assessors might not be cheaper for them than a gross sum awarded by the tribunal. But their efforts in that direction through protests about the extravagance of the American demands, hints of a popular storm in England, and warnings about the danger of making neutrality too onerous came to nothing when a majority of the arbitrators were found to be in favor of giving a gross sum. Gossiping about it among themselves on August 29, the arbitrators found their estimates varied from 15 to 20 million dollars: quite enough, noted Adams. Next day he spoke to Staempfli about it alone, and the Swiss said he was inclined to award $12 million damages, plus interest.

At a formal discussion on Monday, September 2, Bancroft Davis asked for $24 million. Adams and Staempfli were willing to award $18 million, Sclopis $16 million, and Itajuba $15 million. Cockburn announced that he considered Britain liable only for the *Alabama* and offered $4 million. Seeing that he was in a hopeless minority, Cockburn sided with Itajuba, but Staempfli and Adams would not go below $16 million. With Sclopis they formed a majority, and so it would have ended had Itajuba not made an appeal for unanimity on $15.5 million, or £3,200,000. Adams yielded, and the figure was made final. Cockburn, obstinate to the last, refused to sign the public statement.[12]

"I think on the whole you got off cheaply, considering every-

11. Fish to Grant, Aug. 19, 1872, Fish Papers, L.C.
12. Adams Diary, July 22, Aug. 29, 30, Sept. 2, 1872. Tenterden to Granville, Aug. 1, 8, 15, 23, 27, 28, Sept. 1, 3, 1872, Granville Papers, FO 80/106. Telegram from Tenterden to Ripon, Sept. 2, 1872, Ripon Papers.

thing," wrote Henry Adams to his English friend Charles Milnes Gaskell, "and yet I am inclined to think that we have got nearly, though not quite, all we could lay any reasonable claim to."[13] "Thus closed this great experiment," wrote Charles Francis Adams, "with as much of success as could possibly have been expected."[14]

13. Henry Adams to C. M. Gaskell, Aug. 29, 1872, Adams Papers.
14. Adams Diary, Sept. 14, 1872.

CHAPTER 13

Conclusion

Looking back upon the indirect claims *bagatre*, Fish told Bout-well that the pressure brought on him by commercial and finan-cial interests caused him more worry and embarrassment than the British remonstrations.[1] British investors had sunk millions of pounds in American railroads, mines, agriculture, and in-dustry, but the investment itself was more of a safeguard to America than to the capitalists across the Atlantic. Stockholders, of course, would be strongly against war between Britain and the United States, while Americans might think repudiation of their debts was well worth the risk. The real inducement to peace was that America needed more foreign investment. The shortage of risk capital at home guaranteed good relations with Europe, especially England.

During the crisis, Fish was under constant pressure from Levi P. Morton and his London partner, Sir John Rose.[2] Boutwell was so nervous about the U.S. national debt funding operations that he was willing to withdraw the indirect claims first and negotiate afterward during the May crisis over the failure of the supplemental article.[3]

1. Fish to Boutwell, Feb. 10, 1880, Fish Papers, L.C.
2 Rose to Morton, Jan. 27, 1872, Morton Papers. Morton to Fish, Feb. 8, 1872, encl. telegram from Rose to Morton, Feb. 3, 1872; Morton to Fish, March 28, 1872; Telegram from Rose to Morton, April 27, 1872; Morton to Fish, May 4, 1872, Fish Papers, L.C. Fish Diary, April 27, 1872. Rose to William M. Evarts, April 28, 1872, Evarts Papers.
3. "Suggestion," May 9, 1872, Fish Paper, L.C.

Members of Congress were informed of the businessmen's anxiety. Jay Cooke, who was having trouble selling his new Northern Pacific shares, wrote to Carl Schurz urging him to vote for the supplemental article.[4] "See Senator Sumner," ran a telegram to the Massachusetts congressman Oakes Ames, "and secure his influence to advocate amicable adjustment of Alabama question."[5] The nation's loss in gold sales already outweighed anything she might gain from the indirect claims, warned another correspondent.[6]

Nor did public opinion give Fish wholehearted support and encouragement. With the presidential elections approaching, the Democratic journals were busy making the indirect claims into a stick with which to beat Grant.[7] Many of the best independent and Republican papers, already disgusted with Grant, joined in the condemnation. They felt that the administration had got the worst of both worlds by treacherously pressing an unjust claim and then shamefacedly withdrawing it.[8] There

4. Jay Cooke to Schurz, May 16, 1872, Schurz Papers. Henrietta Larson, *Jay Cooke, Private Banker* (Cambridge, Mass.: Harvard University Press, 1936), p. 364.

5. Telegram from George Baty Blake to Oakes Ames, May 17, 1872, Sumner Papers.

6. Arthur Pickering to Sumner, May 20, 1872; also, Naylor and Co. to Sumner, May 16, 1872; Telegram from Israel G. Whitney & Co. to Sumner, March 18, 1872, Sumner Papers. William Hoge to Simon Cameron, May 10, 1872, Cameron Papers.

7. Thornton to Hammond, July 2, 1872, Hammond Papers, FO 391/18. *Atlanta Daily Sun,* Feb. 13, 24, April 3, 1872. *Atlanta Constitution,* May 30, 1872. *Mobile Daily Register,* Feb. 10, 1872. *Savannah Daily Republican,* Feb. 8, 28, 1872. Little Rock *Arkansas Daily Gazette,* May 12, 1872. Washington *Daily Patriot,* Feb. 8, 16, 20, April 5, 18, May 16, 1872. New York *Sun,* quoted in Candace Stone, *Dana and the Sun* (New York: Dodd, Mead, 1938), p. 337. Chicago *Sunday Times,* Feb. 4, May 12, 1872.

8. *Chicago Tribune,* Feb. 5, 8, 12, 24, March 1, May 16, 1872. Washington *Capital,* Feb. 4, 11, April 14, May 26, 1872. Montgomery *Alabama State Journal,* Feb. 9, 16, 1872. Washington *Sunday Morning Chronicle,* May 26, 1872. Prescott *Weekly Arizona Miner,* June 29, 1872. Lawrence *Kansas Western Home Journal,* May 2, 1872.

were, of course, many newspapers and many people who advocated standing fast on the indirect claims and withdrawing
nothing, but an impressive number of distinguished men came
out against Fish. Expert lawyers like William Beach Lawrence,
who had advised Bancroft Davis upon several chapters of the
American case, and R. H. Dana, Jr., ridiculed the concept of
indirect claims. "The feeling here is for the supplemental treaty,"
wrote Edward L. Pierce, Sumner's closest friend, from Boston,
"The work has been done in a slovenly way, but peace ought
to be established." Senator Frelinghuysen, John Pruyn, John
Bigelow, all condemned the administration. Daniel H. Chamber-
lain, the Massachusetts carpetbagger who, as governor of South
Carolina was to come nearer than anyone else to making Black
Reconstruction work, filled a whole column in the Washington
Daily Morning Chronicle with an open letter urging that the
preservation of the national honor and the establishment of the
principle of arbitration were worth infinitely more than any
trumped-up bill of damages. Thornton, in New York for a St.
George's Society dinner, found the absurdity of the official position admitted by everyone. Elihu Burritt, the leader of American
pacifists, appealed to Charles Sumner not to break down the
treaty by working against the supplemental article.[9]

The long dispute over the indirect claims probably weakened
the force of the Treaty of Washington as an example to the
world of two great nations submitting to peaceful arbitration

9. W. B. Lawrence to Sumner, May 16, 25, 1872; R. H. Dana, Jr.,
to Sumner, May 22, 1872; E. L. Pierce to Sumner, May 20, 1872; Elihu
Burritt to Sumner, May 10, 1872; Sam Downes to Sumner, Feb. 12, 1872,
Sumner Papers. Adams Diary, March 2, 1872. Benjamin Rush to Ripon,
May 3, 1872; J. V. S. L. Pruyn to Ripon, Feb. 16, 1872, Ripon Papers.
Cornell Jewett to Fish, Feb. 8, 1872; John C. Hamilton to Fish, Feb.
23, March 1, 1872, Fish Papers, L.C. Thornton to Hammond, April 2,
30, 1872, Hammond Papers FO 391/18. Henry S. Northcote to Sir Staf-
ford Northcote, April 6, 1872, Iddesleigh Papers. John Bigelow to George
Bancroft, July 9, 1872, Bancroft Papers. Washington Daily Morning
Chronicle, May 13, 1872.

instead of fighting.[10] But, though the cause of international peace lost, Anglo-American relations gained. For the first time since the War of 1812, a sizable body of American opinion admitted that Britain was right and the United States wrong. The memories left, the tradition broken, were worth thousands of the facile paeans to international brotherhood inspired by the treaty. In the long run, Anglo-American friendship gained in strength and depth from the testing time of the indirect claims.

The treaty itself proved less important as a precedent than its makers had hoped. Twentieth-century power politics showed up the vague and rose-spectacled visions of nineteenth-century liberalism for what they were. Arbitration can only be employed to settle a dispute when nations genuinely want a just solution, and national interests and national feeling often run directly contrary to such an end. But it was fortunate for international peace that the indirect claims were definitely ruled out of court and not left as a disputed principle to be seized on by every Balkan state. Fish's absurd demand raised the price of neutrality so high that if it had found acceptance, no nation would ever have dared to remain neutral again.

The best that can be said for Fish is that he did realize the desirability of an Anglo-American *rapprochement*. But his timidity, his tendency to quarrel over formalities, his tactless and blundering treatment of Sumner, and his inclusion of the indirect claims in the arbitration (under whatever circumstances) could have wrecked the whole scheme of settlement several times over, had not good luck and British eagerness to end the quarrel prevailed. Admittedly, the treaty might not have passed the Senate without Sumner's conviction that the indirect claims were included in the arbitration, but Fish might advantageously have tried to meet the British halfway when it became obvious that their press and public opinion would not allow them to proceed if the indirect claims were included in the judgment. An American repudiation of the offending parts of their case

10. Fish to Elihu B. Washburne, April 30, 1872, Washburne Papers. Northcote to Disraeli, Sept. 23, 1872, Iddesleigh Papers.

could have occurred in February, perhaps through a face-saving special meeing and pronouncement of the tribunal. If the reputation of Hamilton Fish as secretary of state is to be judged by his policy toward England, it would be slender indeed.

The announcement of the tribunal's award, followed a few weeks later by the German emperor's decision that San Juan rightly belonged to the United States, did not, of course, end the deeply rooted feeling in America against England. It finished an ugly quarrel and removed a dangerous opening for agitation, but the flowering of Anglo-American friendship had to wait until the opening of the new century, a fresh set of international groupings, and changed national circumstances. In 1872 little attention was paid to the award;[11] the election was fought on domestic issues, and after the long and dreary struggle over the indirect claims, few people were interested in the arbitration.[12]

Was there a real danger of war in 1865-1872? Probably not; relations were never as strained as they were in 1861, and the Guards were never ordered to Canada, as they were during the *Trent* crisis. For years after the Civil War, the United States debt was so great that the country's credit would have been wrecked by a prolonged foreign war (quite possibly, the treasury would have found difficulty even in paying the interest), and when the debt was reduced, the Navy had been reduced to a laughing stock.[13]

In the long run, Anglo-American relations were bound to

11. A number of Liberal Republican papers did attack it as a British fraud and a public disgrace: *Chicago Tribune,* Sept. 13, 1872; *New York Tribune,* Sept. 16, 1872; *Hartford Daily Courant,* Sept. 23, 1872; *New York Herald,* Sept. 15, 1872; Chicago *Sunday Times,* June 30, 1872; Frederick *Maryland Union,* Dec. 26, 1872. Administration papers, of course, defended the award; but many seemed curiously reluctant to broach the subject. Possibly with the elections ahead, they did not want to revive memories of the administration's bungling over the indirect claims.

12. Thornton to Ripon, Oct. 8, 1872, Ripon Papers.

13. Oliver P. Morton to Andrew Johnson, Dec. 29, 1865, Johnson Papers. Gideon Welles to John Bigelow, Sept. 21, 1869, printed in John Bigelow, *Retrospections of an Active Life* (Garden City, N.Y.: Doubleday, Page, 1913), IV, 133.

improve after the Civil War, for the conflict gave Americans, for the first time, a tremendous source of national tradition and pride quite divorced from the anti-British overtones of Revolutionary lore.[14] Until America's rise to world power, until Britain was challenged by Germany, Americans found relief from hating Britain only in hating each other.

14. Henry Adams to C. F. Adams, Jr., Feb. 14, 1865, Adams Papers. George Bancroft to Elihu B. Washburne, March 5, 1869; Bancroft to Fish, March 17, 1869, Bancroft Papers. James Russell Lowell, "On a Certain Condescension in Foreigners," in *My Study Windows* (London: Routledge, n.d.), p. 73. Henry Cabot Lodge, *Early Memories* (London: Constable, 1913), p. 205. Curti, *Roots of American Loyalty*, pp. 169-171.

Manuscript Collections

Adams Papers, Massachusetts Historical Society (Consulted on microfilm at Eisenhower Library, The Johns Hopkins University, Baltimore, Md.)

John A. Andrew Papers, Massachusetts Historical Society

George Bancroft Papers, Massachusetts Historical Society

J. C. Bancroft Davis Papers, Library of Congress

N. P. Banks Papers, Library of Congress

N. P. Banks Papers, Illinois State Historical Library, Springfield, Illinois

George Bemis Papers, Massachusetts Historical Society

John Bigelow Papers, New York Public Library, Astor, Lenox & Tilden Foundations

James G. Blaine Papers, Library of Congress

Blair Family Papers, Library of Congress

John Bright Papers, British Library

B. F. Butler Papers, Library of Congress

Simon Cameron Papers, Library of Congress

Zachariah Chandler Papers, Library of Congress

Clarendon Papers, Public Record Office, London

Clarendon Papers, Bodleian Library, University of Oxford

Schuyler Colfax Papers, Rush Rhees Library, University of Rochester, Rochester, N.Y.

J. A. J. Creswell Papers, Library of Congress

Caleb Cushing Papers, Library of Congress

Henry L. Dawes Papers, Library of Congress

Ignatius Donnelly Papers, Minnesota Historical Society, St. Paul, Minn.

William M. Evarts Papers, Library of Congress

William Pitt Fessenden Papers, Library of Congress

Hamilton Fish Papers, Library of Congress

Hamilton Fish Papers, Butler Library, Columbia University, New York, N.Y.

Foreign Office Papers, Public Record Office, London (FO 5/1009-1012, 1061-1065, 1126, 1129, 1187-1192, 1195-1196, 1205, 1296-1302, 1325-1327, 1331-1332, 1334-1338, 1356-1357)

William Lloyd Garrison Papers, Boston Public Library

Garrison Family Papers, Smith College Library, Northampton, Mass.

Giddings-Julian Collection, Library of Congress

Gladstone Papers, British Library

Goldwin Smith Papers, John M. Olin Library, Cornell University, Ithaca, N.Y.

Granville Papers, Public Record Office, London

Edmund Hammond Papers, Public Record Office, London

George Frisbie Hoar Papers, Massachusetts Historical Society

Jacob M. Howard Papers, Burton Historical Collection, Detroit Public Library, Detroit, Michigan

Iddesleigh Papers, British Library

Andrew Johnson Papers, Library of Congress

Reverdy Johnson Papers, Library of Congress

John A. Kasson Papers, Iowa State Department of History and Archives, Des Moines, Iowa

Austen H. Layard Papers, British Library

John A. Logan Papers, Library of Congress

Levi P. Morton Papers, New York Public Library, Astor, Lenox & Tilden Foundations

Alexander Ramsey Papers, Minnesota Historical Society, St. Paul, Minn.

Ripon Papers, British Library

Carl Schurz Papers, Library of Congress

William H. Seward Papers, Rush Rhees Library, University of Rochester, Rochester, N.Y.

William Sprague Papers, Butler Library, Columbia University, New York, N.Y.

Charles Sumner Papers, Houghton Library of Harvard College Library, Harvard University, Cambridge, Mass.

United States Department of State Papers, R.G. 59, National Archives, Washington, D.C. (Diplomatic Despatches, Diplomatic Instructions, Great Britain, 1865-1872)

James Wickes Taylor Papers, Minnesota Historical Society, St. Paul, Minn.

Elihu B. Washburne Papers, Library of Congress

Thurlow Weed Papers, Rush Rhees Library, University of Rochester, Rochester, N.Y.

Bibliographical Essay

The basic materials for this study were the records of the U.S. Department of State in the National Archives, Washington, D.C. (Record Group 59, Diplomatic Instructions and Despatches), and the papers of the British Foreign Office in the Public Record Office, London (FO 5/1009-1012, 1061-1065, 1126, 1129, 1187-1192, 1195-1196, 1205, 1296-1302, 1325-1327, 1331-1332, 1334-1338 and 1356-1357), which were supplemented by the private correspondence of officials and politicans. On the British side, a good deal was gleaned from the papers of two foreign secretaries, Lord Clarendon (the greater part of them are in Duke Humphrey's at the Bodleian Library, Oxford, though there is a smaller, less valuable collection at the P.R.O.) and Lord Granville (at the P.R.O.). The long and detailed letters written to both secretaries by Thornton, the British minister in Washington, D.C., after 1868, are very illuminating and are especially helpful in tracing Hamilton Fish's change of mind during 1870. Thornton also wrote in confidence to Edmund Hammond, permanent undersecretary at the Foreign Office, whose papers are in the P.R.O. There is a certain amount of material in Lord Russell's correspondence (P.R.O.), but I quarried much more from the vast mine of Gladstone Papers in the British Museum. The Museum holds the papers of two of the British representatives on the Joint High Commission of 1871. There is little to detain the investigator in the letters of Lord Ripon, but the diary of Lord Iddesleigh, the *ci-devant* Sir Stafford Northcote, gave such an interesting perspective on the negotiations that one could almost forgive him his atrociously weak and long-winded light verse. Another British Museum collection, the Papers of John Bright, proved rather disappointing.

On the American side, three massive collections provided nearly all the evidence to flesh out the skeleton of the official record. The diary and letters of Charles Francis Adams, part of the Massachusetts Historical Society's treasure trove of Adams Family Papers, gave a view behind the scenes at the Geneva arbitration, as well as supplying details of the diplomacy of the period April 1865–March 1869; details that were all the more valuable because of the paucity of other worthwhile records from that time. Few presidents and few secretaries of state can have left posterity such barren collections of papers as Andrew Johnson (L.C.) and William H. Seward (Rush Rhees Library, University of Rochester). The vast bulk of Charles Sumner's papers are at the Houghton Library, Harvard; most valuable of all was the richly rewarding diary and correspondence of Hamilton Fish in the Library of Congress. It is a scandal of American historiography that no one has ever revived Allan Nevins' pre-World War II plans to publish the Fish Diary, a personal record of politics as valuable for the later nineteenth century as the journals of John Quincy Adams and James K. Polk for earlier years. While it still languishes unpublished, investigators who experience difficulty with Fish's minute and elaborately curlicued handwriting may prefer to use the typewritten transcript prepared by John Bassett Moore and included among the Fish Papers; I found it trustworthy and accurate. Two minor collections, the Bancroft Davis Papers (L.C.) and the George Bemis Papers (Massachusetts Historical Society), supplement the evidence available in the Fish and Sumner Papers. Although I worked through the papers of a large number of other politicians and office holders, I found the results meager; there were a few interesting items in the B. F. Butler, N. P. Banks, and Zachariah Chandler Papers, all in the Library of Congress. There is a little bit more about Butler and his son-in-law, Senator Ames, in the printed collection edited by Blanche Butler Ames, *Chronicles from the Nineteenth Century*; *Family Letters of Blanche Butler and Adelbert Ames, Married July 21, 1870* (n.p., 1957), and there are glimpses of foreign policy discussions in Johnson's cabinet in two published diaries: *The Diary of Gideon Welles,* edited by Howard K. Beale, assisted by Alan W. Brownsword (New York, 1960) and *The Diary of Orville Hickman Browning*, edited by J. G. Randall (Springfield, Ill., n.d.). The pamphlet literature usually repeats arguments already flogged to death in the debates printed in the U.S. *Congressional Globe*, but Reverdy Johnson made a useful contribution with *A Reply to a Recent Speech of Sir Roundell Palmer on the Washington Treaty and the Alabama Claims* (Baltimore, 1871).

J. C. Bancroft Davis wrote two interesting memoirs about the events he witnessed as assistant secretary of state: *Mr. Fish and the Alabama Claims: A Chapter in Diplomatic History* (Boston, 1893) and *Mr. Sumner, the Alabama Claims and Their Settlement* (New York, 1878). Adam Badeau, *Grant in Peace: From Appomattox to Mount McGregor: A Personal Memoir* (London, n.d.), merits attention for some of the letters reproduced in it. Extensive selections from Sumner's correspondence can be found conveniently collected in Edward L. Pierce's *Memoir and Letters of Charles Sumner* (Boston, 1894). Lord Clarendon and Lord Granville still await satisfactory modern treatment, and John Morley's venerable three-decker (London, 1903) remains the best biography of Gladstone.

There is not much to be said in favor of the chapters touching on the Alabama Claims in Glyndon G. Van Deusen's *William Henry Seward* (New York, 1967) or in Martin B. Duberman's soporific *Charles Francis Adams, 1807-1886* (Boston, 1961). Readers seeking an alternative interpretation of postwar events in Anglo-American diplomacy may consult Allan Nevins, *Hamilton Fish: The Inner History of the Grant Administration* (New York, 1937). One of the most impressive of modern American biographies, David Herbert Donald's *Charles Sumner and the Rights of Man* (New York, 1970), deals in definitive fashion with the erstwhile chairman of the Senate Committee on Foreign Relations. Goldwin Smith's *The Treaty of Washington, 1871: A Study in Imperial History* (Ithaca, N.Y., 1941) treats the negotiations from the Canadian point of view, and Brian Jenkins, *Fenians and Anglo-American Relations during Reconstruction* (Ithaca, N.Y., 1969) is concerned with a diplomatic sideshow that reacted upon, and was itself affected by, the negotiations, quarrels, and debates over the Alabama Claims.

Index

Adams, Brooks, 236
Adams, Charles Francis, 17, 44, 48, 68, 168, 219, 226; and amount of damages, 240; on Arbitration, 235; and Arbitration Tribunal, idea of independent action 233, 234; on Britain's wartime behavior, 88; on British opinion during Civil War, 17; character, 30; on Clarendon, 32; confers with Stanley on Dec. 24, 1867, 38-39; discusses Seward's dispatch of Aug. 12, 1867, with Stanley, 37-38; on Fish, 102; and indirect claims, initiates extrajudicial opinion against, 232-233; and indirect claims, offers to help solve dispute, 222; named U.S. arbitrator on Geneva Tribunal, 204; on negotiations of 1866-1867, 39; on Palmerston, 32; resigns as U.S. Minister at Court of St. James, 39; on Russell, 32; on Russell's policy, 31; on Seward's policy over the Neutrality Proclamation, 39; on Sumner's personality, 84; on Sumner's speech, 91; tells Seward that British oppose U.S. annexation of Canada, 37; ultimatum about Laird rams, 17; and war scare of Dec. 1865, 29, 30, 31
Adams, Charles Francis, Jr., 39
Adams, Henry, 36, 52, 63, 168, 239-240
Alabama, 134, 239; career of de-

struction, 15; construction, 88; escape from Liverpool, 16, 26-27, 75, 154-155; puts in at Cape Town, 183; sinking, 15
Alabama State Journal (Montgomery), 82, 88, 187, 195
Alexandra, 18, 134
Alta California (San Francisco), 19
Ames, Adelbert, 200, 201
Ames, Blanche Butler, 200
Ames, Oakes, 242
Anglophobia: and Ben Butler, 147; in Congress, 91-92, 169-170; reasons for, 19-23; stimulated by Sumner's speech on Johnson-Clarendon Convention, 79, 98
Anthony, Henry B., 76, 101, 229 n.54
Argyll, George Douglas Campbell, 8th Duke of, 60, 118

Bancroft, George, 20, 56, 58
Bancroft Davis, John C., 135, 136, 154, 196, 218, 233, 237 n.7; appointed U.S. secretary to Joint High Commission, 170; discusses ways of saving arbitration with Tenterden, 233, 235; named U.S. agent at Tribunal, 207
Bangor Daily Whig and Courier, 88
Banks, Nathaniel P., 160, 223 n.26, 227 n.41; presents anti-British resolutions in Congress, 37, 91-92; produces bill to weaken U.S. neutrality laws, 37-38, 86
Baring, Sir Francis, 69

Laird Brothers, shipbuilders, 15, 88-89
Laird, John, 18, 65
Lawrence, William Beach, 243
Lieber, Francis, 112, 140
Logan Act, 146
Lowe, Robert 228

McClellan, George B., 43
McCreery, Thomas C., 70
McCulloch, Hugh, 57
MacDonald, Sir John, 191; named to Joint High Commission, 170; resists both British and American proposals, 171
Mason, James Murray, 27
Medill, Joseph, 66, 82, 82 n.27
Moran, Benjamin, 49
Morning Post (London), 217
Morrill, Justin S., 162
Morrill, Lot M., 201
Morse, Freeman H., 66, 95 n.84
Morton, Levi P., 163, 213, 218, 229, 231; puts pressure on Fish to abandon indirect claims, 241
Morton, Oliver P., 141, 155, 157, 190, 196, 202; attends conference with Fish, 227 n.41, 229 n.54; wants supplemental article amended, 230
Motley, John Lothrop, 86 n.50; appointed minister to England, 106; dismissed, 131; disobeys instructions 115-116; Fish's instructions to, 109-110; Fish withdraws Claims discussions from, 116; told to spread idea of British withdrawal from Canada, 127; writes memoir on Claims, 107

Nation (New York), 168
National debt, U.S., 245; settlement of Alabama Claims and reduction of, 163
Naturalization, 41, 44, 46, 49, 71; agreement between R. Johnson and Stanley on, 52; protocol approved by Grant, 105; protocol signed, 60; treaty ratified, 134
Nelson, Samuel, 211; named to

Joint High Commission, 170
New York Herald, 64, 68, 81, 83, 89, 189, 195
New York Times, 68, 80, 81
New York Tribune, 68, 81, 83, 88
Nordhoff, Charles, 87
Northcote, Sir Stafford, 173, 191, 194; on Catacazy, 188; entertains Zachariah Chandler, 190; named to Joint High Commission, 170; and objections to second neutrality rule, 203; on Treaty of Washington, 185
Nova Scotia: annexation movement in, 82, 83; annexation sentiment waning in, 138
Nye, James W., 91, 114, 205

Owl (London), advocates preventive war against North, 29

Pall Mall Gazette (London), 88
Palmer, Sir Roundell, 202, 217, 235-236, 238
Palmerston, Henry John Temple, 3rd Viscount, 18; attitude toward Union, 24; death, 32; difficulties in keeping Liberal party united, 24-25, 27; on recognition of Confederacy, 25
Parker, John A., 145-147
Patterson, James W., 157, 158, 194, 196; attends conference with Fish, 227 n.41; persuaded to support Treaty, 199; on supplemental article, 230, 231; votes for Treaty, 204
Peters, John W., 223
Peterhoff, and doctrine of "continuous voyage," 26
Pierce, Edward L., 198, 243
Porter, Horace, 231
Proclamation of Neutrality, British, 17, 27, 50, 97-98, 214; Fish on, 106-107; Motley on, 107-108, 115-116; Seward insists on including in any arbitration, 36-37, 40; Stanley refuses to admit into arbitration, 35, 40; Sumner on, 75-76, 93; treatment of in

The Alabama Claims

Designed by R. E. Rosenbaum.
Composed by Cayuga Press, Inc.,
in 11 point Intertype Baskerville, 2 points leaded,
with display lines in Monotype Baskerville.
Printed letterpress from type by Cayuga Press
on Warren's No. 66 text, 50 pound basis,
with the Cornell University Press watermark.
Bound by Vail-Ballou Press
in Columbia book cloth
and stamped in All Purpose foil.